pop lor i ca (päp lôr' i k ə) *n. pl.* 1. Strange and amusing stories of the unlikely people, inventions, and events that shaped modern American life. 2. Rational explanations for frequently irrational cultural phenomena. (2004: From "pop culture," "lore," and "America")

Poplorica

A Popular History of the Fads, Mavericks, Inventions, and Lore That Shaped Modern America

Martin J. Smith
and Patrick J. Kiger

HARPER RESOURCE
An Imprint of HarperCollins*Publishers*

FIRST EDITION

Designed by Mary Austin Speaker

Library of Congress Cataloging-in-Publication Data

Smith, Martin J., 1956–
    Poplorica: A Popular History of the Fads, Mavericks, Inventions,
and Lore that Shaped Modern America / Martin J. Smith and Patrick J.
Kiger.— 1st ed.
      p.   cm.
    Includes bibliographical references.
    ISBN: 0-06-053531-8
    1. United States—Civilization—20th century—Anecdotes.   2.
Popular culture—United States—History—20th century—Anecdotes.
I. Title: Poplorica.   II. Kiger, Patrick J.   III. Title.

E169.1.S63   2004
306'.0973—dc21

                              2003051054

04 05 06 07 WB/QW 10 9 8 7 6 5 4 3 2 1

Contents

Acknowledgments xiii
Foreword xv
Introduction: How'd Things Get So Weird? xvii

FRANK J. SCOTT'S GREAT GREEN MANIFESTO   1
*In 1870, a little-known landscape architect published a book
that changed the face of America—and continues to ruin weekends.*

THE BIRTH OF COOL   12
*Willis Carrier's 1902 invention affected everything from
architecture to the balance of American political power
to the environment from which it insulates us.*

How Thin Became In   23

*Dr. Lulu Hunt Peters published the first weight-loss bestseller in
1918. Americans have been counting calories ever since.*

Alfred Kinsey's Honeymoon   33

*His research on human sexuality changed the way the world
thought about sex. But long before that, in 1921, he faced
an important moment of truth.*

The Rise of Tacky Chic   45

*In the early 1930s a former billboard artist rediscovered the
ancient technique of painting on black velvet. What followed
was a golden era of bad taste.*

Les Paul's "Log"   58

*Before the solid-body electric guitar transformed music
and became the sexiest accessory in pop culture, it debuted in 1941
as homely, heavy, and utterly ridiculous.*

Wrestling with a Contradiction   70

*In 1947, TV wrestler Gorgeous George strutted in lingerie,
plucked bobby pins from his blond curls, and exuded braggadocio
as intense as his perfume. He also paved the way for
everyone from Muhammad Ali to Kiss.*

THE WAR AGAINST WRINKLES 81

The advent of permanent-press clothing in the 1950s culminated
a five-thousand-year battle against messiness and rescued American
men from almost certain sloth.

THE KING OF LEER 90

In 1952, Robert Harrison's Confidential *magazine created*
a society of voyeurs by prying into celebrities' private lives.

THE WONDER GARMENT 107

Pantyhose was a landmark innovation when it was
conceived in 1953, and eventually grew into a symbol of women's
liberation—or women's enslavement, depending on whom you ask.

THAWS AND EFFECT 119

What to do with 260 tons of leftover turkey? In 1953,
C. A. Swanson & Sons created "convenience food" and revolutionized
the way American families eat—and interact.

HELL ON WHEELS 129

On "E-day" in 1957, Ford rolled out the Edsel as a marvel of
technology, product research, and consumer manipulation. The car
crash that followed forever changed the American marketplace.

The First Angry Mike Man   143
*The combative talk-show host is a raging cliché of modern
media. But in the early 1960s—before Rush and Howard, before Mort,
Geraldo, and Jerry—Joe Pyne was on the air.*

The Supertanker Diaper   155
*Diapers have been around for centuries, but it wasn't until 1966
that two still-unheralded inventors used molecular chemistry to solve
an age-old problem.*

When Mayhem Went Postmodern   165
In 1968, Night of the Living Dead—*the* Citizen Kane *of low-budget,
cannibalistic, zombie thrillers—spawned a new cinematic genre and
helped remake our cultural sensibilities.*

Dawn of the Point-Click Culture   177
*On December 9, 1968, a visionary computer geek showed the world
how man and his machines eventually would interact. And he did it
when Steve Jobs and Bill Gates were still struggling with puberty.*

The Righteous Stuff   189
*In 1976, with one flamboyant feat of athleticism,
Julius "Dr. J." Erving introduced America to the slam dunk—
and professional sports suddenly got funky.*

BETTY FORD'S INTERVENTION 202
*Personal confessions went from anonymous whispers
to public declarations to a steady roar on the talk-show circuit.
It began April 1, 1978.*

FROM *E.T.* TO "ASTROTURFING" 214
*Most people understood the difference between a sales pitch
and real life—at least until 1982 and that adorable alien
with a penchant for peanut butter.*

THE *TOINK!* HEARD ROUND THE WORLD 225
*In 1991, an obscure Southern California golf-club maker
introduced a revolutionary new driver, the Big Bertha. Rather than
lower scores, it raised self-respect.*

Think We Blew It? 237
Chapter Notes 239
Index 271

Acknowledgments

THIS BOOK IS A SYNTHESIS of information gathered by many people during more than a century. We owe them all a great debt. We also extend our sincere thanks to the many repositories of that information that enabled us to connect the dots between present realities and the pivotal moments that led to them. They include: the McKeldin Library at the University of Maryland, College Park; the Library of Congress; the District of Columbia's Martin Luther King Jr. Memorial Library; the Montgomery County, Maryland, public libraries; the City of Baltimore's Enoch Pratt Free Library; and the Los Angeles public library system, in particular the Richard J. Riordan Central Library.

We'd also like to thank our agent, Susan Ginsburg at Writers House, for her early faith in this project, and Toni Sciarra, our editor at HarperCollins, for her incalculable help in giving it final form.

Foreword

People often ask me how history will view certain headline events and people—a war, a president, a Supreme Court ruling. As a historian, I answer, "The truth is, we don't know." The presidential election of 2000 seemed important back then, but the events of September 11, 2001 rendered that controversial election a moot point. In other words, tomorrow's events always color how the historical record will be written.

But I would also like to add that some of the most important things that happen never make the front pages or the top of the evening news. For instance, back in 1905, the war between Russia and Japan surely overshadowed a scientific paper written by an obscure patent clerk named Einstein. Few people could have possibly realized then what a mathematical equation could mean for the world's future.

Yes, it's a long stretch from the theory of relativity to the advent of pantyhose. But not as big a stretch as you might think.

The point is that there are two kinds of history. History with a capital H and history with a small h. The first is what we're supposed to learn in school about dates, battles, elections, and speeches. It is the "HISTORY" in which presidents and politicians change the world's fate.

Then there is the other history, which is all about how we live. It is about convenience, invention, innovation—the unnoticed moments that fundamentally alter the way we function each day and ultimately look at the world.

This is the fascinating history at the heart of this book. With humor and intelligence, Martin Smith and Patrick Kiger have captured some of the most significant moments that never made it into our textbooks and give them their just standing. Not as pieces of trivia, but as moments that made our lives what they are.

After all, ask any parent: What's more important—the Treaty of Versailles or disposable diapers? I think you'll find the definitive answer here.

—Kenneth C. Davis
author of Don't Know Much About History

Introduction

● ● ● ● ● ● ● ● ●

HOW'D THINGS GET SO WEIRD?

THIS BOOK BEGAN WITH that simple question, and what you hold in your hands is our best effort to answer it.

We're guessing that you, like us, have noticed a certain eccentricity creeping into modern American culture. The mere existence of the United States Lawnmower Racing Association should have tipped you off, but there's so much more to it than that. How did we become a culture where the highest-rated talk-show hosts are boorish, insult-spewing loudmouths? When did it become common practice for guests on those talk shows to publicly confess their addictions, dementias, and dark secrets? Why are we so fascinated by the private lives of celebrities that it was considered major news when, for example, professional basketball player Dennis Rodman appeared in public in a wedding dress and announced plans to marry himself?

We also began to wonder how certain present-day realities became an accepted part of American life. If most homeowners hate yard work, why do most suburban homes have lawns? In the best-fed country on the planet, how did thin become in? When did the "convenience" part of "convenience food" become more important than the food?

In trying to answer those questions, we discovered a hidden history of unlikely cultural milestones—people, inventions, innovations, and events that turned out to be pivotal in shaping the way we live today, even if those things went unnoticed or unappreciated at the time. You already know about stock market crashes, wars, and assassinations. You already know about *Citizen Kane*, Elvis, and Enron. But who among us ever stops to think about the profound significance of superabsorbent disposable diapers and TV dinners on the way American families live and interact? Or how Ford's disastrous Edsel changed the way cars are designed, developed, and marketed? Or how the lousy honeymoon of an obscure insect researcher named Alfred Kinsey may have helped spark the sexual revolution?

We sifted through hundreds of possibilities to find the twenty unlikely events we celebrate here, and they include examples from many different areas of culture: sports, film, commerce, design, music, technology, sexuality, health, art, media, food, and fashion. Sometimes, after following a trail of bread crumbs into the past, the milestone we found was a person, such as sixties-era talk-show host Joe Pyne, the belligerent on-air progenitor of Rush Limbaugh, Howard Stern, and the rude brood of modern broadcasting; or First Lady Betty Ford, whose public disclosures about her drug and alcohol problems spurred the recovery movement and made unseemly public confessionals part of the national conversation; or professional wrestler Gorgeous George, whose flamboyant androgyny in the 1940s and 1950s spawned scores of imitators, including big-rebounding, gender-bending Dennis Rodman, the rock group Kiss, and even a young Cassius Clay. Sometimes the milestone was an invention, such as the oversized metal driver, which helped transform the once-exclusive game of golf, or permanent-press fabrics, which freed women from the chore of making their husbands look presentable. Sometimes the milestone was an innovation, such as the solid-body electric guitar or a single, unforgettable slam dunk.

The common thread linking those disparate milestones is that each one reshaped American culture in unexpected and significant ways. And so we offer this Cliff Notes of contemporary culture, a readable resource for people like you with a keen intellect, a healthy curiosity, and a wry sense of humor—people who perhaps were wondering how things got so weird but haven't had the time to sort things out. By design, this book is an eclectic mix, a sampler we hope you'll find provocative, informative, and fun.

We recognize that many of you will think we blew it, that the unlikely events we've singled out are the wrong-headed musings of misguided men. We acknowledge that possibility. So please contact us through our web site, www.poplorica.com, and let us know what *you* consider the most significant—but least likely—events in modern American history. Your suggestion[s] may find its way into an upcoming book.

—Martin J. Smith and Patrick J. Kiger

Frank J. Scott's Great Green Manifesto

In 1870, a little-known landscape architect published a book that changed the face of America—and continues to ruin weekends.

NOTHING SO VIVIDLY UNDERSCORES the peculiar American fascination with the lawn than the Dixie Chopper Jet. At its debut, that custom mower was equipped with a 150-horsepower jet engine designed to help power a Chinook helicopter. It could reach speeds of up to 70 miles per hour. With its fat rear tires and massive power plant, which juts off the back like the business end of an overweight bumblebee, the Dixie Chopper Jet could mow an entire football field in fourteen minutes. It remains the envy of every member of the seven-hundred-member Illinois-based United States Lawn Mower Racing Association.

In any other culture, the mere existence of such a machine would seem like a demented fever dream. In the United States, though, where 46.5 million acres of grass are under cultivation, the

Dixie Chopper Jet achieved a hallowed place among those dedicated souls to whom lawn care is less a duty than a lifestyle choice. Word of it spread not only through news media reports, but the jet-powered mower became somewhat of a celebrity because of its appearances on television shows such as *Good Morning America* and a memorable season finale of *Home Improvement.*

One can't help but wonder what impression the Dixie Chopper Jet would have made on Frank Jesup Scott, the obscure nineteenth-century landscape architect at whose feet we must lay much of the credit, or blame, for the American lawn obsession. How would Scott react to this mower on steroids, or to the stunning reality that, according to the Lawn Institute, a Georgia-based nonprofit organization dedicated to the promulgation of turf, more grass is under cultivation in the United States than any single crop, including wheat, corn, or tobacco? What would he make of Americans' willingness to spend between $25 billion and $30 billion a year on do-it-yourself lawn and garden care, or of the estimated $750 million a year they shell out for grass seed to perpetuate the Sisyphian cycle of mowable new growth? Could the author of a landmark Victorian gardening guidebook ever have imagined that American communities would someday fine or prosecute homeowners whose lawn care was considered inadequate, or that in 1998 the Canadian Center for Architecture in Montreal would mount a massive exhibition about the American lawn that would open with Scott's galvanizing call to arms in the battle to civilize the landscape: "A smooth, closely shaven surface of green is by far the most essential element of beauty on the grounds of a suburban house."

Scott, an Ohio-born student of famed New York landscape architect Andrew Jackson Downing, wasn't pushing a new idea when he published his book in 1870, just pushing it into new places. Grass had been used as a design element since the walled gardens of ancient Persia, and turf areas were part of the Chinese emperor's gardens as early as 100 B.C. The idea spread into Europe, and by the seventeenth century formal gardens featured large stretches of turf, including those at Versailles. Golf began catching on in the British Isles about five hundred years ago, and it's impossible to overestimate the importance that sport played not only in the research and development of grass as a commodity, but in promoting the pastoral ideal through vast stretches of green.

Immigrants brought June grass seeds to the new world, but they did so for strictly utilitarian reasons. They'd brought sheep and cattle as well, and the animals needed pastures to eat. To them, the notion of planting grass to prettify the grounds surrounding a house would have been no more acceptable than the notion of putting earrings on their cows. Well into the late nineteenth century Americans considered lawns a luxury of the upper classes, in that having one required constant tending by scythe-swinging workers or a large flock or herd of ruminants. George Washington, "the father of the American lawn," may have put in a humdinger at Mount Vernon, but then, he had the money and slaves to pull it off.

Frank Scott's book, *The Art of Beautifying Suburban Home Grounds of Small Extent*, brought the grandiose notion of the lawn to the masses at a time when the masses began moving to the suburbs, a movement propelled by urban congestion, improved transportation, and the back-to-nature sketch fantasies of the nation's enterprising real-estate agents, among other things. "To this group, Scott offered principles of design that he believed would achieve the greatest amount of landscape beauty at minimal cost," wrote David Schuyler, a scholar who penned the introduction to an edition of the book reissued more than a century after it first appeared. "Perhaps no other cultural artifact so accurately reflects 19th-century American values than the home, and *Suburban Home Grounds* is an important document of the Victorian era because it celebrates domesticity."

In short chapters and dozens of neat illustrations, Scott imagined the suburban home as the centerpiece of a neatly framed picture. With careful attention to the grounds surrounding even the most modest home, he believed urban refugees could enjoy the same "charms of Nature" enjoyed by emperors and presidents by including a lush carpet of green grass, if on a smaller scale. He also believed—and here's where Scott comes off as a bit of a nineteenth century Big Brother—that for the greater good neighbors should help enforce a social code that required each homeowner to dote slavishly on the grounds surrounding their little corner of paradise.

Scott's career before writing the book was, to be kind, undistinguished. After studying with Downing in New York, he returned to Toledo, Ohio, in 1852 and tried to make a go of it in his chosen field. He apparently practiced there until about 1859, but then joined his father's real-estate business. According to Charles A. Birnbaum's *Pioneers of American Landscape Design*, Scott "continued to think and write about the proper design of the domestic landscape."

But from the moment Scott's weirdly precise and puritan tome rolled off the presses—"an ecstatic paean to the beauty and indispensability of the front lawn," according to one account—he assumed roles as both a true social visionary and the unseen busybody haunting every neighborhood in America. The book not only offered city-sick homeowners specific instructions about how to develop a lawn and gardens, but also spelled out an inviolable code of lawn-care conduct. Scott insisted that "no lawn can be brought to perfection if cut less often than once a week." He decreed that weeds "are to be dealt with like cancers" and removed with "a long sharp knife, and busy fingers." Urging homeowners to restrict shrubs and flowers to the periphery of the lawn, he wrote: "Let your lawn be your home's velvet robe, and your flowers its not-too-promiscuous decoration." He considered fences and hedges divisive, even sacrilegious: "It is unchristian to hedge from the sight of others the beauties of nature which it has been our good fortune to create or secure."

Perhaps Scott's most significant contribution—one which continues to thrive in America's lawn culture—is the sense that each lawn should be a patch in a great green quilt that unites a community and ultimately becomes part of the collective national landscape. In ways both subtle and mildly threatening, Scott argued that proper lawn care is less a matter of individual pride than of civic duty. Do your part, he urged, or your fellow Americans will hate you. The word "slattern" appears prominently in Scott's book, and he reserved it for those with too casual an approach to lawn care.

Scott's book struck a nerve somewhere deep in the national psyche. Sales were brisk enough that new editions had to be printed in 1872, 1873, 1881, and 1886, and it's not hard to find more recent editions for sale on the Internet. It's no coincidence that by 1885— just seventeen years after the United States first granted a patent for a mechanical lawn mower—America was building fifty thousand push mowers a year.

"Scott elevated an unassuming patch of turf grass into an institution of democracy," wrote Michael Pollan in a 1998 issue of *Harvard Design* magazine. "The American lawn becomes an egalitarian conceit, implying that there is no need, in Scott's words, to 'hedge a lovely garden against the longing eyes of the outside world' because we all occupy the same middle class." In his book *Second Nature: A Gardener's Education*, Pollan described the modern mindset that Scott was the first to articulate: "The democratic system can cope with the non-voter more easily than the democratic landscape can cope with the non-mower. A single unmowed lawn ruins the whole effect, announcing to the world that all is not well here in utopia."

And so it began. By the time the real suburban land rush started after World War II, lawns and lawn care were no less a part of the American DNA than Saturdays spent washing muscle cars. Mowers became motorized, adding the male attractive elements of power, noise, and danger to the weekly exercise of cutting the grass. The absurd exercise of mowing is, still, a near-Zen experience for many weekend lawn warriors for whom the sounds, smells, and routines of their weekly chore have insinuated themselves into the American lifestyle like untreated crabgrass. Striving toward Scott's "closely shaven surface of green" became a way for teenagers to make spending money and for parents to teach the values of hard work and reward. Some men built their weekends around the self-perpetuating cycle of fertilizing, watering, and cutting, and their competitive instincts fueled the endless effort to make *their* lawn as lush and weed-free as their neighbors' and, not coincidentally, the lawns that proliferated on television during the 1950s.

Television, in fact, codified Scott's suburban ideals and hard-wired them into the national psyche. As depicted on shows such as *The Adventures of Ozzie and Harriet, Father Knows Best*, and *Leave It to Beaver*, life was supposed to be lived atop a lawn, because each of those shows began with a panning shot that took viewers from the street, across a front lawn, and into the characters' homes. In the 1957 season of *I Love Lucy*, Lucy and Ricky moved to the suburbs and began a lawn-centered life and, in one episode, wisecracked through the building of a backyard barbecue. The formula for a successful American life was expressed in the broadest possible strokes: Nice grass equals domestic bliss.

Maintaining that illusion meant that someone in each house had to spend a lot of time pushing a heavy-reel mower, or behind the crude controls of noisy, fume-spewing foot munchers with names such as Mowamatic, Mulchinator, and Dynamow. Ads for them filled the home-and-garden magazines in the late 1950s and early 1960s, and some lawnmowers even became status symbols. The Mow-Master, for example, was touted as a "miraculous lawn servant" that could "give your lawn that sleek, velvety, professional grooming that will be the talk of the neighborhood." A parade of inventors brought forth machines they claimed would mow a lawn on their own, and the unfulfilled fantasy of effortless lawn care persists even today.

The Vigoro Lawn Food Company touted the slogan "Lawns are to live on" in ads that ran between 1959 and 1962, and there really was something intoxicating about it all. Americans were seduced by visions of a Camelot that included touch football games on the lawn of the Kennedy family compound, and Hollywood did its part to promote the image of the suburban landscape as a place of endless possibilities. Frank Perry's 1968 film, *The Swimmer*, was the story of a man, played by Burt Lancaster, who one hot summer day decided to begin "swimming home" by jogging from one neighbor's pool to the next, sharing memories of his life, all the way across the magnificently grassed Connecticut valley where he lives. It seemed to some a lovely metaphor for one man's death and journey to heaven.

People today who grew up playing on lawns can imagine nothing less for their own children. Americans have identified the smell of freshly cut grass often as one of the most evocative in many surveys, although a Smell & Taste Treatment and Research Foundation study found that the smell of cut grass was a happy connotation mostly for people born before 1960. Those born later often associated it with unwanted work.

By the 1980s, though, the great green metaphor Scott envisioned for suburban democracy was getting a bit weedy and overgrown. Maybe it was inevitable that the lawn—for decades a public projection of a healthy home life—would become a metaphor for illusion. The heavenscape of *The Swimmer* gave way to a vision of suburban decay depicted most memorably in David Lynch's 1986 film *Blue Velvet*. In the promotional poster for that film, for example, a picket fence became the frozen smile masking trouble in paradise, and in its unforgettable opening scenes Lynch portrayed the lawn as nothing more than a clumsy cover for suburbia's dark secrets, like pancake makeup over a battered housewife's bruise. Images of perfect roses, bright yellow tulips, smiling firemen, and safe school crosswalks devolve as Lynch's camera moves from aboveground and burrows into the lush, thick green grass. Beneath the placid lawn Lynch portrays a terrifying, diseased underworld swarming with ravenous black bugs in a ferocious and predatory fight for life. (Lynch returned to the lawn motif in a 1999 film, *The Straight Story*, about a real seventy-three-year-old Wisconsin man who rode a lawn mower on an epic cross-country journey to mend his relationship with his ill and estranged brother.)

The same year that *Blue Velvet* was wowing the avant-garde and disgusting Middle America, the lawn mower emerged in a surprising new film role—the villain. (This was not without some basis in reality, since U.S. emergency rooms treat about sixty thousand mower-related injuries each year.) In Stephen King's 1986 film *Maximum Overdrive*, a passing alien spaceship infects all machines on the planet with an undisguised hostility toward their owners, including a lurking, bloody lawn mower that, after already having dispatched a few homeowners, chases down a passing paperboy. The plot of another King story was used in the 1992 movie *The Lawnmower Man*, which includes a scene in which a mower moves on its own across a lawn while its operator crawls after it, naked, eating the clippings.

Lawn culture weirdness isn't confined to film. In "The Electric Lawn," published in a weighty 1999 collection of lawn-related essays, writer Mark Wigley recounts various oddities, including a man who, dressed in a grass suit, had somebody pushing a lawn mower chase him down a Kansas City street as part of his campaign to "illustrate his feelings about technology and the environment." In the annual Doo Dah Parade in Pasadena, California, one of the traditional entries is the "Toro, Toro, Toro Precision Lawnmower Drill Team." The *Guinness Book of World Records* acknowledges a 14,594.5-mile journey from Maine to Florida (through all 48 contiguous U.S. states and parts of Canada and Mexico) aboard a riding mower. In 1996 the torch for the Paralympics in Atlanta was carried part of the way on a riding mower.

Then, of course, there's the United States Lawnmower Racing Association, which in 1992 brought the strange British sport of mower racing to the land where it truly belongs. The organization was started as a single-race publicity stunt to promote a brand of fuel stabilizer, but during the decade that followed it mushroomed into the National Lawn Mower Racing Series. In 2000, the series featured twenty scheduled races all over the country in which helmeted riders whip around dirt tracks at speeds approaching 60 miles per hour aboard souped-up, decal-covered John Deeres, Snappers, and Lawn Boys with nicknames such as Turfinator, Sodzilla, Geronimow, and Mr. Mowjangles. The star, of course, is the Dixie Chopper Jet, which has been the group's official pace mower and shining star since its inception.

Frank Scott lived to the grand old age of ninety-one, but his death in 1919 came long before his lawn manifesto blossomed into such strange new subcultures. His book remains little more than a footnote in the history of American landscape architecture, and today many scholars in the field are only vaguely familiar with his work. "I regret to say I have never heard of him," replied an editor for the American Society of Landscape Architects when queried about Scott, and landscape scholar Melanie Simo of Bradford, New Hampshire, said, "He's not one of those people who might come up" in a survey of modern landscape designers.

It's also worth noting that by the time a new century dawned, some Americans were engaged in sincere debate about Scott's philosophies and the logic of the lawn. An estimated 30 percent of municipal water in the eastern United States ends up on lawns, according to a 1996 New Yorker article; in the water-starved West, the figure is 60 percent. Some conscientious homeowners began landscaping with drought-tolerant plants and ornamental grasses that required less water, fertilizer, or herbicide. Some even considered letting their lawns grow wild and free, turning the land back to something resembling the pastureland favored by American pioneers. It's worth noting, too, that most people didn't.

Gallons of water required to cover a one-acre lawn with an inch-thick blanket of water, the recommended ration for a single week and one reason some Americans are reconsidering the logic of lawns in areas where water is scarce.

How Clover Became a Curse

Until the middle of the twentieth century, clover was considered a perfectly acceptable part of a lawn and was even included in turf grass mixes sold by industry giant O. M. Scott's & Company (to which landscape architect Frank J. Scott had no relation). It required no fertilizer and, with its roundish leaves and tiny puffs of white flower, clover added an interesting texture to any expanse of grass.

But as author Warren Schultz recounts in his 1999 book, *A Man's Turf: The Perfect Lawn*, the demonization and slow disappearance of clover is "a classic example of the homeowners' perceptions being shaped by the turf industry, specifically the herbicide industry."

The beginning of the end of clover in American lawns began after World War II, when scientists discovered that with minor changes nerve gases created for possible wartime use could be used to kill weeds. Scott's was one of the first companies to offer lawn herbicides to the public, including a weed killer called

Scott's 4-X that wiped out broad-leaved plants but left grass intact. All well and good—except that clover is a broad-leafed plant.

After a weekend dose of 4-X, bare patches of ground quickly replaced those cheery patches of clover. Lawns began to look mangy. But rather than develop an herbicide that would spare the clover in a lawn, Scott's decided to wage a public relations campaign against clover. The company's literature through the late 1950s and early 1960s gradually begins to demonize clover as a plague on a healthy lawn.

The company's disinformation campaign climaxed with the sneering dismissal of clover as a common weed, and naturally recommended certain Scott's products to help get rid of it.

You Want *More*?

- *The Art of Beautifying Suburban Home Grounds of Small Extent*, by Frank J. Scott. Modern editions are available through used booksellers, including a 1982 edition from American Life Foundation and Study Institute, Watkins Glen, New York.
- *A Man's Turf: The Perfect Lawn*, by Warren Schultz, Clarkson Potter, New York, 1999
- *The American Lawn*, edited by Georges Teyssot, Princeton Architectural Press, Princeton, N.J., 1999.
- *Second Nature: A Gardener's Education*, by Michael Pollan, Dell, New York, 1991.
- *Pioneers of American Landscape Design*, by Charles A. Birnbaum, McGraw-Hill Professional, New York, 2000.
- *The Lawn: A History of an American Obsession*, by Virginia Scott Jenkins, Smithsonian Institution Press, Washington, D.C., 1994.

The Birth of Cool

*Willis Carrier's 1902 invention affected everything from
architecture to the balance of American political power
to the environment from which it insulates us.*

IT'S A MEASURE OF WILLIS CARRIER'S peculiar impact upon
modern life that just outside Phoenix, Arizona, in the midst of the
hottest desert in North America, a posh health spa offers its customers use of a Finnish-style sauna. It may seem odd that people
are willing to pay to work up a sweat indoors in a place where they
would perspire heavily for free simply by stepping outside. Summer
temperatures in Phoenix, after all, routinely exceed 100 degrees,
and in July the average daytime high is 106. In fact there was a time,
back in the middle of the twentieth century, when the relatively few
souls who were hardy enough to endure the city's arid local climate
drove around with blocks of ice on their car dashboards and slept in
wet sheets at night in a futile attempt to stay cool.

But today, Phoenix residents are ruled no longer by the sun's oppressive glare. Instead, it's possible to travel from home to work, to a restaurant for lunch, and then attend a baseball game at the forty-nine-thousand-seat Bank One Ballpark at night without ever experiencing more than a few minutes in temperatures higher than the mid-seventies Fahrenheit, the widely accepted benchmark of human comfort. This is all possible because of Carrier's invention, one of the true technological miracles of the modern world: air-conditioning. Because of him, in essence, we can create and control our own artificial climate—and live virtually oblivious to hot climates and seasons—to such an extent that we've made sweating into a form of luxury.

Compared to the lightbulb or the automobile, air-conditioning's impact often is overlooked. Yet just as lightbulbs altered the natural rhythm of day and night, and cars made possible a degree of mobility that changed our sense of distance, so air-conditioning freed us from forces that had constrained humans over much of the planet since the beginning of civilization—heat and humidity. Some see it as one of humanity's most significant inventions.

Though Carrier invented air-conditioning in 1902, it took another half century for his invention to become widely available and affordable. Since then, it has reshaped America in ways great and small. Today, more than 80 percent of the nation's homes are air-conditioned. Air-conditioning has changed the design of our homes and workplaces; influenced where we shop, what sort of movies we see, and how we dress; even altered how we interact with our neighbors. By making life in even the hottest regions of the nation comfortably cool, it induced a massive migration to the fifteen southern and western states known as the Sunbelt. In 1950, those states amounted to 28 percent of the nation's population. Today, according to the 2000 census, they're home to 40 percent. (One of the biggest boomtowns has been the Phoenix area, where the population during the past fifty years has increased tenfold, to more than three million.) The population shift made possible by air-conditioning, in turn, has altered the nation's political balance of power, as conservative-leaning southern and western states gained a controlling share of votes in the Electoral College. Arguably, air-conditioning helped put Ronald Reagan and George W. Bush in the White House.

But while the air conditioner in one sense has freed us from the natural environment, it also exacted a toll—from less social interaction with our neighbors to bizarre new health problems such as Legionnaires' disease and sick-building syndrome. More important, the increasing dependence upon machines to keep us cool burns up electricity and strains our energy supplies. And chemicals that for years were used in air-conditioning units helped damage the Earth's protective ozone layer and increase global warming—the paradox, of course, being that air-conditioning has helped worsen the heat that we depend upon it to control.

It's safe to assume that none of those implications occurred to Willis Carrier in the spring of 1902, when his then employer, the Buffalo Forge Company, assigned him to help a Brooklyn-based printing company solve a vexing problem. Although the twenty-five-year-old Cornell-trained engineer had a reputation for absent-mindedness (he once organized a dinner party at a restaurant but somehow forgot about the engagement en route), he had a relentless focus when it came to engineering challenges. In this particular case, the client complained that when the weather changed, the fluctuations in humidity caused paper to expand or contract, which in turn wreaked havoc with the printing process.

Carrier wasn't the first to try to counter the ravages of summer weather. The ancient Egyptians figured out that when liquids evaporate, they draw heat from the air around them, and they used strategically placed dampened mats and water-filled pots in their houses to make them more comfortable. In the eighth century, the Caliph Mahdi of Baghdad had snow brought down from the mountains and packed into a space between the interior and exterior walls of his summer palace. In the 1850s, Dr. John Gorrie, a physician in search of a way to make his sick wife more comfortable in the Florida heat, got the idea of cooling with ammonia, which absorbs more heat than water as it evaporates. He soon patented the first ice-making machine. By the late nineteenth century other inventors were trying to cool the air inside buildings by using fans or bellows to draw air over blocks of ice, but those devices were cumbersome and not particularly effective.

The methodical Carrier came up with a far more precise system. He knew that just as evaporation could be used to reduce heat, cooling could be used to draw moisture from the air. (That's the reason a glass of ice water accumulates a dew on the glass surface.) In his lab, he took a set of heating coils and circulated chilled water through them, and then used a fan to force air across the coils. He developed the ability to control simultaneously both the temperature and humidity in an indoor space. The following year, he and fellow engineer Irvine Lyle equipped the printing plant with a much larger version of the experimental rig, including an ammonia compressor to chill and rechill the water. The cooling effect on air inside the plant was the equivalent of melting 108,000 pounds of ice a day. In 1906, Carrier won a patent for his "Apparatus for Treating Air." (In the years that followed, engineers would replace the water with chemical coolants such as Freon, which could absorb more heat and make the process even more effective.)

Though air-conditioning was developed for industrial purposes, it didn't take very long for everyone to realize that the ingenious cooling-dehumidifying combo could be used to make humans more comfortable as well. High humidity, after all, makes it more difficult for the human body to cope with heat, because perspiration can't evaporate to cool it—with the result that the person gets even hotter. On Memorial Day 1925, the Rivoli in New York City became the first movie theater in America to offer air-conditioned comfort, thanks to a system installed by Carrier for a then princely one hundred thousand dollars. Adolph Zukor, head of Columbia Pictures, watched in satisfaction as patrons gradually put away the paper fans they'd brought with them to keep cool. Air-conditioned department stores and office buildings soon followed.

But air-conditioning's proponents had even more grandiose ambitions. As journalist and historian Marsha Ackermann notes in her recent book, *Cool Comfort: America's Romance with Air Conditioning*, public health experts of the early twentieth century saw hot weather as a dissipating menace, and an influential Yale geographer, Ellsworth Huntington, popularized a theory that cooler weather makes for smarter, more productive civilizations. As a result, air-conditioning was seen not just as a way to make life more pleasant, but as a means of uplifting the human species. They cheerily foresaw a day in which weather would be irrelevant.

In 1931, Westinghouse Electric engineers designed and built a windowless house inside which temperature, humidity, and ventilation were controlled to simulate "perpetual spring." By the mid-1930s, Carrier—who by then had his own eponymous air-conditioning company—envisioned a world in which the average man would go from his air-conditioned house on an air-conditioned train to his air-conditioned workplace, and would dine in air-conditioned restaurants. "The only time he will know anything about heat waves . . . will be when he exposes himself to the natural discomforts of out-of-doors," he said in a 1936 radio interview quoted in Ackermann's book.

The advent of that air-conditioned utopia was delayed by World War II, but when peace came, affordable window-mounted air-conditioning units became available, and sales soared. In 1946, thirty thousand air conditioners were sold. Within a decade, the annual sales number had climbed to 1.3 million. But by the early 1950s, the real boom was in central air-conditioning systems, which were an integral feature of the new suburban homes that developers were busily mass-producing to fill the sudden demand for low-cost housing created by sixteen million former GIs and their young families. The developers designed tract houses—cramped, minimalist structures built from inexpensive, flimsy materials—and used large windows and sliding glass doors to let in sunlight and create the illusion of space. But the excess of glass made tract houses hot and stuffy in summer—a problem that developers remedied with air-conditioning.

Despite the extra cost of the equipment, builders found they could save money with air-conditioning, because they could leave out all the architectural features that had been used to cool houses in the past, such as wide eaves and high ceilings.

Air-conditioning not only changed the design of the American home, but the lifestyles of its inhabitants. This was particularly true in the South, where it altered the elaborate rituals of dealing with summer heat. Quickly, the old habit of visiting with the neighbors on a shady porch went by the wayside. It was far more comfortable to stay in one's own house with the wall unit going full blast, watching television. But the new "indoor" lifestyle left them feeling oddly isolated.

Those changes may have been disquieting to some native southerners, but air-conditioning also helped reverse prewar population declines in the South, as northerners and midwesterners started moving to places that they previously might have considered too hot for comfort. The technology, after all, made it possible to enjoy the sunshine and mild winters, not to mention cheaper housing and job opportunities, without having to endure brutal summer heat as a price.

The air-conditioning–induced migration had an even more startling effect in the West, where sprawling new metropolises arose almost overnight in the desert. One such place was Phoenix, where residents once had relied on primitive devices called "swamp coolers"—basically, an electric fan that blew air through a dampened pad or screen—and businessmen were known to slip into the handful of air-conditioned movie theaters on hot days for furtive naps. The arrival of true refrigeration-style home air-conditioning in the early 1950s caused a sensation. The Central Arizona Light and Power Co. proclaimed in newspaper ads: "You can manufacture your own weather." As local historian Bradford Luckingham put it in his book *Phoenix: The History of a Southwestern Metropolis*, the city "soon gained a reputation as the most thoroughly air-conditioned place on the planet."

The electronics manufacturer Motorola, a major employer, felt assured that workers from other regions would be able to tolerate the desert climate, and expanded its operations. Acres of new tract houses sprung up. Between 1955 and 1960 alone, Phoenix's population increased threefold, to 440,000 people. Over the next forty years, it would grow another eightfold. By the mid-1990s, developers were erecting nearly thirty thousand new houses each year, and greater Phoenix was spreading outward into the desert at an astonishing rate of an acre per hour.

By the end of the twentieth century, the population of the heavily air-conditioned South and West had caught up to that of the North and Midwest. That shift significantly altered American politics. When John F. Kennedy was elected in 1960, northern and midwestern states accounted for 316 electoral votes, more than the 270 needed for victory. By the 2000 election, states in those regions were down to 253 votes, while the southern and western states had 285. Every elected president since JFK has either been born or made his home in the Sunbelt.

Air-conditioning had an ideological effect as well. After the U.S. Capitol was air-conditioned in the late 1920s, a Democratic congressman from Mississippi rose to complain that the unnatural chill gave the place "a regular Republican atmosphere." He didn't know it, but his words were prophetic. As University of California at Berkeley political science professor Nelson Polsby noted in a 2002 presentation at the American Enterprise Institute, the north-to-south migrants tended to be older and more conservative. The places in which they settled often already had an antiregulatory, pro–property rights, promilitary bent (in part because the economies were bolstered by the presence of military bases and defense contractors). One of the first nationally prominent politicians to spring up from the air-conditioned Utopia was Arizona senator Barry Goldwater, who in 1964 grabbed the GOP presidential nomination away from cold-climate moderates, with the rallying cry that "extremism in the defense of liberty is no vice." He was crushed in that fall's election by another Sunbelt politician, Texan Lyndon B. Johnson, but Goldwater's unabashed conservatism spawned a movement that led to Ronald Reagan, and ultimately to George W. Bush.

By the end of the twentieth century, the air-conditioned utopia that Willis Carrier envisioned in 1936 had arrived. Today, Americans spend 80 percent to 90 percent of their time indoors. The weather outside has become increasingly irrelevant. At the office, we wear long-sleeved garments and jackets, even on the hottest days of summer. When we want to escape the isolation of our homes, we go shopping in an enclosed mall—"the cathedral of air-conditioned culture," as southern historian Raymond Arsenault has written— where the most significant signs of seasonal change are Fourth of July sales and post-Christmas markdowns. We even prefer to exercise in air-conditioned comfort—ergo, the popularity of computerized treadmills, bicycles, and cross-country skiing machines, which simulate the ways we once might have been forced to exert ourselves outdoors.

But utopia is not without its price. For decades, air-conditioning units used chlorofluorocarbons, or CFCs, as coolants. These chemicals have the nasty side effect of gradually making their way into the upper atmosphere, where they trap heat—as much as 7,000 times as much as each molecule of carbon dioxide—and have eroded a hole in the ozone layer that helps shield the Earth from the sun's radiation. Though the use of CFCs was phased out by the United States and other affluent nations by a treaty in the late 1980s, they're still being released in Third World countries eager to imitate our air-conditioned lifestyle. Global warming has made us all the more dependent upon the technology that helped cause it.

Meanwhile, in Phoenix, as the electricity to run air-conditioning burns a hole in residents' wallets—summer electric bills can reach three hundred dollars a month—they're forced to cope with the negative effects of the growth made possible by air-conditioning. Generations ago, people with respiratory problems moved there to take advantage of the clean desert air. Today, Phoenix has ozone and carbon monoxide levels that the federal Environmental Protection Agency rates as "serious" (a distinction shared only by Los Angeles), and the atmosphere is plagued by a peculiar problem—clouds of dust churned up by new construction.

Of course, it's possible to avoid those hazards by staying indoors. In a recently published study, Harvard University medical researchers noted that heavily air-conditioned cities actually have fewer hospital admissions for respiratory problems on days when outdoor pollution is high, compared to other cities without as much artificial cooling. It's not the air-conditioning itself that makes people breathe easier, but rather the closed windows, which prevent them from being exposed to the pollutants outside. The trade-off: Being sealed inside can increase a person's exposure to *indoor* pollution, including fungal spores that accumulate in buildings with improperly installed or dirty air-conditioning filters. A few years ago, according to a local business newspaper, an environmental consultant found that some "sick" buildings had fungal levels 2 to 3 times higher than the outdoors. The warm water that collects inside air-conditioning units can breed *Legionella* bacteria, which can cause a deadly respiratory illness.

The most perversely ironic impact of Willis Carrier's brainchild, though, has been the manner in which it frees us from natural weather, only to imprison us within an artificial world of our own making. In his day, it was believed that hot weather drained civilizations of vigor, but today, it seems that the opposite may be true. As Scott Craven, a writer for the Phoenix-based *Arizona Republic* newspaper, recently put it: "Machine-cooled air has made us weather wimps, running from air-conditioned car to air-conditioned office to air-conditioned home." The occasional spa sauna notwithstanding, we seem to be more vulnerable to heat's ravages than ever.

○ ○ ○ ○ ○

THE OPERATIVE NUMBER: 74

The Fahrenheit temperature that air-conditioning proponents in the 1940s decided was the optimum for human comfort. The number was based upon laboratory experiments in which 15 percent of subjects felt too cold at that temperature, and another 15 percent felt too warm, with everyone else presumably falling in between.

○ ○ ○ ○ ○

Boom Time for Anal Retentives

In 1954, the University of Texas and the federal Building Research Advisory Board created a test project, the Austin Air-Conditioned Village, to study how people lived in twenty-one small houses equipped with units designed by various manufacturers. The idea was to see how they fared in a cooled environment, and how they could be convinced to like it. In most of the houses, the windows didn't open at all.

One of the oddest findings: Though the closed windows kept dirt out and the houses were cleaner, female residents ended up doing more housework rather than enjoying leisure time because the standards of cleanliness became more exacting.

You Want *More*?

- *Cool Comfort: America's Romance with Air-Conditioning*, by Marsha K. Ackermann, Smithsonian, Washington, D.C., 2002.
- *Air-Conditioning America: Engineers and the Controlled Environment, 1900–1960*, by Gail Cooper, Johns Hopkins University Press, Baltimore, Md., 1998.
- http://www.nbm.org/Exhibits/past/2000_1996/Stay_Cool!. html, a Web page describing "Stay Cool! Air Conditioning America," a 1999–2000 exhibit by the National Building Museum.

How Thin Became In

*Dr. Lulu Hunt Peters published the first weight-loss bestseller in
1918. Americans have been counting calories ever since.*

CONSIDERING HOW OBSESSED our contemporary society is with
thinness, it's astonishing to think that a century ago, the ideal of
feminine physical perfection was Broadway actress and singer Lillian Russell. The curvaceous star of productions such as *An American Beauty* and *The Goddess of Truth* carried as much as 186 pounds
on her five-foot-six-inch frame, making her the equivalent of
roughly one-and-a-half Jennifer Anistons or Gwyneth Paltrows.
Instead of banishing carbohydrates or sipping on herbal potions
like today's sexy stars, Russell enthusiastically consumed ten-
course dinners with her boyfriend, the corpulent financier Diamond Jim Brady, and was known to grab a piece of custard pie and
gobble it down as she hurried to catch a train to an out-of-town performance. Admirers were so captivated by Russell's porcelain com-

plexion, the elegant symmetry of her face, and her golden tresses that they scarcely noticed the fleshiness of her arms or the generous expanse of her hips.

Today, of course, a singer with Russell's zaftig figure would be a more likely candidate for liposuction than stardom. What so drastically altered our attitudes about women's bodies, and started our fixation with skinniness?

Arguably, the turning point was a book. *Diet and Health, With Key to the Calories*, written by Lulu Hunt Peters in 1918, was the first best-selling weight-loss manual. Peters, a physician, wasn't the first dieting guru. But she was the first to preach directly to women about the evil of excess flesh, proclaiming that extra pounds were not just unattractive but immoral, and that fat people suffered from a lack of willpower. Peters also advised her readers that reducing and staying slim meant a lifetime of struggle—"no matter how much I exercise, no matter what I suffer, I will always have to watch my weight." And drawing upon then new discoveries about the chemistry of food, Peters was the first to popularize calorie counting as a surefire way to lose weight.

Diet and Health topped the nonfiction best-seller charts in 1924 and 1925 and ultimately sold more than two million copies. More important, Peters's 148-page book helped create a modern world in which women feel pressured to conform to an ideal of svelteness, where finding the right diet is the key to happiness. "Could anyone get any enjoyment out of either being—or looking at—an 'overstuffed' model?" Peters wrote. "I doubt it." While much of her basic dietary advice remains sound even today, the negative, self-loathing beliefs and attitudes that were part of her system helped spawn harmful excesses—from anorexia to the use of dangerous drugs to curb appetite—against which many women now are rebelling.

History's first diet maven may have been the ancient Greek physician Hippocrates, the father of medicine. Circa 400 B.C., he recommended that "those desiring to lose weight should perform hard work before food. They should take their meals after exertion and while still panting from fatigue. . . . They should, moreover, eat only once a day and take no baths and sleep on a hard bed and walk naked as long as possible." Like countless other diet gurus who would follow, unfortunately, he didn't really know what he was talking about.

As a result, in the centuries that followed, those who felt the need to reduce their girth often resorted to similarly bizarre methods. In the eleventh century, for example, William the Conqueror, who apparently had become too corpulent to ride a horse, tried confining himself to bed and subsisting on a liquid diet of alcoholic beverages. In William's day, of course, obesity was a problem mostly for nobles. The masses weren't in much danger of becoming fat, since they had to turn over most of their harvests to their local lord and the church, and had to work long and hard just to keep from starving.

By the nineteenth century, the rise of the market economy and improved supplies of food finally allowed the common folk to accumulate a little surplus flesh. That's about the time that the first self-styled health zealots began to preach the dangers of being overweight. In the 1830s, Presbyterian minister Sylvester Graham preached to Americans that gluttony led to indigestion, illness, sexual depravity, and lawlessness. He recommended a meatless, sugar-free diet of grains, vegetables, and water, and invented a whole-wheat cracker that still bears his name. Another nineteenth-century weight-loss pioneer was William Banting, an elderly London undertaker who, at five feet five inches and two hundred pounds, had such a large belly that he had difficulty tying his shoes and descending staircases. At the suggestion of his doctor, Banting experimented with a diet that consisted mostly of meat, fish, and a few vegetables, supplemented by a half-dozen glasses of wine a day. Though modern nutritionists might frown on that regimen—the alcohol consumption, for example, adds hundreds of empty calories for the body to turn into fat—Banting somehow managed to lose fifty pounds. In 1864 he published a pamphlet touting the protein-and-alcohol diet, "Letter on Corpulence," which sold fifty-eight thousand copies. "Banting," as the method came to be called, went on to become the most common weight-loss recommendation by nineteenth-century doctors.

By the turn of the century the first advertisements for weight-loss products—laxatives, Epsom-salt baths, and preparations that induced vomiting—began to appear, and the diet business had become dominated by charlatans and kooks, most of whom lacked any medical or scientific training. One of the most notorious was Horace Fletcher, a San Francisco art dealer turned nutrition guru. He became known as The Great Masticator for his theory that chewing each bite of food thirty-two times was the ideal way to promote physical well-being and control one's weight. "Fletcherizing" gained a following, including author Henry James and industrialist John D. Rockefeller. Fletcher, who wore a white lab coat to give himself an air of authority, tried to convince actual scientists by mailing them samples of his excrement, whose size and odor he thought indicated good health. Dr. John Harvey Kellogg, better known as the coinventor of the cornflake, augmented the Fletcher regimen with rainwater douches and large quantities of fruit. (He recommended that patients with hypertension, for example, consume as much as fourteen pounds of grapes and strawberries a day.)

Most of these early weight-loss gimmicks were doomed to disappoint their users, since they were based on wishful thinking or salesmanship. But in the 1890s and the early 1900s two chemists made discoveries that offered the promise of a scientifically grounded method of slimming. Wilbur O. Atwater measured the number of units of heat that various foods produced when the body burned them as fuel. The calorie, the amount of heat required to raise the temperature of one gram of water by one degree Centigrade, became the measure. A few years later, Russell Chittenden started measuring exercise in terms of the number of calories burned. Since caloric consumption that wasn't burned was stored as fat, it was a simple jump to the notion that by cutting calories and/or burning more of them, a person could lose weight.

Still, someone needed to convince the masses that calorie counting was the way to lose weight—and more important, persuade them that losing weight really was something important and desirable to do, and not just a delusion practiced by a few health faddists. That salesperson was Lulu Hunt Peters.

Born in Maine, she earned a teaching degree at the Eastern Maine State Normal School before moving west to attend the University of Southern California, where she earned a medical degree in 1909. Even as she began her career as a doctor at local hospitals, Peters continued to struggle with a problem that had bedeviled her since her youth—her weight. As a child in Maine she was, in her own word, "obese," and felt like an outcast. On the day shortly after graduation that she married Louis H. Peters, her weight was 165 pounds, and it zoomed to as much as 220.

Desperate, Peters—who apparently knew of Atwater's and Chittenden's works—cut out the malted milk shakes that she craved and put herself on a tough calorie-cutting regimen. For breakfast, Peters ate a small piece of whole-wheat bread with a bit of butter, and a weak cup of coffee or hot water flavored with lemon juice. For lunch, she ate a corn muffin with butter, another cup of coffee with a tablespoon of cream, and a salad with Roquefort dressing. Dinner was her biggest meal, with a bowl of vegetable soup, a serving of seafood, some vegetables, and another cup of weak coffee. That amounted to just 1,100 calories a day, but sometimes, she would cut down even more. At one point, she fasted for five days straight, drinking only fruit juice. The approach worked, and Peters shed seventy pounds.

According to a 1923 *Los Angeles Times* profile, Peters, who had worked in humanitarian efforts in Serbia and Albania during World War I, initially decided to write about her diet regimen as a way of helping food conservation efforts. (As dieting historian Hillel Schwartz has noted, Peters at one point had proposed the formation of "Watch Your Weight Anti-Kaiser Classes," whose members would show their patriotism by meeting once a week to weigh themselves.)

But even if she was altruistic, Peters was no gentle persuader. She wrote in an informal, wisecracking, slangy style, similar to the one that Dear Abby and Ann Landers would affect decades later, and her message was blunt. With a proven scientific method available, losing weight was a matter of self-discipline rather than genes. "It is not true that [overweight people] cannot help it," she wrote. "They have to work a little harder, that is all." Thus, people who continued to carry extra pounds were weak and deserved scorn, rather than understanding or pity. "Fat individuals have always been considered a joke. But you are a joke no longer. Instead of being looked on with friendly tolerance and amusement, you are now viewed with distrust, suspicion, and even aversion! How dare you hoard fat when our nation needs it?" She occasionally chided characters named "Mrs. Tiny Weyaton," "Mrs. Ima Gobbler," and "Mrs. Knott Little," which supposedly were based upon actual women patients of hers. "You make me fatigued!" she chastised them. At another point, she proclaimed, "How anyone can want to be anything but thin is beyond my intelligence."

Peters's prescription itself was fairly simple. Readers needed to adhere to a 1,200-calorie-a-day diet that was roughly 10 percent to 15 percent protein, 25 percent to 30 percent fat, and 60 percent to 65 percent carbohydrates. She also recommended drinking at least one large glass of water a day. Although she believed it was "practically impossible" to reduce through exercise alone, she prescribed about fifteen minutes of daily physical exertion—either walking or her own regimen of bend-and-stretch exercises, illustrated in the book with stick figures. The key principle was that dieters needed to measure and limit their caloric intake. "Hereafter you are going to eat calories of food," she wrote. "Instead of saying one slice of bread or a piece of pie, you will say 100 calories of bread, 350 calories of pie." She made it easier by advising readers to eat 100-calorie portions, and including charts that showed how much of each food amounted to 100 calories. (According to dieting historian Schwartz, Peters seems to have borrowed the idea from Yale professor Irving Fisher, who devised a similar but less publicized 100-calorie regimen in 1906.)

Once readers had achieved the desired weight loss, Peters did allow them to relent on her stringent regimen—but only slightly. She was one of the first weight-loss gurus to emphasize the notion that staying slim required a long-term commitment and permanent lifestyle changes. "You might as well recognize now, and accept it as a fact, that neither you nor anybody else will be able to eat beyond your needs without accumulating fat, or disease, or both," she warned. She advised every dieter to punctuate the lifetime struggle with an occasional fast, "to show you are the master" of the stomach. She also gave fashion and beauty tips—advising women, for example, on how to massage their necks to avoid double chins.

Peters could get away with her tough-talking approach without offending readers because she readily admitted that she was a former fat person herself. ("My idea of heaven is a place with me and mine on a cloud of whipped cream," she noted.) She was a lot like the preacher who strives to connect with converts by admitting to having once been a sinner. (It hardly was an accident that Peters's book title closely resembled that of Christian Science founder Mary Baker Eddy's 1875 book *Science and Health, With Key to the Scriptures*.) The gospel Peters preached to women was a secular one.

She sold that message with great success. As *Diet and Health* climbed the best-seller lists, Peters found herself in demand. She wrote a syndicated diet column that was published in the *Los Angeles Times* and other papers, and dashed off articles for *Colliers, Ladies' Home Journal*, and a new magazine called the *Health Builder*. By 1923, she had given up her medical practice to become a full-time writer, and in 1924 published a second book, *Diet for Children (and Adults) and the Kalorie Kids*. Her career was cut short in 1930, when she became ill while sailing across the Atlantic to attend a medical convention, and died of pneumonia in London.

In the decades that followed Peters's fame quickly faded, but her calorie-counting method and unforgiving approach to weight loss took on a life of its own. Perhaps inadvertently, the diet doctor had introduced the notion that to be thin is beautiful, and to be beautiful one must suffer. Others would pick up that philosophy and take it to extremes. Even before her death, other physicians had begun to prescribe even stricter diets for patients, and by the 1930s some were limiting them to as little as 400 calories a day, with a menu so sparse that it starved them of vital nutrients. Others tried new gimmick diets devised by hustlers who tried to capitalize on Peters's success. One such fad was the Hollywood Diet, a 585-calorie daily menu that consisted of grapefruits, oranges, melba toast, green vegetables, and hard-boiled eggs. Other dubious regimens were developed by William H. Hay, who insisted that carbohydrates, fats, and proteins had to be eaten separately, and by Gayelord Hauser, who promoted dietary supplements such as brewer's yeast and wheat germ. (His followers included film star Greta Garbo.)

But if the fad approaches didn't work, or Peters's calorie counting seemed too complicated, women of the time simply resorted to lettuce-and-coffee starvation diets. Meanwhile, the excessive, compulsive calorie cutting began to take a toll on women's health. By the late 1930s, one psychiatrist had begun to note a rise in cases of anorexia nervosa, a psychological disorder in which victims literally starved themselves to death.

The obsession abated during World War II, when rationing and shortages turned eating into a precious source of comfort against stress. But in the 1950s, women's magazines again began touting the idea of calorie counting and the virtues of slimness, and *Newsweek* exposed the "Fat Personality"—i.e., the notion that women consumed rich foods to compensate for boredom, unhappiness, and unsatisfying sex lives. In 1959, the *New York Times* proclaimed that 90 percent of significantly overweight people owed their condition to psychological problems. By the 1960s, super-skinny model Twiggy became the rage, and weight loss—sometimes with the help of appetite-suppressing amphetamines—had regained its status as a feminine obsession.

By the early twenty-first century, an estimated 40 percent to 50 percent of American women were on reducing diets. The sale of diet books, food supplements, and other slimming products had turned into a $40-billion-a-year industry. Americans determined to shed pounds consumed three billion doses each year of ephedra, a dietary supplement with stimulant properties, despite the fact that medical researchers had linked its use to dozens of deaths. Still, the struggle for slimness often ended in failure. According to the National Eating Disorders Association, 95 percent of dieters regained the lost weight, and more, within five years. It's a legacy with which Peters no doubt would be disappointed.

THE OPERATIVE NUMBER: 1,718
*Number of books available on Web-based bookstore
Amazon.com that have something to do with "weight loss,"
based on a search for that term in February 2003.*

You Want *More*?

- *Never Satisfied: A Cultural History of Diets, Fantasies, and Fat*, by Hillel Schwartz, Free Press, New York, 1986.

Weight-Loss Shakes

❧

Peters's austere, bland, calorie-counting diet might have worked, but it was something less than pleasurable, and it required considerable self-discipline and persistence. Not surprisingly, generations of diet gurus have sought to tantalize Americans with easy, effort-free reducing methods.

In the 1950s, for example, a popular nationwide chain of salons offered a quick, easy solution for excess pounds: shaking them away. Clients would lie on mechanized tables that shook and jiggled their bodies, with the idea that the fat deposits in their abdomens and elsewhere would be jarred loose and carried away by the bloodstream, to be burned up for energy.

It's not possible to "spot" reduce in such a fashion—except through surgery—but nevertheless, thousands of women visited the salons each day for a quick jiggle, before a tax dispute ultimately forced them out of business. Decades later, mail-order companies continued to peddle vibrating belts, along with dubious gadgets such as plastic weight-loss wraps and special "sauna suits" that trapped wearers' body heat, with the idea of helping them to sweat away unwanted pounds.

- *Fat History: Bodies and Beauty in the Modern West*, by Peter N. Stearns, New York University Press, New York, 1997.
- *Never Too Thin: Why Women Are at War with Their Bodies*, by Roberta Pollack Seid, Prentice Hall Press, New York, 1989.
- "The Art of Wishful Shrinking Has Made a Lot of People Rich," by Donald Dale Jackson, *Smithsonian*, November 1994.
- "Living Off the Fat of the Land," by Michael Fumento, *Washington Monthly*, January–February 1998.

Alfred Kinsey's Honeymoon

*His research on human sexuality changed the way the world
thought about sex. But long before that, in 1921, he faced an
important moment of truth.*

SEX, FOR MOST MEN, isn't a career option. Alfred Charles Kinsey,
on the other hand, vigorously pursued a lifelong infatuation with
sex to become one of the most influential figures in American history. He was so successful at blending his personal and professional
passions that he remains a hero to many men, including Hugh
Hefner, the founding publisher of *Playboy*, who considered Kinsey a
sort of libidinous Neil Armstrong.

Kinsey was a superb, if obscure, research biologist at Indiana
University who for the first two decades of his career focused on the
study of a tiny plant-eating insect, the gall wasp. We now know,
however, that much more than pure science was going on under the
great man's lab coat. Thanks to two weighty biographies published
in the late 1990s, we also know that Kinsey's carefully cultivated

public image as a detached scientist masked the torment of a fero-ciously repressed bisexual voyeur who was uniquely qualified for his late-life career as a sex researcher. That second career, which biog-rapher James H. Jones says Kinsey "approached with missionary fervor," allowed the onetime bug collector to spend his final two de-cades asking intimate questions of thousands of men and women, recording the often arcane details of their sexual histories into a statistical snapshot of mid-century lust, measuring body parts, filming various sexual adventures and anomalies in his attic, even sharing his willing wife with his grad students, all in the name of science.

Today, a man once considered a no-nonsense academic some-times comes across as a creep with credentials, like the guy who, after fondling a stranger's breasts in a bar, explains, "It's OK, I'm a doctor."

But, as Jones wrote in the preface to his nearly one-thousand-page 1997 biography, *Alfred C. Kinsey: A Public/Private Life*, "much of Kinsey's spring-coil vitality can be traced to the inner conflicts and tensions that resulted from secrets he kept hidden from the world, secrets that began in childhood and have remained unknown to all but a few down to the present."

One of those secrets—perhaps the one that ultimately convinced Kinsey to pull back the curtain on human sexuality—was his calami-tous honeymoon.

Kinsey's private life was the subject of much speculation when his landmark studies on male and female sexuality were released in 1948 and 1953, respectively, and landed him on both the best-seller lists and the cover of *Time* magazine. The 1948 report on men—an unlikely hit, packed as it was with graphs, statistical matrices, and desert-dry prose—was denounced by everyone from Billy Graham ("It is impossible to estimate the damage the book will do to the already deteriorating morals of America.") to Margaret Mead ("The book suggests no way of choosing between a woman and a sheep."), but even critics perceived Kinsey as a dispassionate, clipboard-toting statistician. Author and social critic Joseph Epstein wrote that admirers considered the first of Kinsey's studies "in the same class as *Principia Mathematica*, *The Wealth of Nations*, or *Das Kapital*. He was often compared to Galileo, Copernicus, and Freud, scientists who similarly had struggled against an obtuse and belligerent public to bring the truth to light."

The truth, as Kinsey's research suggested, was that ordinary Americans were enjoying a smorgasbord of sexual possibilities, not just the socially prescribed grin-and-bear-it duty of marital intercourse. After crunching the numbers he gathered during years of prodigious Rockefeller Foundation—funded research, Kinsey concluded in 1948 that: the vast majority of American men had sex before marriage; 50 percent had sex with someone other than their wife during marriage; 92 percent of them had masturbated; 59 percent had performed cunnilingus; 69 percent had hired a prostitute; and 37 percent had had at least a single homosexual encounter that ended in orgasm. The homosexuality conclusion alone was enough to trigger fevered hand-wringing in Congress and the media—in those Red Scare years, homosexuals were considered a security risk because of the threat of communist blackmail—and convince FBI director J. Edgar Hoover to launch a program to rid the federal government of "sex deviates."

By the time Kinsey released his 1953 report on female sexuality—concluding, among other things, that 62 percent of woman enjoyed sex enough to masturbate, half of them had engaged in premarital sex, and 13 percent had had at least one orgasmic lesbian experience—Kinsey had become what Jones called "the high priest of sexual liberation." Debate continues about the quality of Kinsey's conclusions and the research methods he used to draw them, but no one denies their lasting impact on a culture so sexually mute that even the *New York Times* chronicled it until the mid-1960s without ever once using the word "penis."

In many ways, though, Kinsey's transformation from bow-tied lab dork into the twentieth century's sexual lightning rod began two decades before, during his honeymoon in June 1921. It was during that trip with his new bride, Clara Bracken McMillen, or "Mac," that the various strands of Kinsey's life began knotting together in a way that profoundly influenced his later work and continues to shape presumptions, views, and attitudes about sex in the twenty-first century.

To understand why that particular moment in Kinsey's life was so pivotal, it's first important to understand the personal demons with which Kinsey was struggling at the time he and McMillen married. Born in 1894 in a particularly grim working-class area of Hoboken, New Jersey, Kinsey was raised by Methodist parents who practiced a fierce brand of Protestant evangelism. As their oldest child, Kinsey grew up beneath the gaze of a god who knew all, saw all, and punished sinners swiftly and without mercy. Kinsey's father—"pompous," by more than one account—was so strict about religious observance that, according to Jones, he once ordered one of Kinsey's aunts from their home for playing the piano on a Sunday afternoon.

Puberty must have been hell for a kid who, perpetually poor and dogged by illness during childhood, was already in a deep hole in terms of self-esteem. Rickets left young Alfred swaybacked and potbellied. Rheumatic fever damaged his heart, making his parents overprotective. His mother claimed his bout with typhoid fever rid him of the rheumatic fever germs, but it also put her son in bed for nine weeks and nearly killed him. Forever the outsider at school, Kinsey's grades suffered and he spent a *lot* of time with those repressive parents, longing for independence.

During that same period of his life, Kinsey, like most children, began experimenting sexually with some of the neighborhood kids. In a mixed group of six boys and girls in the basement of someone's home, Kinsey felt the first prickle of sexual curiosity and attraction—and, always, the unblinking stare of an angry god for having done so.

Life improved for Kinsey after his family moved to South Orange, a suburb of Newark, in 1904. He became an honor-roll high school student, and his health problems vanished. En route to becoming an Eagle Scout he became an avid outdoorsman, and he developed an interest in biology and a lifelong love of field research. He collected things with a passion, including records and stamps, and was described in his yearbook as "a second Darwin" because of his interest in biology. Kinsey was valedictorian of his high school class in 1912.

Nonetheless, we can safely assume that a young man who labored through high school known as "a second Darwin" was not considered a major campus beefcake. Even after he pursued his interest in biology to Harvard, Kinsey apparently managed to grad-uate with his Ph.D. in biology in 1919 without ever having had a date. Although an enthusiastic self-abuser (in more ways than one—reports of Kinsey's nontraditional use of a toothbrush suggest that he was a bit of a masochist), Kinsey corralled his sexual urges, for men and women, into the monastic lifestyle of a serious student.

The Alfred Kinsey who arrived on the Indiana University cam-pus in Bloomington in the late summer of 1920 was both a newly minted twenty-six-year-old junior professor of biology and a bub-bling cauldron of sexual confusion. At an age when his peers were dating and marrying—and at a time when the federal government was jailing sexual pioneers such as Margaret Sanger, who opened America's first birth-control clinic in 1916—Kinsey continued to struggle with his attraction to men, knowing that the impulse made him a social pariah. Soon after settling into his new job, though, Kinsey began dating Clara, a somewhat boyish junior-year chem-istry major who shared Kinsey's fondness for nature. On their first Christmas as a couple, Kinsey took a peculiar stab at romance, giv-ing Clara a compass, a hunting knife, and a pair of Bass hiking shoes. He proposed two months after their first date, and they married on June 3, 1921, in a simple ceremony at her grandparents' home in Brookville, Indiana.

The wedding, to which the couple came as virgins, was the start of a remarkable sexual journey that would last until Kinsey's death in 1956—a disastrously false start, it turned out.

Kinsey approached their union feeling he had much to prove, manhoodwise, and he planned to prove it on their honeymoon. He chose the great outdoors as the venue for their first coupling, perhaps because nature was the one arena in which Kinsey was supremely confident. After perfunctory visits to Niagara Falls and New Jersey to visit Kinsey's parents, they struck out for an extended assault on the peaks of New England's White Mountains that many now believe Kinsey engineered as a personal test for his new bride—and for himself.

"The weather in the White Mountains can be hell in June, and [that] June it was fearsome—with tremendous winds, snow storms, hail, and rain," wrote Jonathan Gathorne-Hardy in his equally exhaustive 1998 Kinsey biography, *Sex, the Measure of All Things*. "One imagines the whole fraught situation, enacted on mountainsides in blizzards, was not helped by anxiety and inhibition on both their parts." Nonetheless, the couple hiked, camped in lean-to shelters, and ate from the food packages that Kinsey carefully prepared (he even pitted the prunes to reduce weight) and shipped ahead to drop points. Kinsey anticipated their lovemaking with equal zeal. Wrote Gathorne-Hardy: "One senses in Kinsey's progress at this point desperate eagerness—and desperate anxiety."

In matters sexual, neither eagerness nor anxiety serve a man well. But, it turns out, those were only part of the problem. Not only were their fumbling attempts at lovemaking hampered by their lack of sex education, but they repeatedly were foiled by a relatively common physical condition: Mac had a thickened hymen that prevented penetration. Years later Kinsey confided to a friend that during the honeymoon—and for two months afterward while Kinsey taught nature study at a girls' camp in Vermont—he and Mac were unable to consummate their marriage.

Although Mac's physical problem was later corrected with minor surgery, both Jones and Gathorne-Hardy concluded that those teeth-grinding early months together were critical in shaping Kinsey's later work. It's easy to hear echoes of personal experience in the words Kinsey used to describe the sexual awkwardness of marriage in one of his fabled reports more than two decades later. Suddenly, he wrote, "husband and wife are supposed to break down all inhibitions. Unfortunately, there is no magic in the marriage ceremony which can accomplish this . . . a very high proportion of females [and] considerable number of males . . . find this very difficult. It can take years to get rid of these learnt inhibitions."

It also took Kinsey years to channel the difficult lessons of his honeymoon into scientific research, but that experience was undeniably significant among those that "both twisted and steeled" the scientist's personality, Jones wrote. "Kinsey clearly was a product of Victorian culture's power to shape and contort character," and he later "translated his inner conflicts and anxieties into a powerful critique of Victorian morality and worked tirelessly to promote sexual liberation."

By the early 1930s, Kinsey was obsessing about sex in letters to a former student named Ralph Voris, upon whom, many believe, Kinsey developed a schoolboy crush. On April 1, 1935, he delivered a lecture called "Biological Aspects of Some Social Problems" to his faculty discussion group in which Kinsey offered a passionate discourse on the importance of sex in human affairs. It was the first public indication that he wanted to use science—the greatest weapon he commanded—to attack the conventional morality that had caused him so much pain.

Three years later, while teaching a controversial university course on marriage (reserved, naturally, for engaged or married students), Kinsey said he first realized how many couples were just as sexually ignorant as he and Mac had been. (Kinsey was not known for his sense of humor, but during one lecture he reportedly asked a female student to name the body part that can enlarge a hundred times. "You have no right to ask me such a question in a mixed class," she replied. Kinsey responded: "I was referring to the pupil of the eye, and you, young lady, are in for a terrible disappointment.") In 1940, Kinsey approached Indiana University's president to help him fund a full-time institute dedicated to sex research, and the Kinsey Institute for Research in Sex, Gender, and Reproduction was up and running by 1947—the same year that the Indianapolis police department labeled comic books, with their shapely superheroes, "vicious, salacious, immoral, and detrimental to the youth of the nation."

Kinsey's 1948 report on male sexuality was followed in short order by an avalanche of change. By 1950, Margaret Sanger had organized funding for research into an oral contraceptive that along with penicillin ultimately made the sexual revolution practical. (It's significant, perhaps, that public officials did not consider arresting her a viable deterrent at that point.) The following year, homosexuals emboldened by Kinsey's study founded the Mattachine Society, devoted to "the protection and improvement of Society's Androgynous Minority." That same year the paperback of J. D. Salinger's classic *The Catcher in the Rye* was published and, with narrator Holden Caulfield's extended discourse on alienation and sex, all hell broke loose.

Former G.I. George Jorgensen underwent the first sex change operation in 1952, becoming Christine Jorgensen, and in 1953, the year Kinsey released his study of female sexuality, Hefner published the first issue of *Playboy* featuring a photo spread of a nude Marilyn Monroe. In 1955, lesbians organized as the Daughters of Bilitis. In 1956—the year Kinsey died—Elvis Presley stepped boldly onto Ed Sullivan's stage and *Peyton Place* was a surprise best-seller. The American publication of *Lolita* followed two years later. By the time the FDA approved the first birth-control pill in 1960, Kinsey's genie wasn't just out of the bottle but was looking for pleasurable ways to use it.

One of Alfred Kinsey's most liberating ideas was the so-called

Kinsey Scale, which was his attempt to quantify an individual's sexual nature and gender preference on a scale of 0 to 6. Instead of looking at a person as either entirely heterosexual or entirely homosexual, the scale, first developed in 1939, offered shades of gray that many feel helped lift the social stigma of homosexuality from the generations that followed.

A 0 rating identified you as totally heterosexual; a 6 rating identified you as totally homosexual. If you were a 3, you were a perfectly balanced bisexual who, as Woody Allen once said, had effectively doubled the odds of getting a date. Ratings of 1, 2, 4, and 5 suggested preferences one way or the other, but a certain lack of commitment. The scale seems a crude measuring device by today's standards, but many homosexuals at the time found great comfort—and courage—in the notion that they were closeted with an estimated twenty million men considered 4s, 5s, and 6s.

Kinsey biographer Jonathan Gathorne-Hardy asked Paul H. Gebhard, who succeeded Kinsey as director of the institute, to apply the scale to Kinsey's own life. He wrote that at the time Kinsey and his bride embarked on their sexually disastrous honeymoon, Gebhard viewed Kinsey as "a 1, perhaps edging toward a 2, on the scale (predominantly heterosexual, but incidental homosexual experience or psychic response)."

By the time Kinsey transitioned from the study of gall wasps into the study of human sexuality in the late 1930s, Gebhard said Kinsey was probably a 3. By the time his first study was released in 1948, Gathorne-Hardy wrote, Gebhard believed that Kinsey was a 4, clearly moving toward the homosexual end of the scale.

But there he remained.

While critics claim Kinsey's sexual preferences skewed his research, it also may have enabled him to approach it with a more open mind. As Gathorne-Hardy noted, Kinsey, as a bisexual, was in "an almost ideal position . . . for someone who was studying sexual behavior in both sexes."

Though they stumbled out of the gate, Kinsey and Mac enjoyed a long and fruitful marriage, as well as a robust and unconventional sex life. They had four children, one of whom died before the age of four, and by all accounts Kinsey was a devoted father. He still found time to pursue a wide range of sexual interests, and some still wonder why he did so much of his research in prisons and gay bars. Kinsey was gone a lot, and Mac was often lonely, but she was supportive to a fault. Together, according to Kinsey's biographers, they often used the attic of their home to stage illustrative sexual tableaux.

For example, a well-known novelist who used to visit the Kinseys in Bloomington once confided to Kinsey that his orgasms were so intense that his body jackknifed at the moment of climax. Kinsey asked permission to film this event, so off they went to the attic so that the writer and his lover could demonstrate. When they were done, according to Jones, Kinsey's wife "popped into the room with a tray of refreshments, along with clean towels so they could freshen up." This was not unusual. At the conclusion of still other filming sessions, according to Gebhard, Kinsey's successor at the institute, Mac "would suddenly appear, literally with persimmon pudding or milk and cookies or something."

Wrote Epstein in his review of the Jones biography: "Has social science ever seemed so, well, social?"

THE OPERATIVE NUMBER: 0

Number of times that fabled sex researcher Alfred C. Kinsey and his wife, Clara, had sex during the first months after their 1921 marriage.

The Kinsey Collections

During his two decades researching the ant-sized gall wasp, Alfred Kinsey, a relentless collector, assembled what remains the largest single collection of insects in the American Museum of Natural History. Of the nearly eighteen million insects in the museum's entomological collections, more than five million are gall wasps collected by Kinsey, many during a yearlong postdoctoral fellowship during which he traversed 36 states and, in the process, logged more than 18,000 miles—2,500 of them on foot.

When Kinsey later turned his scientific attention to sex, his prodigious collecting continued. Today the Kinsey Institute on the Bloomington campus of Indiana University houses the largest conglomeration of erotica in the world. According to Jonathan Gathorne-Hardy, author of an epic 1998 Kinsey biography, the collection he saw was packed into three rooms at the institute. Even if you don't count the material in the institute's unrivaled erotica library, he wrote that the collected material includes:

- a medieval chastity belt
- paintings and etchings by Renoir, Picasso, Matisse, and Chagall
- forty-five thousand processed photographs and thirty thousand unprocessed ones neatly boxed and cataloged (in code) as to physical positions and sexual acts
- numerous statues of copulating couples
- dildos of every size, shape, and color
- one Dingwall's condom in its original eighteenth-century wrapper, and some in condom-shaped vacuum flasks
- erotic toys, including one from which a young rooster springs out and mounts a hen

- various masturbating machines
- books with secret panels for lascivious material
- an 1880s photograph of two dapper gentlemen in tweed, one masturbating the other as they stand in a field
- fifty-five boxes of prison art, crude cartoons, and "comic strip narratives of desperate wish fulfillment"
- Chinese erotic scrolls and paintings "with great, wrinkled genitalia and twinings of indescribable intricacy"

"In a material sense, the collection is in one way the most successful of Kinsey's enterprises," Gathorne-Hardy concluded. "As I write, it is about to be valued for insurance, estimates varying between $20 million and $40 million."

You Want *More*?

- *Alfred C. Kinsey: A Public/Private Life*, by James H. Jones, W. W. Norton & Company, New York, 1997.
- *Sex, the Measure of All Things: A Life of Alfred C. Kinsey*, by Jonathan Gathorne-Hardy, Indiana University Press, Bloomington, Ind., 1998.
- www.indiana.edu/~kinsey, the Web site of the Kinsey Institute for Research in Sex, Gender, and Reproduction.

The Rise of Tacky Chic

*In the early 1930s a former billboard artist rediscovered the
ancient technique of painting on black velvet. What followed
was a golden era of bad taste.*

THE PRECISE DATE THAT TACKY CHIC began is, unfortunately,
lost to history. But as one version of the story goes, it was sometime
between 1930 and 1933, in the city of Papeete on the island of
Tahiti, when an American expatriate painter named Edgar Leeteg
walked into a shop that sold art supplies. Though he was just five-
feet-three-inches tall, a bit pudgy, and something less than well
groomed, Leeteg nevertheless considered himself quite a Lothario
(he once boasted in a letter that he had sex with "a goodly number"
of his female models). As was Leeteg's habit, he flirted with the
young Chinese woman behind the counter. Then he asked her to sell
him some monk's cloth, a type of canvas. "I need it to paint on," he
explained.

"We're all out of monk's cloth," the clerk told him. At that moment—preserved for posterity in James Michener's and A. Grove Day's 1957 nonfiction book, *Rascals in Paradise*—it seemed that Leeteg's goal of becoming a successful artist had suffered yet another setback. He'd arrived in Tahiti a year or so before, equipped with a handful of brushes and some mayonnaise jars filled with paint that he'd stolen from his last employer, a Sacramento outdoor sign company. Though Leeteg had no formal art training, he'd developed the ability to copy human figures from photographs and enlarge them on billboards, and he had a vague notion of plying that trade in the far more alluring surroundings of the South Pacific. But job opportunities proved sparse, and Leeteg's penchant for spending his nights drinking and skirt chasing hadn't exactly helped his prospects. He found himself nearly penniless, reduced to peddling cheap artworks to sailors in bars. Now he didn't even have canvas on which to paint. How could his luck get any worse?

Then the clerk, on the verge of losing a sale, suddenly remembered that the shop's owner had been pushing her to unload an overstock of another type of fabric. "How about some velveteen?" she asked. "Could you paint on that?"

If the clerk had an inkling of the twisted aesthetic that ultimately would spring from her chance suggestion, she might well have urged Leeteg to blow his remaining funds on another boozy binge. Instead, over the next several decades, the simulated knotty-pine walls of working-class and lower-middle-class suburban dens and rumpus rooms across America would come to be adorned with bad black-velvet paintings—myriad images of improbably buxom bare-breasted women, weeping clowns, anthropomorphized canines engaged in gambling, crude copies of Leonardo da Vinci's "The Last Supper," and portraits of Elvis Presley in the full bloom of his latter-day, jumpsuit-straining corpulence. Among the educated and sophisticated segment of society, some called it kitsch, from the German word *verkitschen*, or "to make cheap." Others simply labeled it bad taste because of the cloying nature of the subject material, the often clumsy technical execution, and the colors that glowed like the Bikini Atoll in the wake of an H-bomb detonation, thanks to the fabric's unusual ability to intensify paint hues.

But what really made the intelligentsia chuckle, sneer, and cringe was the way those qualities combined in a perverse synergy that elevated black velvet above Roman brothel frescoes, Victorian bric-a-brac, and other previous affronts to high culture throughout history. Bad black velvet was the visual equivalent of fingernails scraping a blackboard.

This evil twin of modern art simply was too vivid to be ignored. And too popular, in part because it reflected postwar American society in a way that Abstract Expressionism and other genres favored by the cultural avant-garde did not. The market for Tacky Chic was created by postwar America's sudden affluence, in which more people than ever before owned homes—and had more disposable income with which to decorate them. It exemplified the stubbornly egalitarian nature of ordinary Americans, who refused to bow to what professors, bohemian rebels, and the wealthy museum-endowing class told them was art. And if it looked mass-produced and disposable, well, that made it an even more telling symbol of a postwar economic boom built upon ever increasing consumption.

As the ancient Romans were fond of noting, *de gustibus non est disputandum*—roughly, "there is no accounting for taste"—and indeed, the debate over what is tasteful versus what is tacky has engaged humanity throughout history. For centuries, the wealthy and educated minority were the final arbiters, largely because they were the only ones who could afford the luxury of owning art or taking the time to think about it.

But the elite's control of taste was broken in the 1800s by the rise of industrial technologies that made mass production possible. Not only did economic growth give working- and middle-class people a little more money to spend, but entrepreneurs realized that the same methods used to mass-produce barrels or brooms could be used to make figurines, prints, and other bric-a-brac to decorate ordinary people's homes. As art and popular culture historian Peter Ward notes in his book *Kitsch in Sync*, the trend so alarmed the elite that in Great Britain, Prince Albert and other self-styled aesthetes organized the Great Exhibition of 1851 in an attempt to teach the masses what to buy. Their effort ultimately proved futile—in part because it spread the notion that a person qualified as having good taste simply by buying the right things. Manufacturers could easily churn out tacky items designed to make people feel tasteful. That category included engravings of the work of nineteenth-century English painter Sir John Everett Millais, a once acclaimed member of the pre-Raphaelite movement who gave up the pursuit of artistic purity in order to make money painting excruciatingly sentimental but highly popular child portraits. (According to a biographical sketch of Millais on the Web site www.preraphaelites.co.uk, he was denounced by one critic of the time, William Morris, as a "genius bought and sold and thrown away.")

Meanwhile, across the Atlantic, Americans—inventive pioneers that they are—proved even more adept at mass-produced tackiness. In the 1880s, factories full of painters churned out oil paintings of mountains, lakes, and waterfalls that were sold for as little as thirty-five cents apiece. Some of the factory artists produced twenty-five such works a day, and the reputed king of high-speed painting, Gustav Klatt, supposedly could dash off a landscape in eight minutes. In St. Paul, Minnesota, the printing firm of Brown & Bigelow came up with an even more insidious concept. The company hired well-known illustrators and painters such as Norman Rockwell and Maxfield Parrish to create sentimental or humorous works that would be reproduced on calendars, blotters, playing cards, and other items that businesses gave to customers.

Of all the work that Brown & Bigelow commissioned, however,

the images that have lingered irrepressibly are the ones created by an obscure painter named Cassius Marcellus Coolidge. According to a piece by art historian Moira F. Harris in *Antiques & Collectibles* magazine, Coolidge was born in 1844 to a family of well-to-do farmers in the upstate New York town of Philadelphia, and became an inveterate dabbler whose various ventures included drugstores, a newspaper, a bank, and a sign-painting business. Though a ne'er-do-well in commerce, Coolidge clearly was a man of ideas, albeit strange ones. He once wrote a comic opera about mosquito infestation in New Jersey, and apparently invented the photographic caricature, a carnival staple in which a customer's photo is taken while sticking his or her head through a hole in a large painted scene. In the 1880s, Coolidge moved to New York City to embark on yet another career, this time as an artist, and finally began to enjoy some success, doing artwork for cigar boxes and a whimsical advertising poster for a bicycle company that featured a monkey and a parrot going for a ride. But Coolidge's true gift, as revealed in his sixteen paintings for Brown & Bigelow between 1906 and his death in 1934, was for depicting dogs engaging in human activities. Coolidge's anthropomorphism wasn't in the adorable Tom-Kitten-and-Benjamin-Bunny mode of children's book author and illustrator Beatrix Potter. Instead, Coolidge's canines prefer the pastimes and vices of early-twentieth-century American middle-class males. They play baseball, tinker with broken-down automobiles, smoke and drink, carouse on New Year's Eve, deceive their wives about their comings and goings, argue angrily, and even file lawsuits against one another. Coolidge's most famous painting, "A Friend in Need," depicts seven dogs of various breeds playing what apparently is five-card draw poker; in the foreground, a stogie-chomping English bulldog surreptitiously is helping another bulldog cheat the larger breeds, by using his rear left paw to pass him a card under the table.

On first glance, and in many ways, "A Friend in Need" might seem like the ultimate masterpiece of bad art, from the anatomically incorrect limbs on the otherwise realistic canine bodies, to the crass exploitation of the sentimental urge to imagine Rover and Fluffy as having human thoughts, desires, and motives (rather than as, say, domesticated descendants of wolves who might well enjoy devouring us if we were a more convenient size). One problem with this interpretation, however, is the possibility that Coolidge—who, as the author of a libretto about insects, most certainly possessed an offbeat sense of humor—actually may have intended it as satire. After all, if the dogs are replaced with French noblewomen, "A Friend in Need" bears an uncanny resemblance to "The Cheat With the Ace of Diamonds," a 1647 painting by Georges La Tour, who sought to expose the moral turpitude of the upper classes.

"It's a humorous, ironic take, a jab at middle-class America," Alison Cooney, a specialist at Sotheby's auction house, explained to the *New York Times* in 2002. If that's indeed so, the real irony is that Coolidge's sly commentary went over the heads of his audience; where he intended sarcasm, they saw only cuteness. At Coolidge's death in 1934, his obituary in a local paper reported that "he painted many pictures of dogs" during his career. Decades later, Coolidge's canines would resurface again in countless flea markets and shopping mall poster shops throughout the land, as schlock icons rendered on black velvet. That all was made possible by the tacky revolution that Edgar Leeteg helped launch.

Although Leeteg may have stumbled upon black velvet painting by accident, he didn't invent it. The Chinese used the plush fabric as an art medium as far back as the 1200s, and a century later, Marco Polo saw black velvet paintings in India. In Victorian England, black-velvet painting became a pleasant diversion for society matrons, who probably were oblivious to the textile workers driven to madness by the mercury then used in the cloth's manufacture. Few serious modern artists worked with it, in part because velvet had a tendency to soak up paint like a sponge and then cake grotesquely, until a landscape or scene started to resemble an aging hooker's makeup. But Leeteg, who as a youth in Illinois had seen a few Renaissance-era velvet paintings in a museum, had an epiphany. He figured out that thin, light strokes across the fabric would keep the paint from soaking in too deep. His first efforts were female nudes, which had obvious appeal to his drunken-sailor clientele. He sold them for as little as four dollars apiece.

The father of bad black velvet probably would have continued to eke out a living with his depictions of nubile island maidens were it not for a Salt Lake City jeweler named Wayne Decker. According to Michener's and Day's account, Decker happened upon several of Leeteg's velvets in a junk shop in Honolulu while he was vacationing there with his family, and was so taken by Leeteg's work that he subsequently tracked down the artist in Tahiti. Leeteg agreed to do four paintings for Decker, for two hundred dollars and the Hawaiian shirt that the jeweler was wearing. Decker eventually became Leeteg's major patron—the Cosimo de' Medici of black velvet, as it were—giving him a standing order to "send us one of everything you paint." "Edgar, you are the greatest living artist in the world," Decker once wrote to him, in a letter quoted in Michener's book. "I want everyone to see you as great as I do."

Decker's support kept Leeteg going for the next fifteen years, until Leeteg had another stroke of good fortune. A former drinking buddy, an accordion-playing submarine sailor named Barney Davis, moved to Honolulu in 1947 and opened a small art gallery. His customers, who mostly were fellow sailors, kept coming in and asking for velvet paintings like one they'd seen in a certain seedy local bar. Davis went over to inspect it, and discovered that his old pal was the artist. Davis concocted a publicity campaign for Leeteg, dubbing him "the American Gauguin," after the late nineteenth-century giant of French art who had also made his home in Tahiti (though other than a fondness for alcohol, the similarities ended there). Davis helped create the impression that Leeteg was a master by jacking up the price of his paintings, charging thousands of dollars for work that the artist once would have sold for the price of a few drinks. It worked, and by the early 1950s Davis was doing a brisk trade in Leeteg originals. Tiki bars and restaurants were springing up in places like Detroit and Buffalo to capitalize on the popularity of the musical *South Pacific* and on the nostalgia of World War II veterans who'd served in the islands, and many of those establishments bought Leeteg paintings for their decor. Before long, Leeteg could afford to equip his home on Tahiti with an out-house lined with Italian marble and scented by French perfumes. The artist, who in a letter quoted in Michener's book explained that "as long as I'm rutting and drinking I'm not dead," routinely picked up the tab for an entourage on his all-night drinking and carousing marathons and had accumulated multiple mistresses.

Despite Leeteg's sudden wealth, he groused over his lack of acceptance by the art establishment. "Please don't bother submitting any of my work to art societies or museums, as I hold them in contempt," he wrote to Davis, in a letter quoted in Michener's book "Rembrandt and Reubens would get the brush-off if they approached the art guys with their works today." It wasn't just that painting competitions rejected his entries. Some people questioned whether he was an artist at all, suggesting that he merely projected slides of photographs onto velvet and colored them in with an airbrush, like a child following a paint-by-numbers kit. As a result, U.S. customs officials classified his work as mass-produced decorations rather than fine art, and slapped heavy duties on them. (They eventually relented, but only after an art expert visited Leeteg's studio in Tahiti and offered a sworn affidavit that he actually painted his work freehand.) Leeteg's protests were undercut by his assembly-line method. He and Davis established a numerical code for his most popular subjects, so that if Leeteg got a telegram requesting six copies of number 118, he knew to churn out a portrait of a particular Tahitian maiden. He was willing to alter his work to make a purchaser happy. In one instance, for example, he agreed to paint 118 with larger breasts than usual, for an extra fee. He dubbed the resulting work "Girl with the Four-Gallon Tits."

What the artist lacked in subtlety, he made up for with prolific production. At the time of his death in 1953 in a motorcycle accident, Leeteg had dashed off an astonishing 1,700 paintings, an output nearly one-and-a-half times the size of the entire collection of work by American painters in New York's Metropolitan Museum of Art.

Even after Leeteg's demise, black velvet art continued to proliferate. It was cheap and could be made quickly, and the crude images that often resulted glowed with an almost hypnotic intensity—particularly if the viewer was in a darkened room and at least slightly intoxicated. Highbrow critics railed against such mass-produced art—Dwight Macdonald, in his 1953 essay "A Theory of Mass Culture" called it "a cancerous growth on High Culture"—but those warnings went largely unheeded. As Massachusetts Institute of Technology cognition researcher Steven Pinker once explained in a newspaper interview, black velvet art stimulates brain circuitry, unchanged since prehistoric times, that responds to color. "Many of us copy taste from people who we see as prestigious," Pinker said. "We disdain tastes from people who we deem as part of the masses. When you have that factor along with the fact that we have these built-in pleasure circuits, that's why you get people liking black velvet paintings who are too embarrassed to admit they like the things."

By the early 1960s, black velvet paintings had become so popular that a toy manufacturer even marketed a paint-by-numbers kit, whose package blurb suggested—undoubtedly, to the horror of highbrow culture critics—that it would help introduce children to "culture." But most consumers of Tacky Chic preferred to buy it ready-made. Production of black velvet art already had shifted from Tahiti to Mexico. Doyle Harden, an El Paso, Texas—based businessman, began buying truckloads of velvet and shipping it across the border to Juárez, a city that became to black velvet what

Florence was to the Renaissance. Mexican artists, working in art factories at a piece rate of a few dollars per painting, each produced as many as ten works per day. The tiki motif was supplanted by a surfeit of even more cloying themes. *Chicago Tribune* writer Nathan Cobb, who paid a visit to one Juárez art company's operation in the late 1980s, described an adobe warehouse containing "pile after pile of velvet paintings framed in scrap softwood. . . . Oriental gardens, growling lions, Jesus Christs, prowling tigers, American Indians, tropical rain forests, tall ships, German shepherds, bull-fighters, baskets of fruit, bare-breasted women, Virgin Marys, conquistadores, and of course, the ubiquitous unicorns." In addition, Cobb reported, "Juárez's artists churned out portraits of the latest hot American TV and movie stars, such as Sylvester Stallone or Mr. T."

That warehouse also was filled with images of the familiar subject in black velvet art, Elvis Presley, who had certain unique qualifications that elevated him above even card-playing canines and Tahitian nudes as a kitsch icon. Even before his untimely demise at age forty-two, the King already had drenched himself in sentimentality as thoroughly as his trademark Brut cologne. And his profile, from the pouty lips to the sweep of his black pompadour, was so dramatically distinctive that an artist with minimal talent could create a recognizable Elvis. Beyond that, Elvis himself liked tacky art; among his possessions was a massive black-velvet painting of a peacock adorned with hundreds of tiny lights in the tail feathers. Though once ubiquitous at roadside stands and flea markets, "Velvises," as aficionados call them, are increasingly difficult to come by; Mexican exports to the United States largely dried up in the mid-1990s, after Elvis Presley Enterprises warned a major distributor of black velvet art that it considered such likenesses to be copyright violations. Though the company has permitted the King's image to be used on beach towels and golf club covers, none of the more than one hundred Elvis product licensees listed on the Elvis.com web site produces velvet paintings. "Most everything you see of Elvis that's associated with velvet is pretty schlocky," company official Todd Morgan told the *Los Angeles Times* in 1998. "I'm sure if something of high quality were put on velvet, our licensing department would approve it."

By the end of the twentieth century, however, Tacky Chic faced another, more insidious threat to its existence. The highbrow elite, instead of reviling kitsch, had come to co-opt it. "Serious" artists such as Julian Schnabel painted on black velvet and mimicked bad art's imperfections as a means of commenting upon what they saw as the diminishing distinction in the modern world between good taste and bad. Filmmaker John Waters and talk-show host David Letterman tapped into sentimental schlock for comedy material. Bad art filled a valuable function for hipsters, because it enabled them to demonstrate a sense of irony—that is, that they could imbue the tacky and tasteless with an opposite meaning, because they were in on the joke. (As the French novelist Jean Genet noted in his memoir, *The Thief's Journal*, "To achieve harmony in bad taste is the height of elegance.") But even as "A Friend in Need" was reenacted in a recent TV commercial—with actual dogs portraying the poker players—there were signs that Tacky Chic was on the wane. In Mexico, newspaper articles report, the once prolific black-velvet-art factories are slowly vanishing. And in an age where mail-order videos of college girls drunkenly baring their breasts are sold on late-night television, it's increasingly hard to imagine a latter-day Edgar Leeteg titillating anyone with paintings of topless maidens. To be truly enjoyable, bad taste requires a certain amount of naïveté, and in the twenty-first century that seems to be an increasingly rare commodity.

THE OPERATIVE NUMBER: 19.99

*Price, in dollars, that Bruce Springsteen reportedly paid
for a black-velvet painting of himself, after he spotted it in a
store window in his New Jersey hometown of Asbury Park.
The rock star and his wife, Patti, hung the art on a wall
in their home, but had to explain to perplexed visitors
that it was intended as a joke.*

Big Bad Taste

Members of the Artists League of Texas in Abilene painted a 240-square-foot female nude, based loosely on Edouard Manet's "Olympia," in 1988. The effort required several hours of work and eight gallons of house paint.

True Art Endures

Barewalls.com, the Internet art poster retailer, shows "A Friend in Need" ranked 96 on a recent list of its 100 top-selling art reproductions, well behind Vincent van Gogh's "The Starry Night" (number 1) Johannes Vermeer's "Maiden with a Pearl," and Picasso's "The Old Guitarist," but just ahead of Andrew Wyeth's "Christina's World."

You Want *More*?

- *Kitsch in Sync: A Consumer's Guide to Bad Taste*, by Peter Ward, Plexus, London, 1991.
- *Rascals in Paradise*, by James A. Michener and A. Grove Day, Random House, New York, 1957.
- "It's a Dog's World, According to Coolidge," by Moira F. Harris, *Antiques & Collectibles*, March 1997.
- http://www.velvetelvisart.com/pageone.html, a Web site gallery of Mexican black velvet Elvis paintings.

（6）

Les Paul's "Log"

*Before the solid-body electric guitar transformed music and
became the sexiest accessory in pop culture, it debuted in 1941
as homely, heavy, and utterly ridiculous.*

THE PROBLEM BACK THEN, in the early 1940s, was entirely technical. It had nothing to do with revolutionizing popular culture,
creating guitar heroes, or the rise of a phenomenon known as "cock
rock." The man trying to solve it could never have imagined the
release of Led Zeppelin's seminal "Whole Lotta Love" in 1969, or
that Jimi Hendrix would play a snarling electrified version of the
American national anthem at Woodstock that same year to signal an
entire generation's declaration of independence. No, this musical
and cultural revolution began in the makeshift workshop of a tin-
ker, a skinny, jug-eared, redheaded guitarist born as Lester William
Polfuss in Waukesha, Wisconsin.

As he saw it then, Polfuss—who eventually adopted the stage
name Les Paul—electric guitars were the bastard stepchildren

of musical instruments, ill-conceived variations of traditional hollow-body guitars that had been jerry-built with tiny microphones to amplify their sound. For the most part, they were unwanted, uncontrollable, and likely to misbehave. While innovators such as Charlie Christian had demonstrated the possibilities of the electric guitar as a distinctive voice on stage and in the studio, many musicians still regarded them as a misguided effort by uppity rhythm-section players to compete with the drums and the horn section.

"The drummer used to whip us to death," Paul once said. "Everybody killed the guitar player."

But in 1941, Paul talked his way into the Epiphone guitar company's factory on West Fourteenth Street in New York, convincing its overseers to let him use the empty workshop on Sundays. When he emerged a few weeks later he was carrying an instrument soon dubbed, derisively, "the Log." It was to become what a guitar historian called "one of the most fabled instruments in the history of the electric guitar, as much for its oddity as for its sound." The Log today is considered a landmark in the evolution of the solid-body electric guitar, and as such has been exhibited in the Smithsonian Institution and is in the permanent collection of the Country Music Foundation Museum in Nashville, Tennessee. The instrument's ultimate impact on music and popular culture has been as sustained and pure as a Carlos Santana solo.

You'll need quick lessons in guitar history and acoustics to appreciate why Les Paul's Log changed everything about popular music—not just the way it sounds, but who gets paid the most and laid the most—in what has become one of the most dominant art forms of the past century.

Guitars were not always the quasi-phallic, front-and-center sonic beasts they are today. Although existing in various forms since the fourteenth century, and in its modern form since the mid-eighteenth century, the hollow-body acoustic guitar evolved

little until the 1930s. Guitars produced only enough sound to entertain small audiences or provide scratchy backup rhythm for instruments with more distinctive voices. What little noise they did
produce was the result of controlled vibration: A plucked string resonated into a hole cut into the top of the guitar. The hollow space
behind the vibrating string helped amplify the sound. As long as the
string vibrates, it will continue to produce sound. But as the string
vibration weakens and stops, so does the sound. Notes plucked on
most hollow-body guitars have a relatively limited life span, or
"sustain."

For years, Paul and others tried to find ways to amplify the guitar's sounds electrically and sustain them long enough to give the
guitar more personality. Like Paul, many of them were crystal-radio
geeks, precursors of the fish-belly-white electronics hobbyists of
the early 1970s who created the computer revolution. As author
Mary Alice Shaughnessy recounts in her definitive 1993 biography,
Les Paul: An American Original, Paul's first effort was as a teenager.
He was playing for tips as a one-man band outside Beekman's
drive-in barbecue stand in Waukesha, singing into a carbon microphone attached to his mother's radio speaker, strumming his $4.50
guitar, blowing into a harmonica, and thumping the beat on a wash-
tub like a "half-starved fugitive from vaudeville."

While his amplified voice carried across the parking lot, only
those parked nearby could hear his guitar. Paul eventually fashioned a crude amplification system by dismantling his father's Kolster phonograph. He taped its tone arm to the top of his guitar, stuck
its needle into the guitar's wooden top, and fed the sound through
the phonograph's speaker, which sometimes screeched with
uncontrolled electronic feedback. The amplified music and unfamiliar sounds attracted the curious from the produce stand and gas
station across the street, and his tips picked up considerably.

Thus was forged the link between electric guitars, audience
appreciation, and money.

Eventually, Paul and others began experimenting with pickups—tiny microphones placed directly beneath the strings of a conventional hollow-body guitar to amplify the sound electrically. That was when the acoustics got weird. The pickups translated the vibrations of the strings directly into electrified sound. There was no need for a hollow body to amplify those vibrations, and when it did it created a sound that competed with the electrically amplified sound of the strings. When conditions were just right, it sounded about as musical as someone chainsawing a *Tyrannosaurus rex* to death.

"When you've got the top [of the guitar] vibrating and a string vibrating, you've got a conflict," Paul told one interviewer. "One of them has got to stop, and it can't be the string, because that's making the sound."

Bad vibrations weren't the only concern. Dick Dale, one of the first guitarists to recognize ear-splitting sound as a real crowd pleaser, recalled that "no matter what you do to a hollow body guitar—change the thickness of the strings, change electric pickups, whatever—it'll always sound hollow. I always thought that if you could put pickups and strings on a telephone pole, you'd have the biggest, fattest, purest thick sound one could imagine. But you can't hold a telephone pole and play it."

The solution, Paul felt, was to simply eliminate the guitar's hollow body. In 1934, he took his idea to Larson Brothers, a Chicago instrument maker, and asked the company to build him a guitar with a solid, half-inch-thick maple top with no holes in it. "They thought I was crazy. They told me it wouldn't vibrate," Paul recalled. "I told them I didn't *want* it to vibrate."

Paul moved to New York in the late 1930s and began life as a professional musician, eventually landing a regular gig as a player with Fred Waring's famous orchestra, but the impulse to invent and reinvent stayed with him. He had spent many nights in Harlem jazz clubs and seen innovators such as Christian exploring the untapped potential of the electric guitar. So in 1941, Paul talked his way into the Epiphone workshop and began in earnest his quest for "pure string vibration."

What he created was an approximation of Dick Dale's pickup-equipped telephone pole. It was little more than a four-inch-by-four-inch hunk of pine rigged with a Vibrola tailpiece, a Gibson neck with a Larson Brothers fingerboard, and two pickups he'd made using the inner coils of an electric clock. Later, to make it look more like a guitar, Paul affixed a pair of side wings from a used acoustic Epiphone. It didn't much help. The Log was the ugly duckling in a family of instruments known for sensuous curves.

The dead-weight eyesore was utterly impractical for live performances and later mocked—and rejected—by an executive at Chicago Musical Instruments, which made Gibson guitars, as "nothing but a broomstick with a pickup on it." But Paul, the sonic purist, recognized in his creation a beauty that transcended appearance.

"You could go out and eat and come back and the note would still be sounding," Paul once said of the Log's sustain.

Undaunted, he used the Log for studio recordings and continued to experiment. In the mid-1940s, Paul, living temporarily in Waukesha, even went to a local railroad yard in search of the right sound. "I borrowed a wagon and got five kids to help me lug home an abandoned 2 1/2-foot piece of rail," he later told *Guitar Player* magazine. As an experiment, he rigged both the steel rail and a piece of wood as he might a single-string electric guitar, and then plucked the string on each. What he heard from the railroad-track guitar was the aural equivalent of the Holy Grail.

Not everyone was as impressed. "I ran to my mother and I said, 'I got it!'" Paul recalled of that moment. "She said, 'You're nuts. That will be the day, when you see Gene Autry on a horse with a piece of railroad track.'"

According to Steve Waksman, author of *Instruments of Desire: The Electric Guitar and the Shaping of Musical Experience*, Paul returned to New York in 1948 and told band mate Jim Atkins (brother of Chet): "J., that's the most beautiful sound you ever heard. There's absolutely no vibration interfering from any direction, and you get nothing but pure tone. When we can build an electric guitar that can do that, we'll have it made." The following year, Paul teamed up with (and later married) an attractive female guitarist. She took the stage name Mary Ford, and they began performing on stage and radio as a wisecracking duo that played sentimental, melodic tunes. Their performing career took off, eventually landing them on television, sponsored by Listerine.

Meanwhile, on the other end of the continent, another electronics geek with no stage career whatsoever was doing some tinkering of his own. Leo Fender had for years been experimenting with solid-body sound and amplifiers in his radio shop in Fullerton, California. (While Paul and Fender led the parade, even sanctioned versions of Gibson's history acknowledge that many others were close behind, including Paul Bigsby, who was working from suggestions by country guitarist Merle Travis, and designers at Rickenbacker and National.) While Paul focused on his performing career, by November 1950 Fender had built a prototype solid-body guitar that he called the Broadcaster. He soon changed the name to the Telecaster, and while Les Paul and Mary Ford were distracted selling more than six million records in 1951, Fender's Telecaster became the first solid-body electric to go into commercial production.

"No one knows for sure who invented the electric Spanish solid-body guitar," wrote guitar expert Tom Wheeler in the August 1991 issue of *Guitar Player* magazine. "There is not even much consensus concerning the criteria establishing the event. Did it occur when someone strung up a lap steel with six strings at a standard pitch? Or when someone else stuck some frets on an electric Hawaiian guitar? Besides, simultaneous development by independent builders—each with diverse inputs, resources, and influences—is more likely than a straight-line evolution traceable to a single, hallowed First One."

While Les Paul's Log has come closest to achieving hallowed status, let's credit Fender with being the Henry Ford of the guitar industry for bringing reliable solid-body electrics to the masses. The echoes of his Telecaster's first pure notes reached all the way to Chicago, where in 1950 Ted McCarty had become president of Gibson guitar company—the same company whose previous executives had mocked and rejected Paul's crude Log in 1946. Accounts differ about what happened next—the result, almost certainly, of ego-driven historical revisionism—but McCarty and Gibson eventually went looking for the jug-eared inventor who, years before, had brought them his impossibly ugly solid-body prototype.

McCarty claimed Gibson engineers had by then developed a solid-body guitar to compete with Fender's groundbreaking Telecaster and mostly were looking for an endorsement deal from a performer of Paul's stature. Paul, no shrinking violet, claimed the company finally had recognized the brilliance of his solid-body idea and that he was deeply involved with the Gibson engineers in developing the Gibson prototype. What's clear, according to the Shaughnessy biography, is that McCarty tracked down Paul and his wife at a Pocono mountain cabin in the fall of 1951, presented them Gibson's answer to Fender's Telecaster, and—after an all-night negotiating session culminating in a hearty bacon-and-eggs breakfast—they inked a renewable five-year endorsement deal on a page and a half of ordinary stationery. Paul got a cut of every Les Paul guitar sold, and agreed to play only Gibson's guitars in public.

The Gibson Les Paul model that hit the market in 1952 produced something close to the pure tone Paul had pursued with the Log and in his rail-yard experiment. He began employing it to produce a slick pop sound free of feedback and inconsistency.

Even then, though, there were hints that the solid-body electric might become something more than just a pure-toned musical instrument. For example, a 1952 Capitol Records publicity photo of Les Paul and Mary Ford showed Paul with his legs spread and straddling an oversized Les Paul model, its neck jutting up from his crotch. A smiling Ford was perched coyly on the guitar neck in a quasi-erotic, phallocentric pose.

Even if you assume the sexual suggestion was unintended, it certainly foreshadowed some of the dark social undercurrents reshaping America during those years, undercurrents that eventually would move pop music away from pure and inoffensive toward something far edgier. The 1948 Kinsey report on male sexuality had opened a national dialogue about once forbidden topics, and the public was bracing for the much anticipated release of Kinsey's 1953 report on women. The tension wasn't all sexual. The Supreme Court's 1954 *Brown v. Board of Education* desegregation decision set white against black in the South, and Joe McCarthy was spewing anticommunist hatred in Congress.

Suddenly, the toe-tapping music and gentle patter of Paul and Mary Ford seemed hopelessly out of touch with the times. Shaugnessy's book describes how other pop performers such as Doris Day, Bing Crosby, and Perry Como also found themselves struggling to reach young audiences enrapt by films such as *The Wild One* and *Rebel Without a Cause*. Allen Ginsberg and other Beat Generation poets were urging their generation to howl, and Cleveland disc jockey Alan Freed was spoon-feeding black rhythm-and-blues to white audiences, calling it "rock and roll." Bill Haley and the Comets hit number 23 on the charts in May 1954 with "Rock Around the Clock," and ten months later the song, played behind the credits of *Blackboard Jungle*, had young audiences dancing on theater seats and generally going berserk. By 1956, Chuck Berry, Bo Diddley, and Elvis Presley were bigger names than Les Paul ever had been, and the solid-body electric guitar he'd first envisioned in 1941 was becoming his Frankenstein monster, escaped into the world and wreaking a kind of havoc Paul never imagined.

"People like me and [Bing] Crosby were confused," he later told Shaughnessy, "because everything we had learned was just thrown out the window. The music world had taken a different shape and I didn't know what to do about it."

Paul's viability as a performer withered, as did his marriage to Ford. But once an electronics geek, always an electronics geek. He returned to his workshop and in the late 1950s emerged with yet another landmark invention that would have no less profound an impact on the world of music as the electric guitar: the multitrack recorder that enabled studio engineers to separately record and play back each instrument and voice in a song and then blend those parts into a unified whole. That invention alone would be enough to ensure Paul's place in the pop music pantheon. But the fact is, among the finest and most famous electric guitar players working today, there remain primarily two types: those who play the Fender Stratocaster, an evolved version of the original Telecaster, and those who play one of the one hundred or more variations of Gibson's Les Paul model.

Along the way, the solid-body electric guitar became the coolest imaginable pop-culture accessory. In the hands of pioneering performers such as Jimi Hendrix in the United States and Eric Clapton, Jeff Beck, and Led Zeppelin's Jimmy Page in England, it became a "technophallus" that, according to Waksman, was inseparable from "excessive male physicality." Guitar players became the studs of stage and studio, with the sentiment perhaps best expressed by the "Clapton is God" graffiti that appeared on London streets during the guitarist's stint with John Mayall's Bluesbreakers in 1965. By the time Hendrix hit the Woodstock stage on August 18, 1969, and began a set that included his nasty, electrified version of the "Star-Spangled Banner," the guitar hero was a well-established cultural archetype. Adolescent male fantasies have never been the same.

While classic and evolved versions of the Les Paul guitar have never been far from the spotlight—Gibson historian Walter Carter calls the guitars "our bread and butter" and estimates that the company has made and sold about a million of them since 1952—the man for whom the guitar is named did fade from public view for a couple of decades. But by the 1980s, Les Paul's regular weeknight gig at a New York nightclub was drawing a steady parade of acolytes, including some of the biggest names in rock and jazz—the Rolling Stones's Keith Richards, Larry Coryell, Al Di Meola, George Benson, and Eddie Van Halen. Postpunk rocker Billy Idol reportedly came in one night during that period and proclaimed Paul "the real king of rock and roll." During a lavish, star-studded party at Manhattan's Hard Rock Café in June 1987, thrown by Gibson to honor Paul's seventy-second birthday and help heal professional rifts of the past, Paul performed with Jimmy Page, the Doors's Robby Krieger, Rick Derringer, and Paul Shaffer, David Letterman's bandleader.

The following year he was inducted into the Rock and Roll Hall of Fame and Museum, taking his place alongside the Beatles, the Beach Boys, Berry Gordy, Jr., and folk music hero Bob Dylan, whose 1965 decision to "go electric" during the Newport Folk Festival still is considered an epicenter of the rockquake that today includes electrified everything—from synthesized keyboards to electronic drum machines. "Les Paul is an inspiration to a world of guitarists for his playing, for the instruments he created, and his multiple-track recording innovations," Atlantic Records founder Ahmet Ertegun said during that induction ceremony in Manhattan. "Without him, it is hard to imagine how rock and roll would be played today."

Looking out on a Waldorf-Astoria crowd that included Bruce Springsteen, Mick Jagger, and George Harrison, Paul accepted the honor with a brief speech and the wholly unnecessary exhortation to "have fun with my toys."

THE OPERATIVE NUMBER: 20

Estimated weight, in pounds, of Les Paul's "Log," the utterly impractical 1941 prototype that many now consider a landmark in the evolution of the solid-body electric guitar.

Why Electric Guitars Look Like Guitars

Guitars evolved into their traditional shape because they needed a deep, resonant hollow body to amplify the sound of the plucked strings. But an electric guitar is in some ways a much simpler concept, with each string amplified directly by a tiny microphone, or pickup, placed just beneath it. So a solid-body electric guitar doesn't necessarily have to look like a guitar.

But then there's the coolness factor.

Les Paul learned that lesson in 1941 when, after completing work on his landmark Log prototype, he and his trio took it on stage at a New York club called Glady's. The audience saw Paul playing something with a guitar neck and strings and pickups—something that made sounds like an electric guitar—but which made its player look like a man trying to squeeze music out of a wooden anvil.

"I died," Paul told writer Tony Bacon for a story that appeared in the July 2002 issue of *Guitar Player* magazine. "I played the 'Sheik of Araby,' and it was stupid—it just didn't go nowhere."

Disappointed, Paul returned to the Epiphone guitar factory, where he was allowed to use the empty workshop on Sundays, and built two wings for the Log. He clamped them onto the sides of the four-inch-by-four-inch block of pine that served as the Log's body, giving it a more traditional look.

"Then I went back to the very same club, and played the very same song with the same group, and the place just went crazy," Paul recalled. "The whole experience taught me that the audience hears with its *eyes*. And not only was a stick of wood difficult for me to play, but I looked like a geek. From that point, it was obvious that any successful solid-body had to look like a guitar."

Eventually, the outrageous style mandates of disco and funk pushed electric guitar designs in flashy new directions, to the point where solid-bodies assumed the shapes of boomerangs and lightning bolts. But for the most part those were fads and passed, blessedly, into history.

You Want *More*?

- *Les Paul: An American Original*, by Mary Alice Shaughnessy, William Morrow, New York, 1993.
- *Instruments of Desire: The Electric Guitar and the Shaping of Musical Experience*, by Steve Waksman, Harvard University Press, Cambridge, Mass., 1999.
- *Gibson Electrics: The Classic Years*, an illustrated history from the mid-1930s to the mid-1960s by A. R. Duchossoir, Hal Leonard, Milwaukee, Wis., 1994).
- *The Gibson Les Paul Book: A Complete History of Les Paul Guitars*, by Tony Bacon and Paul Day, Backbeat Books, San Francisco, 1993.
- *50 Years of the Gibson Les Paul: Half a Century of the Greatest Electric Guitars*, by Tony Bacon, Backbeat Books, San Francisco, 2002.

Wrestling with a Contradiction

In 1947, TV wrestler Gorgeous George strutted in lingerie, plucked bobby pins from his blond curls, and exuded braggadocio as intense as his perfume. He also paved the way for everyone from Muhammad Ali to Kiss.

PERHAPS THE FIRST THING PEOPLE noticed about George Wagner—besides the peroxide curls on his head, the strains of "Pomp and Circumstance" as he climbed into the ring, and the tuxedo-wearing valet spraying perfume in his path—was the robe. Wrestlers and boxers and other athletes wore robes to break a sweat during their warm-ups, but they were generally big, bulky garments with hoods and usually some rough-hewn nickname or fierce-looking beast with bared teeth emblazoned on the back—the kind of robe a manly man wouldn't be embarrassed to wear. The man who called himself Gorgeous George, by contrast, wore what looked like last weekend's special at the stout gal's shop, a dainty, frilly garment with a cinched waist and a floor-length hem. If you were one of the masses watching the spectacle on an old Du Mont TV, you wouldn't necessarily have realized that it was a garish and provocative shade of purple, but the effect was striking even in black-and-white.

A *Newsweek* writer at the time described Gorgeous George as affecting "a vain sartorial splendor, swishy manner, and effeminate fragrance." That was a tactful understatement. The wrestler strutted and primped like a deranged Miss America contestant. And then there was the way he talked. "Get your filthy hands off me!" he'd screech at the referee like some society matron outraged at her butler's impertinence. He'd take the microphone and spew long, impassioned soliloquies about the details of the torment that he planned to inflict upon his opponent, and wax poetic about his own physical beauty and essential superiority.

"I really don't think I'm gorgeous," Gorgeous George would offer. "But what's my opinion against millions?"

The inevitable cacophony of boos and catcalls didn't faze him. Unflappable in his weirdness, he tossed gold-colored bobby pins into the crowd as souvenirs. (Recipients were expected to swear a pledge: "I solemnly swear and promise to never confuse this gold Georgie Pin with a common, ordinary bobby pin, so help me Gorgeous George.")

Today, of course, none of this would particularly shock or amaze a culture that not only tolerates but almost expects bizarre affectations and posturing by sports figures, entertainers, and celebrities. But in the late 1940s, Gorgeous George was a sensation. It was an era accustomed to the clean-cut, unadorned, reflexively modest, emotionally impenetrable, strong, silent, and virile version of masculinity, of John Wayne and Joe DiMaggio. Gorgeous George—"The Human Orchid," as he was also billed—was an outrageous iconoclast—and a puzzling conundrum to boot. In one sense, he was a certifiable tough guy—a wrestler, 210 pounds of beefy deltoids and pectorals and lats, trained in the ancient and venerable art of bending other men's limbs into painful positions and making them beg for mercy. At the same time, he also affected a persona daringly close to the 1940s stereotype of how an effeminate gay man was supposed to look and act at a time when homosexuality was such a strident taboo that actual homosexuals were deeply closeted and all but invisible. Gorgeous George blended that caricature with an exaggerated machismo. He was both flamboyantly prissy and a swaggering bully whose philosophy was "always cheat." He was a walking oxymoron—the tough sissy—and to audiences conditioned to think about masculinity in simplistic, stereotypical ways, it was an incongruous and incendiary mix. At the arenas where he wrestled, fans sometimes became enraged to the point of rioting.

Though one gay-oriented Web site, outsports.com, has called him "Liberace with muscles," in reality, George Wagner was a heterosexual married man with kids, though he avoided calling attention to that. The boos and derision he provoked, after all, was money in the bank. Most stars reveled in the adulation of their fans. Gorgeous George, in contrast, prided himself on his ability to draw audiences who wanted nothing more than to see him get his perfume-drenched butt kicked. He made a career of playing the character America loved to hate.

And it worked. In the 1940s and 1950s, Gorgeous George not only filled arenas but became one of the first great stars of the then new medium of television. But George's outlandish act had a lasting influence, not just on professional wrestling, whose performers still employ his antics, but throughout popular culture. His macho androgyny shtick has been recycled over the years by male rock stars who wear mascara and teased tresses as they strut the stage proclaiming their virile potency, and by athletes such as flamboyant former pro basketball star Dennis Rodman, who dabbled in cross-dressing and delighted in dropping hints about his sexual ambiguity. Gorgeous George's self-promoting histrionics were copied directly by Muhammad Ali, whose own countless trash-talking imitators in sports, hip-hop music, and other fields likely are unaware of the debt they indirectly owe to the Human Orchid.

Gorgeous George himself had historical antecedents—the ancient Greeks, for example, practiced both wrestling and cross-dressing. The roots of the profession in which he made his living date back to the carnivals and county fairs of late-nineteenth-century America, which often featured wrestlers who would take on local challengers for a price. At the turn of the twentieth century so-called scientific wrestling, in which athletes employed elaborate—sometimes brutal—grappling techniques in a genuine contest, ranked in popularity with baseball and horse racing. In 1909, forty thousand people jammed into a baseball stadium in Chicago to watch Frank Gotch wrestle George Hackenschmidt. But with matches sometimes lasting for hours, the serious competitions eventually lost appeal. The sport devolved into show business, with fixed matches that were carefully scripted to ensure some excitement. Much of the latter came from audience participation—wrestling fans, oddly, still revel in pretending that the spectacle is real. As writer Sam Boal observed in the *New York Times* in 1949, "How else could one explain the phenomenon of elderly women who meta-morphosed into hatpin-brandishing banshees screaming for blood at the sight of a ring villain?"

Even before Gorgeous George, wrestling had a well-established tradition of the bizarre. Promoters often staged shows featuring midgets, giants, and men who wore Turkish fezzes or spiked Pruss-ian helmets and pretended to be foreigners. Some shows featured "lady wrestlers" who wore a lot of makeup and dressed in frilly clothes. They would pretend to go berserk on the canvas and hyster-ically claw at each other—which, as sociologist Michael Ball noted, pandered to the audience's stereotypical view of women as emo-tional and incompetent at "manly" pursuits. By contrast, the heroes in wrestling scripts often are cast as fearsome warriors and virile hunks. The biggest draw of the 1930s was Jim "The Golden Greek" Londos, who made the most of his movie star looks and chiseled physique by buffing his body to a sheen with olive oil.

Those gimmicks worked because they played to audiences' comfortable prejudices and preconceptions. But Gorgeous George's act was even more attention-getting, because he flipped the conventional gender roles and twisted the taboos. Just as important, he did it with an unapologetic, taunting manner that tended to get audiences squirming in their seats. Today, every pro athlete who makes the slash-across-the-throat gesture, or wiggles his posterior after a score to irritate other teams' fans, also is paying homage to the Human Orchid.

The man who pioneered such provocations was born in Nebraska in 1915, the son of a house painter. George Wagner reportedly began wrestling at age thirteen, and twice won amateur championships in Texas before turning professional. Every wrestler needed a gimmick, and since Wagner was handsome, he initially experimented with a sort of dapper, dashing gentleman-about-town persona, wearing spats and a homburg and brandishing a cane. (After all, it had worked for movie star Fred Astaire.)

There are conflicting stories about who influenced him to take his ring character in a more offbeat direction. By her own account in a 2001 interview with an Oregon newspaper, Wagner's first wife, Elizabeth, was the initial inspiration. She made her husband's wrestling garb on her sewing machine. One day, as she recalled decades later in a newspaper interview, Wagner walked in wearing a fancy new robe with satin lining that she'd fashioned for him. "Well hi, Gorgeous George," she joked. Then, the proverbial lightbulb went off in her head. She and her mother bleached the wrestler's naturally dark hair, and the peroxide-blond provocateur was born.

George further developed his flamboyant new ambiance in places such as Oklahoma, where promoter LeRoy McGuirk spotted his potential even though McGuirk's blindness prevented him from fully appreciating George's visual shock value. By the mid-1940s, George had made his way to Los Angeles, where he worked out at the old "Muscle Beach" outdoor gymnasium at Venice Beach and plied his trade at the Hollywood Legion Stadium, the Olympic Auditorium, and other temples of sweat.

Gorgeous George possessed a true gift for inciting audiences. They jeered him with catcalls and wolf whistles and tried to grab his frilly garments and shred them. Once, reportedly, a man even reached through the ropes and burned him on the calf with a lit cigar. George could give it back with gusto. He would march defiantly into the ring, on at least one occasion surrounded by a police escort. His valet, clad in a tie and tails, would spray the ring canvas with a sterling-silver atomizer, spewing a sickly sweet mist that he claimed was Chanel No. 10 (even though the perfume maker made no such scent). When a female fan heckled him, he might taunt her back: "I told you not to come down tonight, Mother." And when the match started, he provoked even more boos with his tactics, which included pulling Georgie Pins from his hair and poking them into his opponent's thighs.

By thespian standards, George may have been guilty of overacting—his routine was closer to Moe Howard than Laurence Olivier—but the broad strokes of his supercilious gender-bending caricature were perfectly suited for the small screen of a then new entertainment medium called television. In the late 1940s, the first commercial TV stations and networks were struggling to find sports programming that would attract the public. They tried everything from baseball to speedboat racing, but the first real spark of excitement came when they set up cameras in wrestling arenas and started showing the weekly card of bouts. As television historian Fred McDonald has noted, wrestling—with its colorful good and bad guys, melodramatic storylines, and rough-and-tumble action—exploited the visual possibilities of the medium to better advantage. In Los Angeles, when newly minted local station KTLA began broadcasting live from the Olympic Auditorium, local sales of TV sets took off, and the man appliance dealers clearly had to thank was Gorgeous George. He became so popular, *Time* magazine once noted, that in Hollywood, bars trying to attract customers by installing televisions put out signs saying GORGEOUS GEORGE, TELEVISION, HERE TONIGHT.

As one of television's first big attractions, George became a bona fide celebrity. Bob Hope sometimes sat ringside at his matches, and he once wrestled Burt Lancaster in a charity event. Outside the ring, George wore clothes nearly as flamboyant as his ring garb—red jackets, yellow slacks, and two-tone shoes—and carried a pocketful of his Georgie Pins, which he handed out as souvenirs to admirers. In addition to wrestling almost every night of the week, he ran a side business, a ranch in Beaumont, California, where he raised his own brand of Gorgeous George turkeys. The busy star eventually drifted apart from his first wife, who became a Jehovah's Witness and moved to Oregon. His second wife, Cherie, took over the role of valet in his act and is credited with creating one of the stock characters in pro wrestling—the attractive female assistant who raises the tension by getting pulled into the brouhaha.

Gorgeous George's success was so alluring that he spawned competitors; at one point, reportedly, there were six different wrestlers using the name Gorgeous George—every one no doubt insisting that *he* was the original. (One of the other Gorgeous Georges even sued George Wagner, but a judge ruled that both could continue using the name.) But just as abruptly as he had risen to stardom, his fortunes began to fade. As they later would do with westerns, game shows, and "reality" programming, television networks had a tendency to jump on a hot trend and overexpose it until viewers fled in droves. By the late 1950s they'd worn out wrestling and started dropping it from their lineups. George tried to drum up more sensation. In 1959, he fought a "hair versus hair" grudge match against a Canadian good guy, Whipper Watson, with the promise that he'd let Watson shave his golden curls if he lost. He did, and TV viewers were treated to the unsettling sight of an electric razor shearing off George's trademark locks.

After his electronic stardom dissipated, George stuck it out for a few more years, continuing to hit the road and play the arenas. It was on one such gig in Las Vegas in 1961—just two years before his death from liver problems—that he was booked as a guest on a local radio show, alongside a young boxer named Cassius Clay. The chiseled, young, former Olympic boxing champion towered over George, and his smooth almond complexion and elegant cheekbones belied the middle-aged wrestler's pretensions of physical beauty. Even so, when it was time to talk about their respective upcoming matches, it became clear who was the master and who was the student. The young boxer, in his soft Louisville drawl, quietly predicted a victory over his opponent. George flexed his still mighty hyperbole. "I'll kill him!" he bellowed about his opponent. "I'll tear his arm off. If this bum beats me, I'll crawl across the ring and cut my hair off. But it's not gonna happen, because I'm the greatest wrestler in the world!"

The future Muhammad Ali was transfixed. He actually went to the wrestling match, where he was amazed to see an arena full of people who'd paid admission so they could scream for George to get pummeled. He realized that talking brashly and acting outrageously could turn him into an athlete who would fill arenas, too. Before long, he was the Louisville Lip, who boasted of his beauty, mocked opponents, and waxed poetic about being able to "float like a butterfly, sting like a bee."

Others may not have imitated Gorgeous George as deliberately as Ali, but over the years his influence has been felt far and wide. In the 1990s, Dennis Rodman, the NBA bad boy, transformed himself from a skilled but largely unnoticed athlete into a household name by dying his hair odd hues, wearing makeup, and dropping hints that he might be gay. He once made news by announcing that he was getting married, and then making a public appearance dressed as a bride. (He once made an annual list of worst-dressed women.)

George, like Rodman, wasn't actually gay. But he was campy in a way that appealed to gay sensibilities. Traces of his flamboyant out-rageousness show up in places such as the films of John Waters. "I love villains in wrestling," Waters said in a 2001 interview with *Index* magazine. "That sport I like because it's not a sport, it's show business. When I was young, Gorgeous George was a huge influence on me."

The Human Orchid's puzzling mix of machismo and effeminacy also bubbled to the surface again and again in popular music. Rock 'n' roll stars altered his formula, replacing the muscular violence with a heterosexual come-on. At the start, there was Little Richard, with his gleaming pompadour, pencil-thin moustache, and pretty cheekbones, screaming lyrics that sounded vaguely dirty. Later, in performers such as Mick Jagger of the Rolling Stones and Steven Tyler of Aerosmith, audiences were treated to the contradiction of long-haired men in sequins, spandex, and makeup, thrusting their pelvises to the beat as they sang lusty lyrics about their prowess with the ladies. Some, including Alice Cooper, were clearly in on the joke; when the woman he's trying to seduce in the song "Be My Lover" asks the singer why he has a feminine moniker, he assures her "you really wouldn't understand." Others, such as the band Kiss, simply played dress-up without a sense of irony. "I'm six-feet-two, and I'd just look like a football player in a tutu," the band's Gene Simmons once explained. "I don't make a convincing homosexual. So to make our statement, we opted for makeup." More recently, Marilyn Manson has opted for the macho androgyny shtick. It's a theme of such enduring popularity that in Los Angeles fashion designer Ryan Heffington has created a Rock 'n' Sissy line of clothing, presumably ideal for today's musically inclined androgynies.

In the beginning, though, there was Gorgeous George Wagner, and it's a safe bet that the man who pioneered this enduring motif would be pleased. As George himself once noted, "I'll never be famous until I'm imitated."

○ ○ ○ ○ ○

THE OPERATIVE NUMBER: 35

*Percentage of Gorgeous George's television viewers who were
women, according to a 1997* Los Angeles Times *story.*

○ ○ ○ ○ ○

But could he "wrassle"?

Despite Gorgeous George's emphasis on theatrics, old-time grap-
plers described him as having some genuine talent at the ancient
art of hand-to-hand combat.

"George could wrassle, don't kid yourself," former wrestler
Gene Kiniski once told a Canadian newspaper. But compared to
some of the towering behemoths that climbed into the ring, he said
George "just wasn't that big" at five-feet-nine-inches and 210
pounds. Despite his lack of stature, George reportedly was strong
enough to have once tossed a 240-pound opponent into a ring
post, splitting open his scalp with a wound that required 130
stitches to heal.

You Want *More*?

● *Sex, Lies, and Headlocks: The Real Story of Vince McMahon and the
World Wrestling Federation,* by Shaun Assael and Mike Mooneyman, Crown, New York, 2002.

- *The Unreal Story of Pro Wrestling*, a documentary narrated by Steve Allen, A&E Entertainment, 1998.
- http://www.wrestlingmuseum.com/home.html, the Professional Wrestling Online Museum.

The War Against Wrinkles

The development of permanent-press clothing in the 1950s
culminated a five-thousand-year battle against messiness and
rescued American men from almost certain sloth.

PERHAPS THE MOST PECULIAR NEW sport of the twenty-first century is something called Extreme Ironing, which could be the premise of a Monty Python skit, except that it's real. Hardy young athletes scale mountainsides, suspend themselves from bridge girders, or float down rivers in kayaks—and then simultaneously, with the help of solar- and battery-powered irons, try to iron the wrinkles from a shirt. Phil "Steam" Shaw, a British factory worker who invented Extreme Ironing in 1997, told the *Toronto Star* newspaper that he dreamed up the sport as a way of adding thrills to "something that was quite boring." Competitors are judged not just by the difficulty of their physical feats, but also by the meticulousness of their creases and smoothness of their sleeves and collars. When asked about the sport's appeal, Extreme Ironing contestant

Matthew "Starch" Patrick deadpanned, "The smell, feel, and look of a freshly pressed garment have a lot to commend them."

That a bunch of predominantly male fun-seekers have turned what once was an onerous household chore into a sport says loads about one of the previous century's oft overlooked technological breakthroughs. Starting in the early 1950s, garments made of wrinkle-resistant fabrics, sometimes referred to as "wash-and-wear" or "permanent press," altered the American lifestyle. Wrinkle-resistant clothing made it unnecessary for Americans—specifically, American women, who traditionally have done the bulk of laundering—to spend countless hours at the ironing board, struggling to turn a crumpled mass of cloth into something resembling a shirt. (Today, according to one recent study, the typical household spends about ninety minutes ironing clothes each week—probably about a tenth of the time it took a half-century before.) The typical American man now can hit the snooze button with impunity each morning knowing that he can pull on those slacks left in a pile on the floor and rush to the office, and yet still maintain the illusion that he is reasonably well-groomed and businesslike. It's no wonder that by the 1990s, wrinkle-resistant clothing amounted to 80 percent to 85 percent of the men's clothing market.

Wrinkle-resistant clothes also have been a force for social change. They appeared on department store racks at a crucial nexus in history, the time when women were just beginning to chafe against the confines of their traditional role as homemakers and make their way into the business world. Wrinkle-resistant clothes gained momentum in the culture right along with the drive for women's equality. Without their wives to do the ironing for them, men might have descended rapidly into sartorial chaos, as surely as the English prep school lads devolved into savages in the novel *Lord of the Flies*. Instead, permanent press helped in a subtle way to iron over a potential source of strife between the sexes and ensured social progress.

We now have the real-life version of the indestructible wrinkle-proof miracle fabric invented by a scientist—portrayed by Alec Guinness—in the 1951 comedy *The Man in the White Suit*. In the film, it should be mentioned, Guinness's character hopes to create a sartorial labor-saving utopia, but instead finds himself pursued through the streets by a crazed mob. Similarly, the real permanent-press revolution had a downside. Once, office workers' rumpled appearance at 5:00 P.M. was a cue to bosses that it was time to call it a day. Today, it's possible to stumble home, exhausted, at the end of a twelve-hour day with nary a crimp in one's wardrobe. "In addition to being easy to care for," a textile-industry web site explains, "wrinkle resistance is also maintained while the garment is worn. So, the slacks you sit in at your desk all day will be less wrinkled by the time you leave the office." Wrinkle-resistant technology has contributed, subtly, to the evolution of a 24/7 working world in which the clock no longer matters.

It's difficult to say precisely why people since ancient times have invested so much effort in trying to keep their clothing crisp and uncrumpled. "Ironed clothes give a perception of power and precision," once theorized Lawrence Salomon, a professor of industrial design at the University of Illinois at Chicago and an expert on the history of ironing. Wrinkled clothing, by contrast, may convey the impression that the wearer is fatigued, or lackadaisical. The aversion to wrinkles is a powerful one; in a 2002 survey of residents of fourteen major American cities by iron manufacturer Rowenta, 45 percent of people said that if they left the house and realized that their shirts were wrinkled, they would go home and change. Crispness, for some, borders upon obsession: 37 percent of the survey subjects revealed that they ironed the T-shirts that they wore beneath their dress shirts, and 5 percent admitted to ironing their socks as well.

Humanity's fixation and frustration with wrinkles may date back to the Egyptians, who began weaving linen garments from flax more than five thousand years ago. The Egyptians also later pioneered the use of cotton, a material whose maddening tendency to take on the appearance of a road map has bedeviled generations of housewives. Untreated cotton fibers don't retain any permanent memory of a shirt's shape or smoothness. Instead, when the wearer's body creates stresses, the chemical chains that make up the fibers adjust by breaking apart and forming new bonds, resulting in the rumpled look. As Haig Zeronian, a professor of textile science at the University of California at Davis once explained to the *Journal of Commerce*, washing exacerbates the problem. When cotton fibers absorb water they bend, forming wrinkles, and stay molded in that messy configuration as they dry.

The ancient Egyptians were such notorious neat freaks that they shaved their scalps and wore wigs because they thought it was cleaner. Naturally, they were the first to try taming the rebellious crinkles and furrows of their wardrobes by smashing down and smoothing the cloth between hard surfaces. In the first century A.D., the Romans got a little more ingenious, loading freshly washed garments into wooden presses and tightening the screw-spindles in an attempt to squeeze out the wrinkle-causing moisture. In the 1500s, the Scandinavians developed an even more complex antiwrinkle device, the mangling board: They wound a damp garment around a roller, ran it up and down the board's surface until it seemed suitably smooth, and then stretched it out to dry.

Eventually, in the thirteenth century, Europe picked up on a Chinese innovation, the use of heat to mold rebellious fibers. The Chinese hot-ironed silk with large metal cups filled with hot charcoal, which did a better job than any of the elaborate cold-pressing contraptions. Hot ironing became the preferred method, but eradicating wrinkles continued to be devilishly difficult. In the 1800s, laundresses boiled buckets of starch and applied it to garments to stiffen the fabric as it hung to dry. Then, they used small but heavy cast-iron implements called sad irons, which had to be heated in a fire and then rubbed with paper or a rag to remove the soot before each use. (The 1887 Edgar Degas painting "Woman Ironing" depicts the meticulous effort that this method required.)

Gas-heated irons gradually replaced fire-heated irons. Those were supplanted in the 1880s by the first electric-heated iron, patented by New York inventor Henry W. Seely. By 1939, the electric iron was second only to the radio as the most common electrical appliance in the home. Of the two-thirds of American households that were wired for power at the time, 80 percent owned an electric iron. In the early 1950s, Sunbeam and other manufacturers introduced electric irons that produced steam. But even with that new gadgetry, ironing remained a grueling task, one that consumed myriad hours of a housewife's time each week. Not surprisingly, a survey by chemical manufacturer Du Pont in the early 1950s showed that 94 percent of women saw ironing—in particular, ironing shirts—as the most loathed of their household duties.

That undoubtedly pleased Du Pont, for which the distaste for ironing was a potential gold mine. The company had licensed a process for creating polyethylene terephthalate—the compound used to make polyester fiber—first developed in 1940 by British chemists John Rex Whinfield and James Tennant Dickson. Unlike cotton and other natural fibers, polyester endured the stress of wear without losing its shape and smoothness, and it didn't absorb moisture the way natural fibers did.

In 1951, Du Pont unveiled its new wrinkle-resistant polyester fabric for fashion reporters in New York, showing them a suit made from the material that had been worn by a research subject for sixty-seven straight days without pressing. Du Pont called it "wash and wear" clothing, the implication being that ironing was no longer necessary. As synthetic fibers historian Susannah Handley has noted, the company hyped its new product by having salesmen cheerfully jump into swimming pools. Phillips–Van Heusen touted the first wash-and-wear shirts with flamboyant ads, such as one that showed workers in a Chinese laundry who were upset that the new garment's disinclination to wrinkle left them with nothing to do.

The new wrinkle-resistant synthetics had some disadvantages, though. Fashion sophisticates sneered at the fabric's slick, not-quite-natural feel. Even the less dandyish had to notice that artificial fibers weren't as comfortable as 100 percent cotton in hot weather, because the synthetics tended to trap heat rather than breathing—giving men a choice between being wrinkled or soaked with sweat. Worrywarts feared that in the event of a fire, their space-age garb would melt and stick to their skin. But Du Pont and the wash-and-wear clothing makers had more potent advantages. They knew that wives purchased 60 percent of men's shirts, and that those same women were falling in love with a new labor-saving device, the electric tumble dryer. Synthetics survived the rigors of the dryer quite well, while the cotton fabrics of the time had a tendency to wrinkle and shrink. Among the men who chose their own wardrobes, Du Pont's market researchers identified another lucrative market niche: traveling salesmen, who often arrived late at night at motels and had to do their laundry in the sink so that they could look presentable for the next day's meetings. For the Willie Lomans of the world, the drip-dry shirt offered at least some small comfort in a life of incessant rejection.

By the mid-1960s, synthetic wrinkle-resistant garments so dominated men's fashion that they threatened economic ruin for the cotton farmers and processors. But just as women were credited for making synthetic fabrics a success, the cotton industry also was to be rescued by a woman. Ruth Rogan Benerito was a rarity for her time: a woman whose strong-willed mother had encouraged her to pursue a career in science. So intellectually precocious that she graduated from high school at age fourteen, Benerito became one of only two female students in chemistry classes at Tulane University, and went on to earn a doctorate from the University of Chicago. She went to work in 1953 for the U.S. Department of Agriculture's Southern Regional Research Center in New Orleans, where she earned fifty-five patents for inventions related to everything from detergents to ceramics.

But Benerito's greatest scientific triumph was her discovery of how to keep cotton garments from wrinkling. In 1969 she patented a method for chemically cross-linking and reinforcing the chains of cellulose molecules in cotton fibers so that they would stay in place under the stress of wear or washing. ("It's sort of like when a woman gets her hair in a permanent wave," she once explained to *Investor's Business Daily*.)

Cotton industry scientists picked up Benerito's lead. From the 1970s through the 1990s, they tinkered with the process for making cotton fiber yarn and other manufacturing steps so that cotton garments would better withstand tumble drying, and developed at least a half-dozen different processes for creating wrinkle-resistant clothing. They also worked to eliminate the use of formaldehyde, a chemical that caused eye and respiratory irritation in textile workers and had been linked to cancer in animals. By the mid-1990s, a multitude of wrinkle-resistant, all-cotton garments dominated the men's clothing field, and one manufacturer, Haggar, was sufficiently emboldened to trademark the term "Wrinkle-Free" for its line of cotton slacks.

Of course, the notion of ending the five-thousand-year battle against wrinkles with absolute victory is a fantasy. Even the cotton industry web site that touts wrinkle-resistant clothing offers the caveat that "certain articles may require a few touch-ups with an iron." Nevertheless, we're inching closer to perfection. The Italian company Corpo Nove, for example, has developed an experimental shirt made from nylon and a "thermal-shape memory" alloy, which essentially irons out its own wrinkles when subjected to heat. Crumple it into a ball and stuff it into a drawer for several weeks, and then blow it with a hair dryer, and it miraculously metamorphoses into a preternaturally smooth garment. The $3,500 prototype shirt is still a bit pricey, but don't be surprised to find such innovations on upscale department store shelves any day now.

In terms of status, wrinkle-resistant attire has come a long way. When it first appeared in the 1950s, it served as an indication of the wearer's relative position in the food chain of corporate America. Executives and senior managers, after all, could afford to send their untreated cotton garments to the laundry. But gradually, even the distinction of class gave way to convenience. By the late 1990s, even Brooks Brothers, that bastion of fashion conservatism, was touting its line of wrinkle-free apparel.

At the dawn of the twenty-first century, clothing manufacturers find themselves faced with a new dilemma. With workplace dress codes unraveling, men have been slowly abandoning the suit and tie and laboring in khakis and open-necked shirts. The crisp, wrinkle-free look no longer is a requirement in the business world, even for diligent young trainees.

That's why manufacturers, desperate to sell more clothes, are backing off from their focus on eliminating wrinkles and are pushing technology designed to neutralize yet another bane of the fastidious dresser—stains. Levi's Dockers brand, for instance, debuted a new type of trousers treated with Teflon, which supposedly allowed a wearer to spill everything from beer to salad dressing on them and have it simply bead up without creating a mark.

○ ○ ○ ○ ○

THE OPERATIVE NUMBER: 17.8

Percentage of U.S. workers in fourteen major cities who— despite traditional societal disapproval—don't mind wearing a wrinkled shirt to work, according to a 2002 survey by iron manufacturer Rowenta. The city with the sloppiest workers was

*Seattle, where 23 percent show up at the office crinkled. In a
similar survey in the United Kingdom by the maker of Bold
detergent, 19 percent of respondents admitted to ironing
just the front side of their clothes.*

Making a Splash

When wash-and-wear clothing debuted in the 1950s, clothing
manufacturers delighted in outlandish demonstrations of its
wrinkle resistance.

Menswear maker Joseph Haspel reportedly waded into the
ocean in his suit at a Florida convention, and then, after he'd dried
off, went to dinner that night in the same attire. Another clothing
mogul, Spencer Witty, liked to entertain visitors by pouring ink or
ketchup over a pair of dress trousers, tossing the garment in a
washing machine, and then hanging it up to dry. An hour later,
he'd proudly display the pants, clean and dry and as crisply creased
as if they'd just been pressed.

You Want *More?*

- *Let There Be Clothes: 40,000 Years of Fashion*, by Lynn Schurn-
  berger, Workman Publishing, New York, 1991.
- *Nylon: The Story of a Fashion Revolution*, by Susannah Handley,
  Johns Hopkins University Press, Baltimore, Md., 1999.

The King of Leer

In 1952, Robert Harrison's Confidential *magazine created a
society of voyeurs by prying into celebrities' private lives.*

FOR A MOMENT, TAKE YOUR mind off the studly young movie
actor who is purported to sport a toupee, the scream-fest on Hollywood Boulevard between one of Tinseltown's formerly most glamorous couples, and the heartbreak of infertility that a popular
daytime TV host supposedly is enduring. Instead, consider one of
the modern world's true peculiarities: Most of us know considerably more about the personal lives of famous people than we do
about our friends and neighbors.

Whether they are movie starlets, rock 'n' roll singers, athletes,
or politicians, celebrities' most private doings—what foods they
binge on, what illnesses they try to conceal, what childhood traumas
or family dysfunctions trouble them, even what sort of sex acts they
like to perform and with whom—invariably become public knowl-

edge. Beyond that, a veritable industry of supermarket tabloids, cable TV shows, and web sites has grown up to satisfy countless millions of celebrity-scandal addicts with a steady diet of titillation.

What's most amazing, however, is that there was a time, a half century or so ago, when this traffic in the tawdry didn't exist, when society's glitterati largely had the power to dictate how they were depicted in the media. That all changed thanks to Robert Harrison, a twisted genius who became the patron saint of prurience, the progenitor to today's purveyors of celebrity sleaze. In December 1952, Harrison launched a new magazine, *Confidential*, which almost overnight radically and indelibly altered the American concept of celebrity. The magazine's motto was "Tells the Facts and Names the Names," and it did so with the mischievous glee of the lad proverbially pointing out the emperor's nudity. While other magazines and newspapers of the time published timidly fawning articles on famous people, *Confidential* brashly laid bare their sexual kinks, drug habits, and Communist party connections. Harrison's publication ran stories with titles such as "Picasso Is an Opium Addict!" "Errol Flynn and His Two-Way Mirror," and "Why Liberace's Theme Song Should Be 'Mad About the Boy.'" It exposed actor Rory Calhoun's prison record and the voracious sexual appetites and hard drinking of major league baseball heroes ("These Yankees Had a Ball!").

Time magazine once labeled Harrison "The King of Leer," and with good reason. In *Confidential*'s heyday in the mid to late 1950s, the magazine achieved a circulation of roughly four million, and as actor Humphrey Bogart once cracked, "Everybody reads it, but they say the cook brought it into the house." *Confidential*'s phenomenal popularity in supposedly prim-and-proper 1950s America was a shock to society's self-appointed guardians of propriety. The mainstream news media derided it as trash, the U.S. postmaster general sought unsuccessfully to ban it as obscene, and California legislators even held hearings to ponder *Confidential*'s menace to the privacy of the rich and powerful. Hollywood studio heads pondered setting up a special task force to refute its exposés. Eventually, through a slew of libel lawsuits by movie stars and a politically motivated criminal prosecution, Harrison's opponents did succeed in forcing him out of the celebrity scandal business. But by then it was too late. *Confidential* had bared a dark side of the American psyche: our collective urge to sacrifice our idols, or at least to stare with hypocritical disapproval at their feet of clay.

An eccentric dandy who favored white fedoras, silk cravats, and alligator shoes, Harrison hardly invented the human craving to be shocked and scandalized. In the seventeenth and eighteenth centuries, ballads—single-sheet publications that told news events of the day in verse—pandered to their readers by focusing upon grisly murders and the excessive pomp of royal weddings. In the 1920s, tabloid newspapers in New York pumped up their circulation with sensationalized crime coverage and headlines such as "Famous Killer's Girl to Wed Society Man."

The most blatantly trashy of the New York tabs was the *Daily Graphic*, owned by Bernarr Macfadden. The "Pornographic," as wags called it, invented a device called the "cosmograph," in which pieces of photos were pasted together to create an image of an event at which a *Graphic* photographer hadn't actually been present. When silent film heartthrob Rudolph Valentino died, for example, the Graphic published a cosmograph of the actor on the emergency room operating table, followed a few days later by a depiction of Valentino being greeted at Heaven's gate by Saint Peter and the angels. Another of the *Graphic*'s attractions was Walter Winchell, whose slang-laden tidbits about the comings and goings of Broadway actors were the genesis of the modern gossip column.

The *Graphic* also gave Robert Harrison his start in the publishing business, as an office assistant, against the wishes of his Latvian immigrant father, whose dream was to see young Robert learn a trade such as plumbing. As journalist Tom Wolfe wrote in his lengthy profile of Harrison for *Esquire* in 1964, the *Graphic*'s tawdry sensibilities had a powerful influence upon the future *Confidential* publisher: "Okay, it was bogus. It was ballyhoo. It was outrageous . . . but by god, the whole thing had style."

Harrison had to keep his penchant for sleaze close to the vest when he moved on to a new job, working for the *Motion Picture Daily* and *Motion Picture Herald*. The papers were published by Martin Quigley, a Catholic activist who had played a key role in forcing Hollywood studios to accept the "production code," a set of rules that barred anything beyond a hint of sex in movies. On the sly, however, the ambitious Harrison began staying after hours and using his straight-laced boss's office to work on a personal side project, a magazine called *Beauty Parade* that featured photos of scantily clad models. Quigley eventually got wind of Harrison's moonlighting, and as the story goes, fired him on Christmas Eve. Nevertheless, *Beauty Parade* sold well at newsstands, and Harrison soon followed it with a slew of other successful skin mags, with names such as *Wink* and *Flirt*. As Wolfe noted, Harrison's contribution to the genre was the concept of arranging sexy pictures around some story line, such as "Models Discover the Sauna Baths."

Harrison might have become an obscure footnote in the history of erotica but for another event: television broadcasts of congressional hearings on organized crime, chaired by Senator Estes Kefauver, who subpoenaed scores of notorious hoods and compelled them to submit to his combative, theatrical interrogations. As Sam Kashner and Jennifer MacNair wrote in *The Bad and the Beautiful*, a history of Hollywood in the 1950s, the Kefauver hearings fascinated the nation in the same way that the O. J. Simpson murder trial would four decades later. They also inspired Harrison: If the public craved sordid revelations, why not create a new magazine to fill it? The ever creative publisher added one tangy twist. Instead of the criminal underworld Kefauver was exposing, Harrison decided to focus his new brainchild, *Confidential*, on another powerful, secretive group of malfeasants—Hollywood stars.

Harrison's notion was a brash one. In 1952, with the exception of a few powerful—and carefully pampered—columnists such as Winchell in New York and Louella Parsons and Hedda Hopper in Los Angeles, studios and their press agents virtually dictated the stories that newspapers and magazines printed about stars. They got away with it because they controlled access to their clients. As writer Lee Server noted in his biography of actor Robert Mitchum, when RKO Warner decided to make the husky young actor into a teen heartthrob, the studio's publicity department concocted an official biography in which the marijuana-smoking, profane ex-hobo from hardscrabble rural Delaware became a former child vaudeville star with a degree from Duke University "who likes people and is a great kidder." It might be widely known in the business that a macho leading man was gay, or that a leading lady was addicted to diet pills, but reporters didn't dare write those stories, and the mainstream media wouldn't have published them even if they had.

Confidential broke that self-enforced code of silence. Harrison's fledgling publication wasn't part of the club, and it didn't have a prayer of receiving invitations to studio press conferences or getting authorized access to a star. So *Confidential* went another route, bypassing the Hollywood publicity machine altogether. Instead, the magazine got its scoops from Hollywood Research, a California-based company that Harrison apparently set up as a front to make it more difficult for people to sue him. Hollywood Research spent one hundred thousand dollars a year buying the services of Tinseltown informants, ranging from police officers to prostitutes. One of its most prolific sources of dirt was a beautiful former actress who lured various movie stars into bed so that she could capture their conversations with a hidden microphone. The magazine also employed a herd of roaming freelance photographers who hid in the shrubbery outside restaurants and used other bizarre tricks to get candid and often unflattering photos of the stars.

Postwar technological advances—miniature tape recorders, smaller cameras that could be equipped with telephoto lenses—aided *Confidential*'s spies in their reportorial trickery. *Confidential* also quietly paid retainers to journalists from mainstream media outlets such as United Press and the New York *Daily News*, in exchange for tidbits their bosses might have thought too sleazy to publish. Many of *Confidential*'s stories, in fact, were based on information that mainstream reporters knew about but didn't print.

The classic *Confidential* article was fifteen hundred to two thousand words of alliterative, slangy, double entendre–laden prose. The Liberace article, which described the pianist's supposed attempt at a homosexual seduction, noted "the pudgy pianist's many faithful fans would have popped their girdles if they had witnessed their idol in action last year in an offstage production that saw old Kittenish on the Keys play one sour note after another in his clumsy efforts to make beautiful music with a handsome but highly reluctant young publicity man." (The pianist, who strived to keep his sexual orientation a secret, sued the magazine and won a financial award.) An article in the May 1955 issue, "Robert Mitchum: The Nude Who Came to Dinner," detailed a party at which the "brawny star" supposedly took off his clothes, doused his body with ketchup, and proclaimed, "This is a masquerade party, isn't it? Well, I'm a hamburger!" The September 1957 issue contained a first-person story by a transvestite who claimed to have fooled a then popular male star: "You told Maxine that I was a 'lovely girl' and added the Audrey Hepburn bit. And pretty soon, you and I were dancing to Calypso music, remember? That's when you really turned on the beautiful hunk-of-man charm."

While *Confidential*'s painfully purple prose wasn't going to win over fans of *The New Yorker*, the public ate it up. *Confidential*'s first issue, in December 1952, sold 250,000 copies. By 1956, *Confidential* claimed a circulation of 4.2 million, which Harrison gleefully boasted was greater than that of any publication since the Gutenberg Bible. That translated into cash, and *Confidential* virtually printed money, generating profit margins in excess of 50 percent.

Harrison once explained his success by observing that Americans like to read about things that they are afraid to do themselves. But in a 1956 article for the highbrow Catholic literary journal *Commonweal*, Gonzaga College professor John P. Sisk theorized that part of the magazine's appeal was a uniquely American resentment of celebrities:

> Another man's success only spotlights one's own hopeless mediocrity, especially in America, where the fruits of success are so tantalizingly near. The American is not protected from envy by an aristocratic order that makes certain kinds of success unthinkable. With luck, he might have been the one sunning himself with the unbelievable blonde on the private beach. It is some comfort, then (and cause to congratulate himself on his own virtue) to learn that it is the wrong blonde and that there will be hell to pay.

At the same time, Sisk argued, there were more complex, murky feelings at work as well. The public saw celebrities as living out ordinary people's fantasies of wealth and power, which culminated in unlimited, orgiastic sex: "The sin is all that humanizes the celebrity for the non-celebrity [because] celebrityhood as such is beyond the reach of his imagination." The studio publicity departments' puzzling insistence that movie idols were paragons of clean living only left a fan feeling more frustrated and unfulfilled—and eager for the real dirt.

In fairness, *Confidential* wasn't totally without merit. In a fashion comparable to the Internet rumor mill of today, it occasionally broke news that the respectable mainstream media, for whatever reasons, wouldn't touch. It exposed the brutal treatment of juvenile delinquents in an Arizona "Devil's Island for Boys" and, presciently, detailed how tobacco companies were lying to the public about the dangers of smoking. Its stories on corruption in the gambling and garment industries aroused the ire of mobsters, who on one occasion apparently took Harrison for a ride and threatened him with death. (By his account, he escaped by convincing them that he was already dying of incurable cancer.)

But *Confidential* would never have received a laurel from the *Columbia Journalism Review* for its ethics, either. Early on, for example, *Confidential* curried favor with powerful columnist Winchell, who would plug the magazine on his TV show in return for the magazine's hatchet jobs on his enemies. ("It got to the point where we would sit down and rack our brains . . . we were running out of people, for Christ's sake!" Harrison would later recall.) Insensitivity was another *Confidential* hallmark. In stories such as "The Lavender Skeletons in TV's Closet" the magazine gleefully outed gays and lesbians in an era when they faced career ruin and even prosecution if their sexual orientation became known. As Kashner and MacNair recount, tennis great "Big Bill" Tilden died of a stroke shortly after a *Confidential* piece revealed that he'd done jail time and repeatedly had been blackmailed over the years as a result of his homosexuality.

Over time, the magazine even developed a clandestine relationship with some movie moguls. In an era when their once tight control over actors was slipping, leaking unflattering information about a star to *Confidential* offered them a way to punish those who were too brazenly defiant. On other occasions, the magazine allowed the studio to choose whose reputation would be savaged. According to Kashner and MacNair, one studio, for example, fed the magazine info about actor Rory Calhoun's prison record in order to get Harrison to spike a piece about two bigger and more valuable stars, Rock Hudson and Tony Perkins.

Ultimately, however, *Confidential*'s virulent success at celebrity scandal-mongering proved to be its undoing. Former editor Howard Rushmore left the magazine after a bitter falling-out with Harrison. Harrison could replace Rushmore, but he also had to contend with the ire of the powerful people his magazine tormented. The publisher found himself dodging bullets from celebrities—sometimes literally, such as the time he went on a hunting trip in the Dominican Republic and was shot in the shoulder by one of his companions while the two were arguing about a story that Harrison had run on the man's actress ex-wife. (Both men later insisted it was an accident.) Other celebrities viewed him and his magazine as a threat to the insular world of privilege they once had taken for granted. *Confidential* infiltrated the class of supplicants that celebrities had come to depend upon—from wardrobe ladies and bartenders to cops and reporters—and convinced them to violate the code of silence that covered up stars' embarrassing misbehavior. *Confidential* also posed a larger danger to the profitable illusion of moral character that Hollywood had nurtured by churning out all those ponderous epics, saccharine romances, and heartwarming family dramas. Somebody had to stop Harrison before he hipped middle America to the disturbing truth that the movie and TV industries—the same ones who fed them sanctimonious messages about the right way to live—were actually filled with people who felt no need to follow those rules. Something had to be done about *Confidential*.

The government, always eager to help the rich and powerful, tried first. The U.S. postmaster general briefly barred Harrison from sending *Confidential* through the mails on the grounds that it was obscene, but Harrison hired rainmaker attorney Edward Bennett Williams and forced him to back down. A federal prosecutor in Chicago indicted the magazine (but not Harrison or his staff, oddly) on obscenity charges after it ran an article on the then taboo subject of abortion; at trial, the magazine was acquitted. The stars themselves began filing defamation lawsuits. Mitchum, for example, took the magazine to court over the "nude hamburger" article (even though, as his biographer points out, the anecdote actually was a tamer version of a story that the actor himself told to friends). Maureen O'Hara, Dorothy Dandridge, and Liberace, among others, also sued. The magazine might have been able to fight them off individually, but the cumulative pressure of so many lawsuits became a burden.

Things got worse. In the spring of 1957, a Los Angeles grand jury indicted *Confidential*, Harrison, and assorted underlings. The case reeked of politics; then California attorney general Edmund G. "Pat" Brown was eyeing a run for governor, and deep-pocketed movie industry potentates were valuable supporters. The main charge—conspiracy to commit criminal libel—came from an obscure, antiquated section of the California code that made it a crime to publish a falsehood that damaged a person's reputation unless the publication had some justifiable motive. A couple of decades later the law would be tossed out as unconstitutional, but at the time it guaranteed a virtual automatic conviction, since it was difficult to argue that *Confidential*'s keyhole peeking had any redeeming social value.

The proceeding turned out to be as lurid as anything *Confidential* ever published. One defendant, who was accused of collecting gossip on a wrist microphone, fled to Mexico and attempted suicide. A prosecution investigator also tried to kill himself—and succeeded. A subpoenaed witness, Mae West's chauffeur, died under mysterious circumstances just before the trial began. In August 1957, hundreds of spectators crowded the Hall of Justice in downtown Los Angeles, hoping to catch a glimpse of Mitchum, Mae West, Dick Powell, and other movie stars Harrison had hinted he would haul into court as defense witnesses. Ultimately, he didn't make good on that threat, in part because some celebrities reportedly chose to be out of town so they couldn't be served with subpoenas. A few, including actress Maureen O'Hara, called Harrison's bluff by taking the stand for the prosecution.

The state's surprise witness turned out to be *Confidential*'s embittered former editor, Howard Rushmore. Rushmore testified for two days, laying out the magazine's reporting and editing methods in sleazy detail. For the studios, however, his appearance backfired, because he inadvertently dropped names of stars that they'd hoped to keep out of the mess. (In addition, he testified that one of the reporters covering the trial, Florabel Muir of the New York *Daily News*, had been on a secret retainer to supply stories to *Confidential*, although she subsequently denied it.) And the movie power brokers undoubtedly cringed when another prosecution witness, a Hollywood madam, described how she arranged a meeting for one star with a pair of prostitutes to "bring up to date" an old story about her own sexual encounter with him years before.

After two weeks of deliberation, the jurors were fighting bitterly, in part because some of them didn't want to read the stack of racy novels that *Confidential*'s lawyers had introduced into evidence to show that the magazine wasn't any more obscene than the rest of the newsstand. They were hopelessly deadlocked, with five jurors holding out for acquittal. *Confidential* managed to beat the rap, but the cost was too great, and Harrison still faced the prospect of a dozen lawsuits by various celebrities. He cut a deal with prosecutors: All of the charges except for two minor counts of obscenity were dropped. In return, Harrison announced that *Confidential* was changing its editorial focus and no longer would delve into celebrities' private lives.

Denuding *Confidential* of celebrity sleaze took away the magazine's main appeal to readers, and sales dropped. Eventually, Harrison was forced to sell the magazine. *Confidential* actually survived for another two decades under various owners, filling its pages with less risky revelations, such as exposés of hippie drug use. When Tom Wolfe tracked down Harrison a few years later to do an *Esquire* profile, he was living at a hotel under an assumed name and publishing a considerably tamer tabloid called *Inside News*, which featured stories such as "Castro's Sex Invasion of Washington." In 1978—the same year that his former magazine, *Confidential*, finally bit the dust—Harrison died in his office at age seventy-three.

Though the Hollywood establishment was able to chase *Confidential* out of the scandal trade, it proved to be a hollow victory. The public had been tantalized by that brief glimpse, and it was eager for more. The rules of the game had been forever changed. *Confidential*'s successors proved more adept at avoiding the legal traps into which Harrison's publication had fallen. In the 1960s, the *National Enquirer*, a Hearst tabloid taken over by a former Central Intelligence Agency officer named Generoso Pope, Jr., pushed the boundaries of print propriety. As author S. Elizabeth Bird notes in her study of supermarket tabloids, *For Enquiring Minds*, the *Enquirer* mixed lurid accounts of crimes (headlines such as "Kills son and feeds corpse to pigs") with accounts of drunken misbehavior by celebrities. When Elvis Presley died in 1977, the *Enquirer* showed how far tabloid journalism had advanced beyond the *Daily Graphic*'s cosmographs by actually obtaining a picture of the star in his coffin.

By the late 1980s, the celebrity scandal business had mushroomed far beyond anything that Harrison could have envisioned. The *Enquirer*, the *Globe*, the *Star*, and other tabloid weeklies lined the racks of every supermarket in the nation; the six biggest papers had a combined circulation of ten million readers. The new scandal sheets used updated versions of *Confidential*'s tactics; at least one paper, for example, had informants who regularly went through the trash outside celebrities' homes in Beverly Hills to glean revealing details about their private lives. In 1997, the *Globe* ran a cover exposé of Frank Gifford's tryst in a New York hotel, complete with surveillance pictures of the football great embracing a blonde who obviously was not his wife, TV personality Kathie Lee Gifford. (In a subsequent lawsuit, it emerged that the tabloid had promised the woman money beforehand for her story and photos.) Most brazen, perhaps, was *Celebrity Skin*, a magazine that specialized in obtaining and publishing photos of celebrities in the nude. (Its motto: "Stripping Tinseltown Bare since 1979.")

Beyond that, *Confidential*'s sleazy sensibilities spread to the mainstream media. In the 1970s, Time Inc. actually started a gossip publication, *People*, which became a phenomenal success. In the mid-1980s Condé Nast launched *Vanity Fair*, which mixed coverage of international business and politics with grisly true-crime stories and tawdry tell-alls about celebrities such as Michael Jackson and actor Steven Seagal. Even *Esquire*, once the paragon of literary journalism, ran a cover story on actor Kevin Spacey that insinuated he might be a closeted gay (though, in fact, he was not). Mainstream news reporters developed an ingenious technique for being tawdry while still retaining the facade of high-mindedness: If a story was too tasteless to touch, they waited until it was broken by a tabloid, and then reported about the subsequent uproar.

Ultimately, however, that increasingly faint distinction between legitimate news and prurience became unnecessary. In the late 1990s, the politically orchestrated investigation of then president Bill Clinton's affair with a young White House intern resulted in publication of an official document, the so-called "Starr Report," that contained explicit sexual details that *Confidential* never would have dared publish.

The society of sleaze that *Confidential* wrought has evolved in other ways. The entertainment business has discovered, to its surprise, that the public actually likes the idea that their favorite stars had tawdry secrets in their closets. It made them seem more human, more sympathetic. That led to the rise of confessional journalism, exposés in which the subjects were willing, even eager, participants. As Jack Levin and Arnold Arluke noted in their book, *Gossip: The Inside Scoop*, in roughly 40 percent of the *National Enquirer*'s celebrity stories, the subjects cooperated and gave sit-down interviews. Ultimately, the trail blazed by Harrison led to "reality" TV shows, in which the celebrity stars allowed camera crews into their homes with the intent of documenting their most embarrassing behavior for millions to see. The King of Leer would certainly be proud.

THE OPERATIVE NUMBER: 35

Number of the row at Grauman's Chinese Theater in Hollywood in which a Confidential *story claimed that actress Maureen O'Hara engaged in "heavy kissing" with a male companion. O'Hara claimed the incident was made up, and although* Confidential *produced two theater employees who claimed to have witnessed it, they didn't agree on some details. At one point in* Confidential's *criminal trial in 1957, the jury actually took a field trip to the theater to probe the story's plausibility for themselves.* New York *Daily* News *reporter Theo Wilson, who went along, later recalled that one of the bailiffs had to pry a corpulent male juror out of a seat in row 35, where he'd gotten stuck "trying to see if it was physically possible to do in that seat what* Confidential *claimed Maureen was allegedly doing with her beau."*

The Most Poisonous Pen

To render his racy gossip into readable prose, Robert Harrison bypassed the journalistic mainstream. His somewhat bizarre choice for editor was Howard Rushmore, a gangly six-feet-five-inch, emotionally troubled former communist and onetime movie critic for the *Daily Worker*, where he'd been forced out after showing insufficient zeal in condemning *Gone With the Wind*.

Rushmore had metamorphosed into a fanatical anticommunist investigator, hosting a radio show called *Out of the Red* and working briefly as a research aide for Senator Joseph McCarthy. After the FBI discovered that some of his revelations were figments of his own feverish imagination, he fell out of favor with the communist witch-hunting set, and was on the skids and drinking heavily when Harrison met him at a nightclub. Rushmore hoped to use *Confidential* as a soapbox for his anticommunist crusade and as a comeback vehicle, but what Harrison really wanted was movie-star sleaze. Swallowing his pride, Rushmore adopted pen names such as "Brooks Martin" and switched from exposing fellow travelers to probing issues such as whether seemingly busty actress Zsa Zsa Gabor actually wore falsies.

Rushmore continued to harbor hopes of regaining his stature among the red-baiting political right. To that end, he wrote articles praising J. Edgar Hoover and anonymously mailed them to the FBI. When that didn't work, as Hollywood historians Kashner and Mac-Nair recount, Rushmore tried a more desperate gambit. In July 1955, shortly after appearing on a local TV talk show in Chicago, *Confidential*'s editor vanished. When police searched his hotel room, they found his wallet, keys, a plane ticket back to New York, but no sign of where he had gone. His wife told them that he'd told her that he was on "a real hot story," and that he was to meet a mysterious source named "Larry." The latter supposedly was a communist who had proof that Navy Secretary James Forrestal, who'd plunged to his death from a hospital window in 1949, had been murdered.

Rushmore's disappearance became national news, and Harrison had to print additional copies of *Confidential* to meet the newsstand demand. Eventually, however, an anonymous phone call led detectives to another hotel in Butte, Montana, where Rushmore was staying under an assumed name. Rushmore claimed the hoax actually was designed to conceal his real plan, which was to help the FBI expose communists in the miners' union in Montana. J. Edgar Hoover instructed his agents that Rushmore was "a nut," and that the bureau should avoid contact with him. The incident effectively trashed whatever hopes Rushmore had of resurrecting his career as a semilegitimate right-wing political commentator.

In 1955, he bitterly parted ways with Harrison when the two quarreled over Rushmore's desire to use *Confidential*'s pages to bash popular liberal icon Eleanor Roosevelt.

Rushmore's appearance as a prosecution witness at his former employer's criminal trial didn't exactly lead other publications to deluge him with job offers. Reduced to working at cheap pulps such as *True War*, he began drinking more heavily than ever, and his wife left him. A year after the trial, he forced his way into a Manhattan cab in which she was riding and shot her to death, and then turned the gun on himself. It was a particularly perverse coda: In death, Rushmore turned himself into the sort of lurid tale in which the magazine he'd come to despise had once specialized. In a perverse sort of tribute, Harrison would later publish an exposé suggesting that the conspiracy theorist actually had been murdered as part of some dark cabal.

You Want *More*?

- *The Bad and the Beautiful: Hollywood in the Fifties*, by Sam Kashner and Jennifer MacNair, W. W. Norton, New York, 2002.
- *Dish: The Inside Story of the World of Gossip*, by Jeanette Walls, Avon/Spike, New York, 2000.
- *For Enquiring Minds: A Cultural Study of Supermarket Tabloids*, by S. Elizabeth Bird, University of Tennessee Press, Knoxville, Tenn., 1992.
- *Winchell: Gossip, Power, and the Culture of Celebrity*, by Neal Gabler, Knopf, New York, 1994.

The Wonder Garment

*Pantyhose was a landmark innovation when it was conceived in
1953, and eventually grew into a symbol of women's liberation—
or women's enslavement, depending on whom you ask.*

IF YOU'VE BEEN LISTENING CLOSELY to the media murmur
during the past decade, you've probably heard not just the soft
grumble of growing consumer discontent among American women,
but a much more complicated story. It includes conflicting themes
of freedom and oppression; soaring scientific and technological
innovation and insoluble problems; women's changing role in society and an expanding generation gap; and the death rattle of a social
revolution. The topic?

Pantyhose.

What for decades had been a source of irritation and complaint
among American women exploded into national debate in early
1993 following the publication of *Why Women Pay More: How to Avoid
Marketplace Perils*, a book by former *New York Times* consumer

reporter Frances Cerra Whittelsey and consumer advocate Ralph Nader. The book argued that the makers of cosmetics, clothes, and cars, among other products, routinely charge women higher prices than they charge for comparable products for men. But what really got people talking was an accusation—leveled during a January 1993 telecast of Phil Donahue's talk show featuring the book's authors and other consumer advocates—that the tendency for pantyhose to snag and run was part of a calculated master plan to sell women an inferior product that would self-destruct in a ridiculously short amount of time, sometimes before its first use.

"You are getting so ripped off on your pantyhose!" Donahue told his national television audience after several women in the studio lifted a skirt to show evidence of the conspiracy. "They fall apart. You're paying all kinds of money for them. You're not doing anything about it."

Donahue's show sparked a flurry of interest among consumer reporters around the country. By the spring of 1994, fifteen television stations had aired "investigative" stories critical of pantyhose makers—this at a time when, according to one report, more casual styles already had the U.S. hosiery market "shrinking like a pair of wool socks in hot water." The National Association of Hosiery Manufacturers, now the Hosiery Association, responded with a $250,000 media counterattack designed to educate women about *why* pantyhose had the approximate life span of a camera flash. While claiming that its efforts had nothing to do with the unfolding public relations nightmare, the group distributed video clips and brochures to the mainstream and fashion media touting the proper care of pantyhose. An industry group spokesman argued that women had created the problem by clamoring for increasingly sheer synthetic leg coverings since the introduction of nylon stockings in 1940. They simply needed to understand that "the lighter and sheerer the hosiery is, the more delicate it is, and the more care it requires."

Not many fashions have ever triggered that level of contention among the general population—the monokini and the leisure suit do come to mind—but this was a passionate dispute about a fashion *accessory*. It continues to this day. How did something designed for so simple and intimate a purpose engender such zealous public debate?

The answer is that from the moment it was first conceived in 1953, sheer pantyhose was never simply a convenient antijiggle solution for women's legs. True, on one level, it was designed to instantly smooth, shape, and tan a woman's less-than-perfect legs without her ever having to don a running shoe or step into sunlight. Women have long understood the appeal of a perfect leg to the typical male, and a sheer leg covering allows them to offer a tantalizing glimpse of naked leg flesh, only better. On another level, pantyhose was intended to liberate the fashionable female office worker from the onerous chore of stuffing herself into a girdle, garters, and other "foundation garments" that were as highly engineered as a suspension bridge and required her to dress with no less rigor than a medieval knight girding for battle.

"It was a wonderful invention," said Alison Lurie, author of a 1981 study called *The Language of Clothes*. "You have no idea what it was like to be a woman before pantyhose. There was all this hardware and scaffolding you had to wear. There were straps and elastic and rubber and wire, and with all that paraphernalia, there were still very large areas that were cold and unattractive."

"And no more embarrassing moments when your dress got caught in a breeze!" agreed Knoxville, Tennessee, newspaper columnist Ina Hughs, referring to those flukes of breeze or passing snags when "that pudgy flesh between the top of the stocking and the bottom of your britches" was unveiled to the world.

Alas, the miracle wonder garment was not without flaws. "Every woman over ten years old has a pantyhose horror story," Hughs wrote. "Bad hair days are nothing compared to having the elastic on your pantyhose give way as you start down the aisle on a Sunday morning. By the time you get to your pew, you're taking baby steps to keep from tripping over yourself, and everyone lifts their eyes from the hymnbook and wonders if you need to visit the ladies' room, or if you have just been arrested and put in ankle restraints."

Author L. C. Van Savage's complaints were more to the point: "They chafe, they bind, they roll, they creep, they sag, they snag, they hurt, they barber pole, they burn, they freeze." As Savage and countless other pantyhose wearers have concluded, pantyhose *had* to have been invented by a man, perhaps the Marquis de Sade himself.

But the real story of how pantyhose was invented and eventually became such a polarizing cultural lightning rod is worth repeating. There's simply no way to tell it without weaving together threads from some of the most significant social and industrial movements of the past century—a fact that puts pantyhose squarely among the landmarks of twentieth-century innovation.

The story has many beginnings. One version starts in the early 1930s, when Du Pont, the chemical giant, set a team of researchers to work developing a durable synthetic fiber that would replace delicate silk as the stocking material of choice—"an epoch-making invention," according to Susannah Handley, author of *Nylon: The Story of a Fashion Revolution*. That story climaxed in 1940, at the Wonder World of Chemistry exhibit at the New York World's Fair, when nylon stockings made their public debut to rapturous applause. With World War II approaching, nylon stockings promised to free the nation's legs from the grip of the Japanese silk industry. Another version starts on what was hyperbolically dubbed "N" Day—May 15, 1940—the first day that nylon stockings went on sale in the United States and created the kind of public sensation that decades later would be associated with a Beatles American tour or a new *Star Wars* movie. Yet another version begins on February 11, 1942, when Du Pont, in order to make parachutes, ropes, tents, uniforms, flags, and other materials needed for the effort to win World

War II, turned all of its nylon production toward that end and forced American women to make what some considered the ultimate sacrifice for their country. (With no silk from Japan and no nylon from Du Pont, some American women resorted to drawing a "seam" down the back of their legs to create the illusion that they were wearing stockings, which were intended to create the illusion that they were wearing nothing on their bare legs. Follow that?) Still another version of the pantyhose story begins in 1965, when London designer Mary Quant outfitted Twiggy, the first supermodel, in a miniskirt that required nothing less than pantyhose to keep the doe-eyed waif from becoming the first mass-media porn star.

But perhaps the most significant moment came in 1953, in the textile town of Altamahaw, North Carolina, without fanfare or any public notice at all. Ethel Gant, the pregnant wife of the president of Glen Raven Mills, was trying to reconcile her desire for fashionably smooth legs with her expanding belly, which in those postwar baby boom years also was pretty fashionable. Her girdle-and-garter options were limited and uncomfortable, and her husband, Allen Gant, Sr., saw an opportunity in his wife's dilemma. Innovators at another North Carolina textile company had in the late 1940s developed a way of twisting nylon yarn in a way that made it stretch. According to a Glen Raven Mills corporate history, *The Raven's Story*, Ethel and Allen began toying with the idea of making a sheer version of theatrical tights for day and dress wear. Ethel supposedly liked the idea so much that she stitched together a prototype using two nylon stockings and a pair of her underpants.

Clearly, refinements were needed. Early efforts included versions that stretched to the wearers' chins, and it took Glen Raven researchers until the spring of 1959 to perfect a way of making the first commercial version of pantyhose. By today's standards those early models would be considered crude and unsightly—not to mention unhealthy, since moisture-trapping nylon sent yeast infection rates skyrocketing, until the advent of the cotton crotch years later—

but the company's trademarked Panti-Legs were hailed as a revolutionary step in fashion when the company introduced them in 1960. Like the brassiere, another landmark fashion accessory, they were able to create the illusion of nudity beneath clothing. Pantyhose became the ultimate fashion tease, with a look-but-don't-touch quality that even appealed to fabled look-but-don't-touch fan dancer Sally Rand, who wrote to Glen Raven Mills praising Panti-Legs and pleading for a version without seams. That refinement soon followed.

Pantyhose arrived in the marketplace at a time when the world was changing fast. Americans could once again afford little luxuries after years of wartime sacrifice. Older women who had settled into domestic lives after the war gradually began returning to the workforce they'd bolstered while America's men were serving in Europe and the Pacific theater, and they had more important things to do than spend their mornings trussing themselves into foundation-garment armor.

Also, by 1963, with the so-called youthquake underway in Europe and heading for the United States, younger women were emulating the mod styles that Quant and French designers André Courrèges and Pierre Cardin created—styles modeled by Twiggy, Jean Shrimpton, and other fashion icons whose hemlines crept ever crotchward. (Quant caused a stir in 1967 when she arrived at Buckingham Palace in a miniskirt to be honored by the queen.) Sales of pantyhose rose in direct correlation to hemlines, and that was the beginning of a great generational divide that continues today between older women who remember the bad old days before pantyhose and younger women who grew up oblivious to the inconvenience of stockings. By 1970, the year Hanes began selling its L'Eggs brand pantyhose in plastic eggs on supermarket shelves rather than through department stores, pantyhose sales accounted for 70 percent of the women's hosiery market.

Du Pont, for its part, was taking nylon into new fashion frontiers. It began producing variations of the fiber and marketing its synthetics to the high-fashion couturiers using sexy nonchemical names such as Sparkling, Qiana, and Cantrece. Those and other synthetic fibers not only revolutionized couture but wove their way into everything from wedding dresses to the space suits the Apollo 11 astronauts wore when they planted a nylon American flag on the moon's surface in 1969.

There was a playful sexiness to it all. Clothes got clingier. Legs became fashion statements unto themselves as designers experimented with colors, patterns, and sparkles. As the cost fell women began assembling entire wardrobes of pantyhose instead of coddling one good pair of stockings.

"In the beginning we couldn't get enough of them," said novelist Rebecca Forster, a former advertising executive specializing in women's fashion. "We collected L'Eggs eggs, and we crossed our legs more because sexy wasn't as explicit."

Playfulness also became the hallmark of pantyhose marketing, which reached a memorable high in 1973 when Hanes approached New York Jets Super Bowl hero Joe Namath with an idea. Namath was notoriously sexy—in a hairy-chested, nail-anything-that-moves party boy way—but he possessed a pair of crumbled knees that bore countless scars from his long career in football. The pantyhose company convinced Namath to sheath his fabled legs in a pair of Hanes's Beauty Mist—brand pantyhose and recline seductively while a television camera panned from his toes, past his elegantly smooth calves, battered knees and thighs, then past his disorienting chest, and finally to his startling and familiar face. The commercial showed how pantyhose could make even Namath's legs appear fetchingly attractive, and it remains the hosiery industry's most memorable statement of purpose, if also a turning point in Namath's reputation. (Years later, the football legend recalled a disillusioned man from Alabama who approached him and said, "You know, Joe Willy, I don't mind you wearing those there pantyhose like that, but Lord, son, did you really shave your legs?")

Oddly, the Namath commercial also was somewhat of a turning point in the history of pantyhose. Pantsuits came into fashion about the same time, and working women welcomed the chance to shuck their pantyhose for knee-length sheer nylon socks and other hosiery options. Once liberated, many found that they enjoyed not wriggling into those sausage skins each morning and feeling a waistband's bite throughout the day. In the years that followed, the popularity of "casual Friday" in the workplace would deal another blow.

The hosiery industry had no intention of going quietly. It introduced specialty products, some of which carry an unmistakable whiff of desperation. The world's women today have the opportunity to wear pantyhose that supposedly massage, moisturize, and provide "aromatherapy." L'Eggs markets "anti-cellulite" leg wear designed to make even the cottage-cheesiest leg flesh look as toned as that of an Olympic athlete, and one brand, Spanx, is aimed at women who like their pantyhose without feet. One company began marketing Gloveez, a novelty spandex-nylon glove with textured vinyl fingertips designed to help women don their pantyhose without damaging them, and at one point Hanes, claiming, "Good looks start with good health," began packaging its hose with inserts and photographs demonstrating the proper technique for conducting a breast self-exam.

Perhaps the most remarkable recent innovation was begun by a generations-old Midwest hosiery company that noted the number of orders it received from cross-dressers and other men and now makes and sells a line of men's pantyhose called Comfilon using the derivative marketing slogan "Comfilons are not your mother's pantyhose." Even Wolford, the Austria-based luxury hosiery company, sells an expensive cotton-velvet men's pantyhose under a brand name calculated to be less feminine. Rather than ordering pantyhose, male buyers can simply ask for the "Waistsock."

Pantyhose also have found their way into everyday usage without any marketing effort whatsoever. After an 11,070-foot volcano called Mount Spurr spewed a cloud of ash over Anchorage, Alaska, in 1992, there was a citywide run on air filters to keep cars, trucks, and buses running. Unable to find filters to equip its trucks, an Anchorage food company put pantyhose over the intake valves in the air filters of its delivery trucks and conducted business as usual. Competitive swimmers in Australia began wearing them to combat lactic acid buildup after training. In a flurry of letters to syndicated advice columnist Abigail Van Buren, a plumber recommended using pantyhose as a lint trap for washing machines, a seamstress recommended old pantyhose as the perfect stuffing for quilts, and a portrait photographer said pantyhose make a fine lens filter that can soften the appearance of a subject, especially older women with wrinkles. One Dear Abby reader took the opportunity to resurrect a bit of classic pantyhose humor. He recounted a moment in the locker room at his local gym when a curious male colleague watched him pull on a pair of pantyhose and asked when he'd begun wearing them. His answer: "Right after my wife found them in the glove compartment of my truck."

Still, between 1986 and 1992, the percentage of women who said they'd bought one pair of pantyhose within the previous six months declined from 82 percent to 75 percent. In 1992, 1.6 billion pairs of pantyhose were sold in North America. By the year 2000, that number reportedly had slipped to 1.2 billion.

One other curious phenomenon should be noted. These days, it's not hard to find wistful commentary in the media and on the Internet that recalls the good old days of silk stockings and nylons despite the onerous contraptions that made them practical. In a lengthy discourse called "Where Have All The Stockings Gone?" writer Anne Schlitt once recounted the memorable seduction scene in the film *The Graduate* in which actress Anne Bancroft, playing

Mrs. Robinson, seduces her daughter's boyfriend, Benjamin, played by a young Dustin Hoffman. When Benjamin threatens to back out of the hotel room encounter, she reels him back in by slowly, teasingly rolling her stockings from her ankle up to her thigh. The scene was so sexy that the film's producers used it on the movie poster.

"If Mrs. Robinson were living in modern times," Schlitt wrote, "what final plot would she have pulled? Slipping one's foot into a shoe, while pretty, doesn't have the same languorous appeal as pulling on a stocking. She most certainly couldn't have struggled with pulling on a pair of pantyhose; whatever excitement was building would have dissipated. . . . If Mrs. Robinson hadn't worn stockings in the hotel room, Benjamin would have left and our graduate would have never learned the lessons of love."

But, naturally, there's even some debate about the relative sexiness of stockings versus pantyhose. A couple of years ago, a British men's magazine, *Mondo*, conducted a survey in which a majority of British men it asked said they no longer found a woman in stockings as big a turn-on as a woman in sheer pantyhose. The magazine then asked three high-profile writers to explain why they preferred one type of hosiery more than the other. While David Thomas of Chichester, West Sussex, described pantyhose as "disgustingly practical [and] hosiery's answer to the flat shoe," the majority of surveyed men agreed with Quentin Letts, a political columnist for London's *Daily Mail*.

"Your jaws may drop," Letts wrote, "but men do have the ability to think for themselves. It may have taken us a while, but we have reached the conclusion that stockings and their attendant appendages are absurd and at least half a century out of date. It has dawned on us that they are a misery for a woman to wear. If you really love your sweetheart, you do not want her to walk around all day with a draught whistling up her skirt." He argued that pantyhose prevent such discomforts, "are far kinder to the Rubenesque figure," and "cover your darling's bottom in a nice peachy way and mean she can wear a skirt as short as a Milan taxi driver's temper." They are, in short, "modern [and] equitable."

In Letts's passionate defense of pantyhose, women may detect evidence of an even more profound revolution.

THE OPERATIVE NUMBER: 8

Average number of wearings that hosiery manufacturers claim a pair of sheer pantyhose will last.

When Chemistry Seemed Sexy

The portion of Du Pont's Wonder World of Chemistry forum at the 1940 New York World's Fair touting the connection between nylon fiber and great legs became a surprise hit and was celebrated by one observer as the fair's "sexiest corporate show." And according to Susannah Handley, author of *Nylon: The Story of a Fashion Revolution*, the company's elaborate effort to weave its revolutionary nylon into the world of fashion was an unrivaled success.

The world premiere of "Nylon: This Chemical Marvel," with its display called "Chemistry Serves the Realm of Fashion," included a knitting machine that knit nylon stockings right in front of the gathered crowd and a pair of mechanical hands that stretched a nylon stocking to its longest length and snapped it back, around the clock, to prove the durability of the synthetic fiber.

But according to Handley's account, the real stars of the show were models known as the Test-Tube Lady (also known as the Princess of Plastics) and Miss Chemistry of the Future. The Test-Tube Lady emerged from a giant test tube wearing an expensive prototype ensemble made entirely of artificial materials. Miss Chemistry strutted around the stage in a lovely—but then commercially unavailable—lace evening gown, stockings, "satin" slippers, and undergarments made entirely of nylon.

Conspiracy-minded women have suggested for years that pantyhose *must* have been invented by a man, and in a broad sense, they're correct. For the first time, Handley wrote, "the masculine world of molecular chemistry was portrayed as leading fashionable women forward."

You Want *More*?

- *Nylon: The Story of a Fashion Revolution*, by Susannah Handley, Johns Hopkins University Press, Baltimore, Md., 1999.
- *Plastic: The Making of a Synthetic Century*, by Stephen Fenichell, Harper Business/HarperCollins, New York, 1996.
- *Why Women Pay More: How to Avoid Marketplace Perils*, by Frances Cerra Whittelsey and Ralph Nader, Center for Study of Responsive Law, Washington, D.C., 1993.
- "The History of Hosiery," by Sid Smith, http://www.bluechip-socks.com/reserves/history/hist.html.

Thaws and Effect

*What to do with 260 tons of leftover turkey? In 1953,
C. A. Swanson & Sons created "convenience food" and
revolutionized the way American families eat—and interact.*

AMID THE SHOW-BUSINESS GREATS and not-so-greats commemorated in concrete outside Mann's Chinese Theater in Hollywood, perhaps the oddest tribute was a block of sidewalk containing
the impression of an aluminum frozen-food tray. It was made to
honor a man named Gerry Thomas, who is credited with helping
create a seemingly humble invention, yet one that subtly but pervasively helped reshape American culture: the TV Dinner.

The TV dinner was one of the first examples of "convenience
food." It was designed to require almost no effort, either in the
preparation or the actual consumption. It also was the first food that
was consciously intended to facilitate another experience—television watching. In accomplishing all that, it radically altered the traditional social experience of the evening meal. As a newspaper

headline on the anniversary of the TV dinner's creation once proclaimed, only half-facetiously: "It Came, It Thawed, It Conquered."

The story of the TV dinner actually starts before TV even existed. In the 1910s, Clarence Birdseye, a college dropout, went to arctic Canada as a nature researcher for the U.S. government. Birdseye noticed that fresh fish caught by Arctic natives, when thrust into extremely cold seawater, quickly froze. Later, when it was thawed and cooked, it still tasted fresh, because freezing food quickly prevented the formation of large ice crystals that damaged the fish flesh and ruined the flavor. Birdseye returned to the United States, and in 1923 he spent seven dollars on an electric fan, buckets of brine, and some cakes of ice. With those materials he developed a system of packing food into cardboard boxes and "flash-freezing" it. In 1930, the first frozen meat, fish, and vegetables hit the market. So that stores would have a place to display those wares, Birdseye also developed refrigerated display cases for grocery stores and leased cooled boxcars to transport frozen food around the country. Around that time, appliance manufacturers began to create the first home refrigerator-freezers cooled by Freon gas, which gave consumers someplace to store frozen foods until they could be thawed and eaten. The devices didn't become common in American homes, however, until the mid to late 1950s.

There have been varying accounts of the TV dinner's development in the early 1950s by Omaha, Nebraska-based poultry processor C.A. Swanson & Sons. (One version, for example, has Gilbert Swanson, one of the scions of the founder, cooking up the idea after he watched guests at his home balance dinner on their laps while watching "The Ted Mack Family Hour.") But in recent years, an even more strangely serendipitous story has emerged. In this version, which is disputed by some, turkeys had reproduced more enthusiastically than usual, thanks to a warm breeding season, resulting in an oversupply of meat. Swanson found itself stuck with a lot of unsold turkey—260 tons of it, to be precise. The company didn't have enough room in its warehouses to store it. To keep it from spoiling, the company had no choice but to load the turkey into ten refrigerated boxcars and ship it back and forth across the country while Swanson figured out what to do with it.

One of the staffers assigned to come up with a solution was Thomas, a Swanson sales executive. He had some vague notion for a new, labor-saving product, an instant dinner that wouldn't require much in the way of preparation. The World War II vet still remembered the Thanksgiving dinner he'd once hastily consumed on a rainy battlefield in Okinawa. The sliced turkey, dressing, and potatoes all came in a neat little container. The problem was that the various items got all mashed up and mixed together, so that when you opened it in the rain, it turned into an unappetizing stew. That wouldn't sell. A short time later, Thomas traveled to Pittsburgh for a sales call. He saw a new container that Pan American Airlines had devised to serve dinner on long flights: an aluminum tray with compartments to separate the meat, potatoes, vegetables, and dessert.

Thomas had an epiphany. He asked if he could stick one of the trays in his overcoat pocket, and on the flight home sketched on an envelope a design for a tray with compartments for the meat and side dishes. When he got back to Omaha, he says he showed it to Clarke Swanson, another of the founder's sons. "Look," Thomas explained, "what if you put frozen turkey in here and cornbread dressing in there and sweet potatoes in there? Stick the whole thing in the oven, and in less than half an hour—no fuss, no bother—you've got a meal!"

The notion of freezing a pre-cooked meal wasn't totally new—a New York company, W. L. Maxson, had first manufactured them for the Navy during World War II, and frozen pizzas and steaks already were on the market. Swanson itself already had developed a heat-and-serve chicken pot pie that was a strong seller. Even so, the genre of convenience food was still a dicey concept. In the early 1950s, America hadn't yet evolved into the fast-paced, impatient culture that it would later become. Most people still ate food cooked from scratch, and the menu varied distinctly from region to region (and in the big northeastern and midwestern cities, with their immigrant ethnic populations, sometimes from neighborhood to neighborhood). Dinner was an institution that played a central role in American family life, not just as a source of nourishment, but as a social ritual. It often began with a prayer, and the passing around of serving bowls and platters of steaming food piled high enough to reassure people of their comfortable prosperity (that held true even in poor households, where the platter might contain only a pile of hog maws or spaghetti and sauce). Between mouthfuls, conversation among family members provided news and entertainment. The time-consuming labor of finding, preparing, and cooking the meal usually was left up to a family's women members, a convention that helped reinforce the traditional division of roles among the sexes.

The company produced an initial run of five thousand dinners, with an assembly-line of workers ladling the food into each tray by hand. The woman who supervised the cooking came from Alabama, so the side dishes that came with the sliced turkey—corn-bread dressing and sweet potatoes—had an oddly southern feel for a product from the Midwest with a Swedish surname on the box. (Later, Swanson replaced those items with white-bread dressing and mashed white potatoes, which were geographically indistinct.) The list price: ninety-eight cents. A grocery store chain in Oakland, California, promptly bought one hundred cases of the product. The chain's manager was undecided about whether convenience food would ever become popular, but he was sure that the trays themselves would be prized by women shoppers—as a way to store buttons.

But he and other skeptics apparently hadn't noticed the early signs of the changes that would soon sweep American society. Swanson's new, instant meal-in-a-box had arrived at a pivotal moment. During World War II, many thousands of women workers took over jobs to replace men who'd been inducted into the military, and in the postwar economic boom many of them had remained in the workforce. "The timing was marvelous, but who knew?" Thomas told a reporter for the Newark *Star-Ledger* years later. "The way I figure is this: There had just been an upsurge of women working outside the home. But they were still expected to fix dinner. They wanted to work, but still provide a satisfactory dinner for the kids." The Swanson product, which took just twenty-five minutes to cook, made that easily possible.

For men, the concept apparently was a bit tougher to swallow. "I got a lot of hate mail from them," Thomas recalled in the *Star-Ledger* interview. "They said we were ruining family life. Men said they would divorce their wives if they were served our dinners. They wanted them to fix meals from scratch. But that wasn't going to happen anymore, and we caught the trend early."

A bit too early, in one sense: In the 1950s, refrigerators with freezer compartments were still rare, so most of the women who bought Swanson's new product had to shove it in the oven when they got home and cook it for consumption that evening.

Even so, Swanson managed to sell ten million TV dinners in the first year, because Thomas—who got a one thousand dollar bonus for his initiative—had devised a product almost perfectly in sync with the rise of another technology that was in the process of transforming American society. "Television was becoming popular," Thomas once explained to the New Orleans *Times-Picayune*. "So I thought we could attach ourselves to this very popular thing. And that's how the name was coined."

To make sure nobody missed the connection, the first TV dinner boxes were designed to look like televisions. A picture of the food was displayed on a wood-grain "cabinet," complete with illustrations of knobs and buttons. It was only logical for Swanson to go that route. The 1950s was an era—perhaps the last era—when there was an unabashed belief in the wonder of progress, and giving products spiffy space-age-sounding names was a popular marketing gimmick. (The plethora of products with "atomic" as part of their packaging is prime evidence.) By 1953, network television had only been around for seven years, but more than half of American homes already owned sets, and it was evident that the medium had taken hold. Swanson, in fact, already had a connection with television: The food company was the sponsor of "The Ted Mack Family Hour," one of the most popular shows in the early days of network broadcasting.

But the TV dinner went beyond simply exploiting a connection with its namesake. The food product actually worked in synergy with the still new medium to help turn television watching into an American compulsion. Arguably, the TV dinner played an even more significant role in the rise of television than another development, the La-Z-Boy chair (which was developed by Edward M. Knabusch and Edwin J. Shoemaker in the spring of 1928, months after Philo Farnsworth developed the first primitive TV set in September 1927.) As neuroscientists would later discover, television was a passivity-inducing medium; research subjects showed reduced alpha wave production while their eyes were glued to the tube. If a person made the small effort of turning the set on and sitting down, TV did the rest. The TV dinner was a complementary passive experience. It required little effort to prepare, or to consume. A diner didn't even have to avert his eyes from the screen to eat, since the food items were partitioned on the plate.

The sensuous experience of eating was no longer a distraction, even after fried chicken and Salisbury steak were added to the frozen menu. "There were few ways to wreck a TV dinner, even fewer ways to make it taste good," as *San Francisco Chronicle* columnist Steve Rubenstein once observed. Since all the items were on one tray, vegetable side dishes and the meat course had to be baked for the same twenty-five minutes, an imprecision that tended to wipe out nuances of flavor. Some of the early recipes for TV dinners were created not by a master chef but by Betty Cronin, a college-trained bacteriologist who was pressed into service after hours to develop recipes that would withstand the rigors inflicted by convenience. It reportedly took eighteen months, for example, to develop a fried-chicken breading that wouldn't fall off. The only thing about the TV dinner that interfered with the TV experience was having to sit at the dinner table to eat it, since the aluminum tray was too hot from the oven to balance on one's lap. That was quickly remedied by the invention of the folding TV table-tray, which enabled diners to position themselves in close proximity to the screen.

In just a few short years, dinner was transformed from a communal ritual into an experience that people barely noticed, save for the vaguely satisfied sensation of having their stomachs full. That metamorphosis is depicted dramatically in the 1990 Barry Levinson film *Avalon*. In the early part of the film, which spans the decade after World War II, a second-generation immigrant family's boisterous meals are filled with elders' rambling storytelling and arguments over the potatoes around a crowded, brightly lit dinner table. Near the end of the film, the next generation of the family eats, silently, in a suburban living room that is dark save for the pallid reflection of the black-and-white television upon their expressionless faces.

One could argue that the trade-off for that alienation was freedom for women from the laborious responsibility of cooking. In truth, however, the culture of convenience that the TV dinner helped foster didn't necessarily make a homemaker's life much easier. The TV dinner helped set an expectation of speed and ease that food cooked from fresh ingredients couldn't possibly match. (One recent survey found that in a third of all food choices made by American consumers, convenience became the most important factor.) So the cook of the house increasingly relied upon canned soups, Minute Rice, and cake mix. As a consequence of the migration of the next generation of immigrant families to the suburbs, the old style of kitchen work in which several generations of women shared the labor—and gave advice and comfort—began to die out. The new role model and influence was the stylishly coiffed, tastefully clad fictional homemaker Betty Crocker, whose cookbooks pictured Jell-O molds and chiffon cakes as neat and symmetrical as the portions on Swanson's aluminum trays. That unattainable ideal of seemingly effortless instant perfection imposed another sort of tyranny upon women—one that a few additional minutes couldn't alleviate.

By the 1960s, when Swanson dropped the "TV Dinner" moniker from its products, the notion of eating in front of the tube had become so ubiquitous that it no longer had the same marketing clout. Indeed, the portion of Americans who ate dinner while watching television continued to rise steadily over the next several decades, so that by the end of the twentieth century it amounted to 66 percent of the population. Many of those people were eating reheated frozen meals, of which half a billion packages were sold each year. As microwave ovens became popular in the 1980s, Swanson ditched its classic aluminum tray—an example of which was donated to the Smithsonian Institution in 1986—and replaced it with plastic. Swanson itself underwent change, being acquired by a succession of parent companies. In 2002, the latest owner, Pinnacle Foods, closed the Omaha plant where the company launched its creation. (Thomas retired from Swanson in 1970 and moved to Arizona, where he founded a gourmet pet food company. In 1998, he was inducted into the Frozen Food Industry Hall of Fame.) But the Swanson name lives on, and Swanson's Hungry-Man is still the second-best seller in the frozen dinner market, just behind ConAgra's Healthy Choice brand.

The influence of Thomas's invention continues to be felt. By the early twenty-first century convenience food was an ingrained part of the American lifestyle. "For the World War II generation, the attitude can be summed up as, 'I'm glad I don't need to cook anymore,' " market researcher Ronald N. Paul told *Food Engineering*, a trade magazine, in 2000. "For Baby Boomers, it's been, 'I wish I had time to cook.' For Generation X, it's, 'What, me cook?' Generation Y wonders, 'What's cooking?' " Nearly a half billion dollars' worth of refrigerated dinners were being sold each year.

But just as another twentieth-century innovation, the personal computer, was on its way to being supplanted by handheld portable devices, so the TV dinner seemingly was on the verge of obsolescence, due to the acceleration of the trend it had helped create. Eating from a tray required a person to sit down and use utensils. As the twenty-first century dawned, food packagers had developed a concept that required even less effort to prepare and consume—a cardboard tube filled with frozen macaroni and cheese, scrambled eggs, or another soft food. Consumers could shove the product in the microwave and then eat with one hand, squeezing a plunger that expelled the food into their mouths, while they drove a car, manipulated the joystick on a video game, or punched up a new song on their MP3 player. Meanwhile, the instant meal of the 1950s had become the subject of nostalgia. Ike, a Manhattan restaurant with a retro theme, began servicing its très chic patrons reheated TV dinners—at six dollars a pop.

THE OPERATIVE NUMBER: 74

Percentage of women who say they serve TV dinners and other prepared foods to their families because they're too busy to cook, according to research by Nestlé Frozen Foods.

The Vanishing American Meal

❧

According to a 1998 article in *Psychology Today*, three-quarters of American families no longer eat breakfast together, and the typical family sits down for dinner together just three times a week. This reflects not just declining family interaction, but the fact that the concept of three meals a day is itself becoming extinct. Instead, increasingly, Americans eat by "grazing." Research indicates that the typical upper-middle-class consumer nibbles on food items about twenty times in the course of a day.

You Want *More*?

- *Pickled, Potted, and Canned: How the Art and Science of Food Preserving Changed the World*, by Sue Shephard, Simon & Schuster, New York, 2001.
- http://www.affi.org, Web site of the American Frozen Food Institute.

Hell on Wheels

On "E-Day" in 1957, Ford rolled out the Edsel as a marvel of technology, product research, and consumer manipulation. The car crash that followed changed the American marketplace.

ON SEPTEMBER 4, 1957, AMERICA was caught up in the sort of anticipatory frenzy usually reserved for the latest buxom blonde movie starlet or hip-wiggling rock 'n' roll singer. In Cambridge, Massachusetts, a marching band led a congratulatory parade down the city's main avenue. In Richmond, California, a helicopter stretched a giant banner across the San Francisco Bay. In Shelby, North Carolina, a throng eager for a glimpse of the new star jammed the streets, so that police had to be called in to direct traffic. It's strange to think that the inspiration for all this pandemonium wasn't a person, but a car.

Not just any car, mind you. Ford Motor Company, in a bold bid to wrest a sizable chunk of market share from rival General Motors, had sunk $250 million—the equivalent of $1.6 billion today—into the development of a wonder car. Ford had combined revolutionary new automotive technology with styling intended to be a radical, eye-catching departure from anything else on the American road. Just as important, the new car was a first-ever attempt to combine modern psychology, marketing-research techniques, and mass media in an elaborately orchestrated campaign to create an instant sensation—an *über*pitch that reached into consumers' souls and touched the very essence of their self-images, dreams, and desires, so potent that it was capable of causing hundreds of thousands of them to abruptly switch their brand preference. *Fortune* magazine called Ford's new car "the most thoroughly planned product ever introduced." One automotive writer speculated that it might well become the first new brand of any sort to achieve $1 billion in annual sales—in its first year.

That day, nearly three million people crowded into dealers' showrooms to see what the excitement was about. Their curiosity had been aroused to a fever pitch by months of carefully planned leaks and rumors planted in the press, and by tantalizing commercials that showed the ghostly blur of the mystery car racing down a country road. Indeed, as Ford public relations official C. Gayle Warnock told another executive, the car maker had convinced the public that "it was going to be some kind of dream car—like nothing they'd ever seen."

The car they gazed upon was very, very different, from its unorthodox vertical oval grille and flattened tail—a marked contrast to shark-tooth grilles and fins on other 1950s cars—to the futuristic push-button transmission controls mounted in the middle of the steering wheel, to an innovative speedometer that could be set to flash warning signals when the driver exceeded the speed limit. But perhaps the most distinctive thing about the car was its odd-sounding name: the Edsel.

It was a brand name that would become an enduring icon in American culture, though not in the way Ford intended. Instead of dominating the marketplace, the Edsel became one of the quickest, biggest flops not just in automotive history, but in the history of product marketing. In doing so, it became the quintessential symbol of failure, a clunker whose name alone is still capable of evoking snickers a half century after its embarrassing demise. (When Dunkin' Donuts wanted to inject some humor into its TV commercials a few years ago, for example, it showed Satan driving up to try a new iced-coffee drink—in an Edsel.)

The Edsel, in some ways, was the ultimate product of its times. After World War II, the U.S. economy grew explosively, creating prosperity of a sort that previous generations might not have dared to dream about. But even as manufacturers of consumer products raked in phenomenal profits in the 1950s, there was an air of uneasiness. In order for the economy to keep growing, the public had to keep buying new houses and washing machines and automobiles—whether they really needed them or not.

Product designers, market researchers, and advertising executives set out to solve that problem by harnessing new ideas in psychology and methods of gathering and analyzing information. Led by experts such as Viennese émigré psychoanalyst-turned-advertising consultant Ernest Dichter, companies began to use questionnaires, interviews, and other tools to peer into the minds of their customers and study their aspirations, fears, desires, and self-image. (Among Dichter's clients was a major soap company, whose ads invited consumers to "wash your troubles away," after the psychoanalyst discovered through interviews that for many people, washing was a subconscious attempt to rid themselves of guilt.) Many in corporate America came to believe, as Dichter put it, that consumers' psyches could be shaped and manipulated to develop "a need for goods with which the public has been unfamiliar—perhaps even undesirous of purchasing."

When a Ford ad proclaimed that the Edsel was the result of "what we knew, guessed, felt, believed, suspected—about you," those words had a deeper meaning. By the early 1950s, middle-class Americans were purchasing seven million new cars a year, and as author Vance Packard noted in *The Status Seekers*, the automobile had become not just a means of transportation, but a way of defining one's identity. Automakers such as Ford believed in an economic continuum, in which young families started with the lowest-priced cars and strived to move up the ladder to flashier, more expensive models as they became more prosperous. Thus, in 1954, when an internal report recommended the development of a new, moderately priced vehicle to grab that growing segment of the automotive market, Ford didn't focus on mundane matters such as fuel economy or whether the trunk was roomy enough for an extra bag of groceries.

Instead, the designers who were assigned to what was then called the E-Car ("E" for "experimental") set out to create a status symbol. They analyzed photographs of all nineteen of the domestic car models on the market, with the aim of designing a car that would look dramatically different. As a result, instead of the horizontal grilles that most cars had, the E-Car had an unusual oval grille. As automotive historian Thomas E. Bonsal has noted, its vertical silhouette intended to evoke the elegance of the Rolls-Royce and other European luxury cars. Under the hood, the E-Car had a huge V-8 engine, with far more horsepower than its potential owners would ever be able to use. Its interior was equipped with a dazzling array of space-age gadgetry—an automatic transmission operated by push buttons mounted in the center of the steering wheel and designed to be so sensitive to the touch that they could be depressed with a toothpick. In addition to the alarm-laden speedometer, the dashboard also included a push button that opened the trunk and a device that allowed the driver to lubricate the chassis with a twist of a knob. Instead of the hard-to-read gauges that most cars had, the E-Car featured a console with "idiot lights" with messages such as "service engine" or "door ajar."

But the car's startling styling and futuristic features were only a part of the package, and not necessarily the most important part. After marketing studies contributed to the successful launch of the Thunderbird in 1954, Ford decided to pull out the stops for a car that it hoped would be an even bigger hit. Marketing research director David Wallace, who was assigned to develop the E-Car's marketing image, believed there was little real difference among various makes of cars, and that quality or performance had nothing to do with why people picked, say, a Chevy over a Ford. "Cars are the means to a sort of dream fulfillment," he told *New Yorker* business writer John Brooks. "There's some irrational factor in people that makes them want one kind of car rather than another—something that has nothing to do with the mechanism at all but with the car's personality, as the customer imagines it. What we wanted to do, naturally, was give the E-Car the personality that would make the greatest number of people want it."

In an effort to figure out what psychological buttons to push, Ford hired Columbia University researchers to probe the minds of sixteen hundred recent car purchasers in Peoria, Illinois, and San Bernardino, California. Instead of asking what sort of features the subjects preferred or which cars they thought performed the best, the researchers asked them to describe the person they envisioned behind the wheel of a particular make. Chevrolet owners were described as older males, less assertive but wiser, while the Buick was a car for middle-aged wives of lawyers and doctors, and the Mercury driver was perceived as a young buck who loved to put the pedal to the metal. The researchers also asked myriad questions unrelated to automobiles—for example, what sort of drinks the subjects preferred. (Middle-class car buyers, it was discovered, tended to stick to martinis and Manhattans at home, rather than more exotic concoctions, because they "do not have much confidence in their cocktail-mixing ability.")

From that mountain of data, Ford developed a snapshot of the typical personality for customers in the moderate-priced market segment that the E-Car was intended to snare. They would be young adults who liked to see themselves as rising executives or professionals ("millions pretend to this status, whether they can attain it or not," a Ford report noted), but who deep inside weren't quite so confident. They would tend to be conservative ("spirited but responsible"), family oriented, and most important, concerned about how others perceived them. ("Recognition by others of the owner's good style and taste," the report noted, was a major potential selling point.)

Wallace believed that if a customer's own personality clashed with the perceived personality of an automobile, the person would probably choose another make. Thus, despite the new car's cutting-edge appearance and features, Ford oddly opted to craft a personality for the new car that wasn't *too* distinctive. Instead, it would aim to be deftly vague and protean, a psychological blank slate of a car for people who, deep down, wanted reassurance more than thrills. It would project the message, Wallace wrote to Ford executives, that "The E-Car has faith in you, son—we'll help you make it!"

Ford became so obsessed with using psychology to craft every detail of the car's marketing that the project began to struggle under the weight of its voluminous research. When assigned to come up with a name, for example, Ford's advertising firm, Foote, Cone & Belding, amassed eighteen thousand possibilities, ranging from the usual military and nautical-inspired choices (Pacer, Ranger, Corsair, Citation) to oddball monikers such as the Zoom, the Zip, the Drof (Ford, spelled backward), and the Simplex. Researchers were deployed in the streets of several cities, where they surveyed passersby, asking them what associations various names brought to mind. (Oddly, they never told subjects that they were considering names for a car.) After a year's effort, the list was reduced to a single sheet of paper containing sixteen names, including the marketing experts' recommendation, Corsair, which not only scored high in the sidewalk interviews but had a faintly adventurous ambiance that seemed perfect for the E-Car customer's personality.

At that point, however, the data-driven approach finally collided with Ford's old-fashioned corporate hegemony. Executive vice president Ernest Breech, who ran the meeting in the absence of company president Henry Ford II, didn't like any of the final sixteen choices. Instead, he abruptly resurrected a possibility that had been discarded early in the selection process—Edsel, the first name of company founder Henry Ford's only son. "Why don't we call it that?" Breech said. The researchers were dismayed; they'd tested that name and found that in consumers it evoked associations such a "pretzel," "weasel," and "hard-sell." (According to one account, 40 percent of the consumers reportedly responded with "What?") Breech was not to be dissuaded. Before long he'd tracked down Henry II, who was on holiday in Nassau, and obtained his approval by phone.

The new car's strange name was an early hint of the complicated dilemma that would prove to be the Edsel's undoing. Though it was supposed to be the first research-driven car, in actuality the Edsel was anything but scientific. Instead, the car was developed using a mix of assumptions—flawed ones, as it turned out—and research gathered with the intent of persuading people to want the car Ford had developed, rather than trying to figure out what sort of car they actually wanted. But even when the studies' conclusions were valid, they couldn't trump the inclination of Ford's entrenched bureaucracy to ignore data when it suited them.

Now that the car had a name, Ford spent a lavish $50 million—more than $300 million in today's dollars—for an advertising and promotional campaign the likes of which the world had never seen. Over a two-year period prior to E-Day, Ford kept the E-Car/Edsel shrouded in mystery. When it came time to shoot commercials, the car maker hired a film production company used by the Atomic Energy Commission for security purposes, and required the actors allowed on the closely guarded Hollywood soundstage to swear oaths of secrecy. Simultaneously, however, the company selectively leaked bits and pieces of information about the car's revolutionary design and gadgetry in the press, with the aim of creating an air of intense anticipation. When the Edsel finally was unveiled to the press in the late summer of 1957, automotive-beat reporters were taken to Ford's test track, where they were startled to see stunt drivers putting a fleet of the new cars though various daredevil maneuvers—leaping from ramps and whizzing around one another in crisscross patterns at 70-miles-an-hour speeds. It was as if Ford couldn't resist showing off.

Ford followed up the rumor campaign with extensive advertising, heavily concentrated in the still new medium of television. Edsel became sponsor of *Wagon Train*, a popular Western series. The car maker also underwrote "The Edsel Show," an October 1957 variety special featuring Bing Crosby, Frank Sinatra, Rosemary Clooney, Louis Armstrong, and Bob Hope that attracted fifty-three million viewers. Amid all that show business glitz, the actual pitch for the Edsel was surprisingly low-key. Ford's advertising agency designed the car's ads to sound quietly self-assured—a quality that might resonate with the aspirations and insecurities of the target audience. "They'll know you've *arrived*, when you drive up in an Edsel," a typical ad told them.

But even Ford publicity man Warnock feared that the company might be outsmarting itself by setting hyperbolic expectations that the Edsel would be unable to meet. As he later recounted for journalist John Brooks, "I said [to a Ford executive], 'When they find out it's got four wheels and one engine, just like the next car, they're liable to be disappointed.'"

Unfortunately for Ford, Warnock turned out to be right. Hordes of curious Americans jammed dealerships on E-Day, but the curious weren't so quick to buy. Instead, Ford soon began getting ominous reports, such as the call from a dealer in New England who reported that two customers walked into the showroom, took a look at the Edsel, and then went next door to order Buicks. Ford's projections called for selling 200,000 cars a year, which meant that dealers had to peddle 600 to 700 cars a day. By the first week in October, they were only selling half that number.

By November, sales had dropped to 220 cars a day, and Ford executives were in a panic. In December 1957, the company sent letters to 1.5 million owners of medium-priced cars, offering them eight-inch plastic scale models of the Edsel if they only would stop by a dealership for a test drive.

Later, at least one Ford official would blame the sluggish sales on the Soviets' launch of the Sputnik, the first space satellite, which shattered Americans' sense of technological superiority and incited a backlash against the sort of space-age consumer gadgetry with which the Edsel was laden. Others would point to the Edsel debut's coinciding with the start of an economic recession—although another new car introduced at around the same time, American Motors' Rambler, had strong sales.

But there were more tangible problems—for example, the negative public buzz that quickly developed about mechanical and quality-control problems. Instead of building new plants to manufacture Edsels, Ford had tried to save money by simply speeding up assembly lines in its existing Ford and Mercury plants. Too often, however, the result of that haste was a car with a hood that didn't open properly or a door that rattled from a loose bolt deliberately hidden inside it by a frustrated autoworker as a none-too-subtle protest about his increased workload. The innovative push-button transmissions had a 50 percent failure rate within three months of use. In response, as historian John A. Byrne has written, Ford executive vice president Robert McNamara imposed a quality-control system. McNamara assessed points for each flaw—twenty points for a missing part, a tenth of a point for chipped paint—and allowed only cars with a score of less than thirty-five to be sold. While it probably sounded good on paper, that solution arguably made the problem worse, since the company was in effect giving itself permission to send dealers defective cars. (McNamara eventually left Ford in the 1960s to become U.S. secretary of defense, a post in which he oversaw an even more disastrous project, the Vietnam War.) By early 1958, Ford had to use an old plant in New Jersey to store the returned inventory. It became an elephants' graveyard for thousands of vehicles, many of them missing parts because dealers had been forced to cannibalize them to fix other Edsels.

Another Ford miscalculation was the Edsel's styling. The vertical oval grille was intended to evoke a European limousine, but Americans, who weren't really that familiar with the Rolls-Royce look, projected their own interpretations onto it, with the odd result that the car wrapped in psychological research itself became a sort of Rorschach blot. Some joked that the grille looked like a toilet seat, or "an Oldsmobile sucking a lemon." But at a time when a popular best-seller, journalist Vance Packard's *The Hidden Persuaders*, made it trendy to look for the hidden sexual content of advertising, others inferred a more lascivious symbolism. In his book, *The Edsel Affair*, former Edsel public relations man Gayle Warnock recalled that one irate member of the public wrote to him, complaining that Ford had gone too far "by designing a car with a front like a female vagina." The noted linguistic philosopher (and future U.S. senator) S. I. Hayakawa even wrote a scholarly article denouncing Ford, whom he accused of designing "a car that would satisfy customers' sexual fantasies and the like," and said prospective buyers could get the same titillation from a copy of *Playboy* magazine at far less expense. (Though Ford wasn't actually trying to use erotic cues, the company probably didn't help matters with unintentional double entendre advertising slogans such as "The one car that can look you in the eye and say you never had it like this before.")

As Edsel sales in 1958 and 1959 continued to dwindle, Ford grew even more desperate. The automaker tried to convince the public to ignore the loser image the car had developed with magazine ads that repeated the phrase "The Edsel is a success" like a mantra. At one point it gave dealers ponies, so that they could lure in families by offering free rides to children. But nothing seemed to go right—when then vice president Richard Nixon took an Edsel with him on a diplomatic junket to South America, protesters pelted his car with tomatoes and eggs.

Eventually, Ford jettisoned some of the car's more gimmicky features, and in the last model year, even gave the trademark grille a nose job. But none of those changes staved off the brand's doom. In 1959, just forty-five thousand Edsels were sold—fewer than consumers had purchased in the first three months after the car's debut, and about a quarter of what the company originally had envisioned selling. That December, just as the former wonder car's details had been leaked in tiny, tantalizing doses to the press, so Edsel's discontinuation was leaked, in the form of a footnote to a Ford Foundation financial report.

Some critics took the Edsel's embarrassing failure as a sign that the use of psychology and marketing research to design products—what *Time* magazine at the time derided as "motivational mumbo-jumbo"—was a sham. The real problem, however, wasn't that Ford relied on research, but the sort of research that Ford did and the way that it chose to use the information. The car maker believed—as it turns out, naïvely—that if it identified and pushed the right buttons in consumers' minds, it could create the desire to buy a product, regardless of the product's features. For all its questioning of consumers about word associations and the relative masculinity of various car makes, Ford's researchers never thought to ask a simpler question: What sort of car would people really like to own?

If Ford had asked the public that question, the company might have discovered that American tastes in the mid 1950s were in the process of shifting: Instead of another big, fast, flashy sedan, what people really wanted were small economy cars. The imported Volkswagen Beetle, with styling no less peculiar than the Edsel, saw its sales triple from 1955 to 1957. The Rambler, a domestic small car, sold 200,000 vehicles in 1958—almost twice the 110,000 Edsels purchased in the latter's two-year existence. "This was an area that Edsel research overlooked," Ford marketing guru Wallace later admitted. In an odd irony, at the time of the Edsel's cancellation, Ford had a compact version, the Edsel B, on its drawing boards. That design instead became the highly successful Mercury Comet.

From the Edsel, automakers learned that they couldn't dictate consumer tastes. But instead of abandoning research, they shifted their focus and began trying to use data about consumer likes and dislikes to design better products, ones that people were more likely to want.

By the early 1990s, the development and marketing of General Motors' Saturn, the first new car brand since the Edsel, showed just how much had changed. Saturn's chief executive, Skip LeFauve, reportedly gave copies of a book on the Edsel to his management team, and instructed them to learn from Ford's mistakes. Rather than simply build a car that GM executives liked, Saturn's designers used consumer survey data to fine-tune even the car's smallest details, such as the location of the radio control knobs on the dashboard and the sound made by the engine and exhaust. And instead of trying to use psychological wiles to manipulate middle-class Americans' desires and insecurities, Saturn's marketing touted the tangible benefits of choosing the new car—such as a dealer network focused on providing good service, and "no-haggle" pricing.

The emphasis on understanding consumer wants and needs has spread beyond the auto industry. In the restaurant field, for example, the Applebee's chain relies upon extensive consumer research—rather than executives' tastes—to decide what new dishes are included on its menus, and uses a sophisticated computer system to track and analyze what its customers seem to like best.

Intriguingly, the Edsel's parent company, Ford, goes to perhaps the greatest extremes to understand what customers really want. As a recent *Washington Post* article detailed, Ford researchers virtually move in with selected consumers and follow them around the clock, riding along to the supermarket and children's soccer practices in an attempt to understand exactly how cars fit into people's lifestyles. The company used the mountain of research data to create two fictional average customers, Lewis and Kathy, and to write detailed life stories for them, so that car designers could see exactly whom they are trying to please. As one Ford executive promised: "We'll go wherever the consumers want to go." In that change of attitude, the Edsel's influence continues to be felt.

THE OPERATIVE NUMBER: 24,900
*Current estimated value, in U.S. dollars, of a 1958
Edsel Citation convertible (original price, approximately
$3,500) in excellent condition, according to a
car collectors' web site.*

How the Name Could Have Been Worse

At one point, the poet Marianne Moore was enlisted by Ford to come up with possible names for the new "E-Car." Her list of creative but unusable suggestions included Adante Con Moto, Pastelogram, Intelligent Bullet, and Utopian Turtletop.

You Want *More*?

- *The Fate of the Edsel, and Other Business Adventures*, by John Brooks, Harper & Row, New York, 1963.
- *The Edsel Affair*, by C. Gayle Warnock, Pro West, Paradise Valley, Ariz., 1980.
- *Disaster in Dearborn: The Story of the Edsel*, by Thomas E. Bonsall, Stanford University Press, Stanford, Calif., 2002.
- http://www.edsel.net includes an extensive collection of Edsel photographs, historical information, sound clips of commercials, and various memorabilia cleverly presented through the format of a fictitious Edsel dealership, the Smith Motor Company.

The First Angry Mike Man

*The combative talk-show host is a raging cliché of modern
media. But in the early 1960s—before Rush and Howard, before
Mort, Geraldo, and Jerry—Joe Pyne was on the air.*

IN THE SCHIZOPHRENIC LANDSCAPE OF modern American
media, it's hard to imagine the undistinguished period from the
1950s through the early 1970s, when the primary mission of most
radio and television talk-show hosts was simply to be nice. Programming executives trying to snag a share of the massive,
detergent-scented audience of postwar homemakers pinned their
hopes on pleasant, likable hosts such as Arthur Godfrey, Betty Furness, Art Linkletter, Garry Moore, Mike Douglas, Merv Griffin, and
Dinah Shore—a veritable parade of potential Prozac spokespeople.
Regis Philbin, heir to their essential niceness, still clings to the
notion that "the likability factor is enormously important." In a
video documentary about talk shows released in 2000, he said,
"When you get right down to it, the personality of the person who is

conducting that show is the chief selling factor in making it a success."

Right you are, Rege: Personality is critical. But likability? How does that explain the over-the-top success of conservative flamethrower Rush Limbaugh, the three-hundred-pound gorilla of the talk-show genre who once referred to Ross Perot as "a hand grenade with a bad haircut" and who disconnects liberal dissidents by performing a "caller abortion," complete with vacuum-cleaner sound effects? Or the huge and rabid fan base of shock jock Howard Stern, who once joked on the air about his then wife's miscarriage and dispatched correspondent-provocateur "Stuttering John" Melendez to ask an unsuspecting Oliver North, "Did you ever have a nightmare where your penis gets caught in a paper shredder?" What role did likability play in the brief but spectacular success of the late Morton Downey, Jr., who routinely blew cigarette smoke into the faces of his guests and dismissed one by saying "Don't call me a prostitute, you fat, ugly slime."?

By the 1990s, many talk shows had metastasized into the broadcast equivalent of bear-baiting, with the host chosen not to promote pleasant on-air conversation but rather to provoke the kind of dramatic—better yet, embarrassing—public spectacle that would generate a little buzz in the crowded modern-media marketplace. The format reached a notable nadir when TV sleaze monger Jerry Springer pretty much dropped the "talk" from the talk-show format altogether and began pitting his trash-talking guests against one another like fighting cocks, packaging exploitainment for mass consumption or, when things got too medieval for broadcast, selling the choicest outtakes for $19.99 on uncensored videocassettes such as *Too Hot for TV (Deluxe Edition)* and *I Refuse to Wear Clothes!*

Yes, in broadcasting near the end of the twentieth century, nothing succeeded quite like excess. For every likable Jay Leno, David Letterman, Larry King, and Oprah Winfrey, there seemed a contemptible—and often highly rated—evil twin.

But if you follow the trail of staged showdowns, corrosive conversation, and dismissive insults backward from the reigning monarchs of the genre, you'll find yourself in a tiny radio studio at station WILM in Wilmington, Delaware, where in 1949 a chain-smoking, conservative loose cannon named Joe Pyne invented the whole shouting-head genre with his first call-in talk show, *It's Your Nickel*. The Chester, Pennsylvania, native was still in the early stages of a career that already had included the U.S. Marine Corps, where he won three battle stars and lost his left leg, as well as stints as a tobacco auctioneer, nightclub emcee, and radio D.J., and he was looking for an outlet for his many strong opinions.

He found it in *It's Your Nickel*, a precursor of the now familiar calls-of-the-riled format. Because the technology at the time made it difficult to broadcast callers' voices, though, listeners heard only the acerbic Pyne as he repeated each caller's question or point. Pyne's translations invariably included his own bare-knuckled points of view about local politics, public officials, and the issues of the day, and callers he found dull or disagreeable soon found themselves disconnected, often with a parting insult. (Pyne eventually developed a familiar repertoire of insults that included his trademark, "Go gargle with razor blades!" as well as "I could make a monkey out of you, but why should I take the credit?" and "I hope when you go home your mother runs out from under the porch and bites you on the leg.")

Pyne's combative style came along at a time when television was stealing radio's once massive audience, and radio needed something fresh and outlandish with which to compete. Television also was stealing many of radio's established performers. "At the 1950 point, there was a great, powerful suction, you might say, from television, which suddenly needed hundreds of people," recalled talk show pioneer Steve Allen in a video documentary called *It's Only Talk—The Real Story of America's Talk Shows*. "They had nobody. There had never been television before, so how could they have veterans? So they pulled in people from radio, vaudeville, circuses, God knows what."

Pyne stayed in radio through the 1950s, talking his way from smaller markets to larger ones. He succeeded everywhere he went, and programmers began to understand, as the ancient Greeks did, that conflict is the essence of drama, and drama is what prevents people from touching that dial. Pyne made clear that a protagonist without an antagonist is duller than a Mister Rogers's soliloquy. Spontaneity, unpredictability, and uncontrollability—the energizing chance that, at any moment, things could get interesting, weird, or go horribly wrong—were effective lures for audience and advertisers alike.

"Mr. Pyne was in no sense an entertainer," Allen said. "He never claimed to be able to charm his audience. He was just a rough talker, a fighter."

Talk shows had always been cheap and easy to produce, and remained so even after they migrated to television. ("It's simple," Philbin once said. "You want a talk show? Two chairs and a camera, and you've got a talk show.") Pyne eventually talked his way into national radio syndication on 254 stations around the country. He followed that success into television, where *The Joe Pyne Show*, which ran from 1965 to 1969 with a live studio audience, was eventually syndicated to 240 stations across the United States. While Pyne's reach and impact changed radically from his humble start, though, his essential shtick stayed pretty much the same.

But the story of Pyne's rise from obscurity to fame, or infamy, is about much more than one man's success. It is, in many ways, the story of a nation living through one of the most traumatic and transforming periods in its history and grasping for ways to cope. Never mind that the mercurial Pyne predated by more than two decades many of the imitators who followed. His real contribution may have been to serve as a national mood ring at a time when America was undergoing a total personality change and needed to talk through its issues.

Part of Pyne's appeal was that he seemed just as angry and confused as many of the people who tuned in. Not only had he lost that leg, but the country he had defended on the battlefield was suddenly getting strange on him. What were he and listeners to his early radio shows supposed to think about rock 'n' roll? Racial foment? Americans dying in Korea? After Pyne moved his act to Los Angeles in 1957, he and his fellow Americans watched as President John Kennedy was murdered in Dallas, police unleashed dogs against civil rights protesters in Birmingham, and young Americans were shipped off to fight in yet another obscure Asian country. He wanted answers, he wanted them now, and pity the caller or guest who stonewalled, waffled, or lied.

It's clear now that the arc of Pyne's broadcasting career—from small audiences to larger ones, from local radio to national television syndication—precisely parallels the country's growing need to vent. Reasoned analysis? Not a chance. Pyne tuned his radar to the issues that would make his audience react rather than think. "The subject must be visceral," he once told *Time* magazine. "We want emotion, not mental involvement."

Pyne and the culture finally reached a twisted codependence in the early 1960s. In the recent *It's Only Talk* documentary, talk-show host Montel Williams said that media coverage of cataclysmic events during those years, especially the aftermath of the Kennedy assassination, "opened up America to saying, 'I want to see it all, I want to hear it all, I want to know it all.' From that point forward, coverage of the Vietnam War changed, coverage of the riots and the race situation changed. From that point forward, television and news changed. The stories got deeper and deeper and deeper, and we started [talking about] issues that we as a nation had refused to talk about."

Maybe it's coincidental, but author and protocol expert Letitia Baldrige blames the dissolution of civil public discourse on that period in the country's history. "The level of conversation went down," she said. "The level of kindness and niceness went down. People stopped writing thank-you notes. People stopped saying 'Thank you' and 'Please, may I?' The whole world changed. Television reflects it."

Reflecting the country's dark mood was not a job for someone nice. It was a job for an antihero, someone perfectly in tune with the times, someone willing, as Pyne was in 1965, to punctuate a post–Watts riots conversation with a militant black guest by pulling a gun during his show and shouting "Let 'em come! I'm ready for 'em." It was a job for someone so confident that he could stare into a television camera and welcome viewers by saying, as Pyne once did, "Good evening. It's time once again to play chicken."

Some guests were better at it than others. Segregationist governor Lester Maddox was one of the many who simply walked off Pyne's set when the going got rough. (The conservative Pyne refused to shake Maddox's extended hand as the old racist left the set, a scene which must have given prosegregation conservatives a moment's pause.) Others resorted to equally bare-knuckled insults, as flummoxed fellow talk-show host David Susskind did when addressing Pyne's studio audience: "Never in one time and place have I seen such an assembly of slack-jawed, thin-lipped, beady-eyed political morons." The especially quick-witted sometimes were able to best Pyne on his own terms, as rock guitarist Frank Zappa did the day Pyne began their on-air conversation by declaring "I guess your long hair makes you a woman." The counterculture poster-boy replied without missing a beat: "I guess your wooden leg makes you a table."

Pyne's fist-in-the-mouth approach to interviewing guaranteed his audience at least a glimpse at the personality behind each guest's public image, and as in the Zappa exchange, occasionally rose to the level of art. "No one conducts the straight, hard-hitting interview as well as Joe Pyne," wrote the *Los Angeles Times* in a 1967 article that dubbed Pyne "the master showman of the talk realm."

Some of those who followed Pyne's lead often had no interest in listening to their guests, or in elicting true character, and others took his style to increasingly bizarre extremes. At times, the fist-in-the-mouth technique became more than just a metaphor.

"You have to understand that they are not there for comfort; they are there to afflict," said broadcasting expert Michael Marsden of Eastern Kentucky University, who traces a direct line from Pyne to the broadcast provocateurs of today. "They are there to keep us on pins and needles. They play with our fears and, in some ways, reinforce the sense that life is out of control." Marsden once told a newspaper reporter that the best talk-show hosts know how to push listeners and the boundaries of taste to the limit, but not beyond. "Less talented people don't know how far they can go. What you end up with is a lot of racism and sexism, the underside of American life."

Actually, we've ended up with a lot more than that, including madness, mayhem, and at least two talk show–related murders. (White-power miscreants gunned down belligerent Jewish talk-show host Alan Berg in his Denver driveway in 1984, inspiring Eric Bogosian's play *Talk Radio*, and in 1996 Jonathan Schmitz shot friend Scott Amedure to death after Amedure confessed his crush on Schmitz during a nationally televised *Jenny Jones* appearance.) We've ended up with a media landscape full of noxious talk-show celebrities such as Geraldo Rivera, Sally Jessy Raphael, and Laura Schlessinger. We've ended up with Howard Stern's books as *New York Times* best-sellers and Watergate conspirator-turned-radio-personality G. Gordon Liddy urging his listeners to shoot intrusive federal agents. ("Head shots, head shots—kill the sons of bitches!") We've ended up with Limbaugh, a failed rock 'n' roll D.J. who *Mother Jones* magazine dubbed "The Wizard of Ooze" as a de facto national policy adviser; Christian talk-show host Pat Robertson as a presidential candidate; and pro wrestler-turned-talk-show host Jesse "The Body" Ventura as the governor of Minnesota. (Robertson and

Ventura certainly aren't the first and only people to step from a mass-media pulpit into electoral politics. Michael Deaver, Ronald Reagan's media adviser, once credited Reagan's election as president to the fact that after leaving the California governor's mansion in 1975, the Great Communicator took a commentator's job on the Mutual Radio network and "was on the radio every day for nearly five years, talking to 50 million people a week.")

We've also ended up with an unfortunate cultural fascination with "reality" television, which relies on calculated staging to create the same sense of unpredictable spontaneity that Pyne pioneered decades ago. That, in turn, has led to an unfortunate blurring of the line between entertainment and reality, as when a Worchester, Massachusetts, man attacked a woman dressed as Barney the dinosaur several months after syndicated shock jock Tom Leykis's infamous on-air "killing" of that popular children's television character. ("Why are you doing this to me?" Deborah McRoy pleaded with her attacker, who continued to hit her in the face even after the oversized Barney head fell off.)

Joe Pyne died of lung cancer in 1970, long before things really got out of hand, and one can't help but wonder what he'd think of the broadcasting mayhem he unleashed. Would Pyne have condoned Morton Downey, Jr.'s, behavior the day he and pop artist Mark Kostabi actually came to blows on the set of Downey's TV show? Could he have imagined a day when Downey, his advertisers losing interest and his career in freefall, would get so desperate to generate publicity that he apparently scrawled swastikas on his face and clothes in a bathroom at San Francisco International Airport and blamed the attack on skinheads who hated his show? (Downey, whose show was canceled shortly after that "attack," defended himself on a rival TV talk show—where else?—telling nice-guy host Phil Donohue: "If I'm lying, I'm obviously already in mental jeopardy and need a rubber room.") Would Pyne have approved of the hall-of-mirrors talk-show moment when Downey shoved Stuttering John to the ground when the Howard Stern hit man asked him, "Would you let your wife dance topless in clubs for money if you really needed it?"

By the turn of the twenty-first century, with certain talk shows snorkeling deeper and deeper into humanity's cesspool, Steve Allen, as a spokesman for the Parents Television Council, was running full-page newspaper ads denouncing TV as a "moral sewer," and professional virtue czar and high-stakes gambler Bill Bennett was asking, "Is this vulgar, degraded, and coarse material absolutely necessary?"

Perhaps not. But by then, the volume knob that Joe Pyne first cranked was stuck on eleven. Talk shows had created a new and prevailing language for public discourse, providing what *Los Angeles Times* writer Patrick Goldstein once called "the megaphone for the new voices of America." Sunday morning discussion shows had become predictable shouting matches. Pundits who behaved like pit bulls got regular, well-paying gigs. Programmers began creating public-affairs programs that played *Hardball* in the *No-Spin Zone*. Producers even began looking for hostile hosts for the least controversial television formats, including game shows such as *Weakest Link*.

Washington Post media critic Howard Kurtz says America has become a "a high-decibel culture in which a lot of incendiary sound bites get thrown back and forth, but real ideas sometimes take a back seat." Even Mike Wallace, the fabled *60 Minutes* attack dog, eventually found himself clamping his hands over his ears. "It's noisy," he once said. "And I like opinions. But . . . *quiet down*."

One of the more curious ripples from the Pyne splash is the ongoing migration of personalities between media and politics. Since politicians and talk-show hosts often succeed based on the same skill set—the ability to deliver opinions convincingly, or at least loudly—they have begun trading places from time to time. Recent history is replete with examples of talk-show hosts winning political office—in the fall elections of 1994, nine talk-show hosts ran for Congress—and don't even try to count the number of politicians who found employment as talk-show regulars after leaving their elected post. (Hats off here to Jesse Ventura, who managed a brief career as a commentator for the XFL football league while still working as Minnesota's chief executive.) It's telling that no one seemed particularly surprised in August 2002 when reports surfaced that former Oval Office vulgarian Bill Clinton had discussed with two major networks the possibility of hosting an afternoon TV talk show.

Looking back, it's clear that Joe Pyne stood at a crossroads of broadcasting history, a point at which the talk-show host archetype divided neatly in two. Hosts who followed Pyne's lead either took the high road or the low road in their search for an audience. Some simply took the gutter. In 2002, *Talkers* magazine named the twenty-five greatest radio and TV talk-show hosts of all time and put Limbaugh atop the radio heap and Larry King as TV's number 1—a split decision, you might say, between the forces of nasty and nice.

So what's the future? Hard to say, but it's worth noting that by early 2003, programming executives at MSNBC were trying to decide what to do about a new talk show hosted by one-time talk titan Phil Donahue. Since the 1970s Donahue had been a paragon of intelligence and empathy on the talk-show scene, but low ratings had clearly doomed his resurrected show. MSNBC needed another talk show to take its place, and began casting about for a host. The network's choice to replace the King of Kind?

Jesse Ventura.

THE OPERATIVE NUMBER: 22

*Percentage of Americans who in early 2003 told Gallup
pollsters that they get their "news" every day from talk-radio
programs—twice as many as four years before. The trend
troubled even talk-show hosts such as talk-radio pioneer
Michael Jackson, who said, "I wouldn't want my most ardent
listeners to think of me as their major source of news."*

There's Honor Among Sleaze

Joe Pyne's combative style spawned countless imitators, many of whom never developed Pyne's ability to walk the fine line between being provocative and, say, felony assault.

Some, such as Morton Downey, Jr., made their reputations by being physically aggressive toward guests. (In fact, "the Official Morton Downey Jr. Web site" features video clips of Downey's most memorable fistfights and shoving matches—none of which are nearly as appalling as aspiring singer Mort's rendition of the song "Teach Your Children" on the same Web site.) Others, such as Jerry Springer, simply goad their guests to violence and leave the mop-up to overmuscled bouncers.

But among the perpetrators, there's a code of honor that may not be apparent to the casual viewer. In 1998, long after Downey's brief run on national television came to an ignominious, swastika-scrawled end, "television's ultimate loudmouth" was asked to comment on the frequent comparisons of his show to Springer's.

Downey—the man who delighted in dismissing guests as "pablum puker" and "scum bucket"—looked down his nose and clarified the difference:

"Everyone says, 'Springer's doing your show now.' That's not true. I didn't do sleaze. There were times when I did things that were a little sleazy, but I didn't do shows on my neighbor's collie dog having sex with my neighbor's wife."

Just in case you missed the difference.

You Want *More*?

- *It's Only Talk—The Real Story of America's Talk Shows*, documentary narrated by Fred Willard, Actuality Production for A&E Home Video, 2000.
- *Inside Talk Radio*, by Peter Laufer, Carol Publishing Group, Secaucus, N.J., 1995.
- *Can We Talk? The Power and Influence of Talk Shows*, by Gini Graham Scott, Insight Books, New York, 1996.
- Web sites with good Joe Pyne biographies: http://broadcastpioneers.50g.com/pyne.html and http://www.laradio.com/about.htm
- For video clips of modern talk-show mayhem, try http://mortondowneyjr.com and http://www.jerryspringer.com.

The Supertanker Diaper

Diapers have been around for centuries, but it wasn't until
1966 that two unheralded inventors used molecular chemistry
to solve an age-old problem.

BABIES LEAK. IT'S NOT A design flaw, per se, just a reality that
humans have struggled with, in various ways, since our species first
slithered from the primordial muck and decided that dry was better
than wet.

Until recently, though, the preferred method for dealing with
the leakage problem was roughly the same as it had been for centuries. How different, really, were the cotton diaper or the early
generation disposable paper diaper from the Native Americans'
milkweed papoose liner, the moss-packed animal skins preferred
by Eskimos, or the string-tied cloth squares used by mothers in
Elizabethan times? Same concept, same result: wet, uncomfortable
babies whose diapers leaked like the *Exxon Valdez*.

But in 1966, two competing scientists laboring in corporate

obscurity—Carlyle Harmon at Johnson & Johnson and Billy Gene Harper at Dow Chemical—filed virtually identical patents that brought the odd notion of high performance to diapering. Their innovation, the result of advanced research involving the molecular behavior of materials called polymers, not only solved the age-old leakage problem, but has since influenced everything from the mobility of young families to expensive industrial transportation problems; from a supermarket shelving dilemma to debate about the impact of diapers on the global ecosystem.

By making the only truly significant leap in diaper technology in history, one might assume those innovators assured themselves a hallowed place in history and the eternal gratitude of a drier mankind. And yet, when Harmon died in 1997, his obituary in his local Utah paper was only four hundred words long and barely mentioned an accomplishment that has profoundly influenced commerce and the lives of people all over the world.

"We tend to credit those who create an idea, not those who perfect it, forgetting that it is often only in the perfection of an idea that true progress occurs," wrote Malcolm Gladwell in a 2001 *New Yorker* story that gave Harmon and Harper long overdue credit for solving the diaper leakage puzzle. "The paper diaper changed parenting. But a diaper that could hold four insults [the diaper industry term for baby pee] without leakage, keep a baby's skin dry, clear an insult in twenty seconds flat, and would nearly always be in stock, even if you arrived at the supermarket at eight o'clock in the evening—and that would keep getting better at all those things, year in and year out—was another thing altogether. This was more than a good idea. This was something like perfection."

Perfection, in this case, involved sprinkling a handful of chemical flakes into critical sectors of a disposable paper diaper. These flakes were an early form of what later became known as a superabsorbent polymer, which is a thirsty little chemical structure able to absorb up to three hundred times its weight in liquid. The salt typically found in urine reduces the absorption rate to about a quarter of that amount, but even that represented a diapering breakthrough of staggering proportions. Harmon and Harper, in near simultaneous eureka moments, concluded that polymers—the preferred type today is sodium polyacrylate—not only could absorb a baby's entire overnight output, but also quickly converted fluid into a more solid gel that stayed in the diaper.

Until that moment, the pantheon of diaper innovators included precisely two people, Marion Donovan Butler and Victor Mills, whom *U.S. News & World Report* hailed as no less "pioneers of women's liberation than Betty Friedan and Gloria Steinem." Butler was a *Vogue* magazine editor turned post–World War II housewife who, like other mothers of her generation, had worked outside the home during the war years and developed a distaste for washing and folding diapers—perhaps the most onerous chore ever devised for a new parent, one that came with the numbing awareness that it would all have to be done every day, multiple times a day, for a couple of years. Butler's first foray into diaper innovation came in 1946 when she attacked the cotton-diaper leakage problem by assembling a prototype reusable diaper cover from an old shower curtain. She later conceived the idea of a disposable diaper made of absorbent paper.

Butler's work earned her accolades as the "mother of disposable diapers," and preceded by more than a decade the work of Mills, a Procter & Gamble engineer whose 1997 *New York Times* obituary lauded him as the "father of disposable diapers" for heading the team that developed the world's first commercially successful disposable diaper, Pampers.

Mills had come to the Pampers project with a long history of innovation at Procter & Gamble. He'd played leading roles in improving manufacturing techniques for Ivory Soap, Duncan Hines cake mix, and Jif peanut butter, and might well have gone to his grave known as the man who gave the world stackable Pringles potato chips had he not also been assigned to the disposable diaper task force. Using insights he gained while watching his new grand-child, Mills and his team took Donovan's basic diaper innovations—a waterproof plastic outer layer and an absorbent-paper inner layer—and combined them. They refined the inner layer idea by making the paper crepey, and therefore more absorbent, and sent their disposable diapers into the marketplace.

Here was a product that made a new parent's life instantly less gross. Rather than having to shake, scrape, and rinse a loaded dia-per before adding it to that malodorous, malevolent pail of diapers waiting to be washed, these could simply be thrown away, forgotten. But it was more than that. For the first time, mothers who couldn't afford expensive diaper services were able to step off of the thank-less laundry treadmill. Extended day-care was suddenly practical. A two-income family was no longer beyond imagination. The experi-ence was like stepping from black-and-white Kansas into a color-saturated Oz. Once you'd used disposables, it was very hard to go back.

While they'd solved the disposability problem, the leakage problem proved more stubborn. Like the cloth diapers that pre-vailed at the time, those early Pampers had to be pinned on. Their effectiveness depended on a parent's skill at fitting the bulky, rec-tangular diaper precisely to the nonangular undercarriage of a squirming child. The whole exercise could be rendered pointless by a child who simply rolled, kicked, crawled, or walked in a way that shifted the diaper's paper wadding away from the source of the anticipated leak. And babies are notoriously unreliable target shooters.

Pampers hit the market in 1961 as a veritable Model T compared to the Lamborghini diapers of today. Procter & Gamble and innova-tors such as Kimberly-Clark and Johnson & Johnson began to tin-ker with diaper designs in the years that followed, making small refinements that minimized some of the problems. They tailored the diapers more closely to the typical baby's shape. They elasticized the leg openings to reduce leaks. They began shredding the absorbent paper rather than making it crepey in a valiant effort to solve the "pressure" problem, a confounding reality mostly involving a toddler's tendency to plop down on its bottom. (If a diaper was soaking wet at the moment of squishdown, it tended to release all those carefully collected leaks like a squeezed sponge.) Engineers eventually began adding more and more paper, to the point where diapered babies began to get comically bottom-heavy, wet or dry.

It wasn't just a question of style or comfort. Bulky, old-style disposable diapers created problems at every stage of their existence because, frankly, size does matter, and in ways you probably never imagined.

For example, with each diaper containing so much shredded paper—"fluff," in diaper-speak—not many of them could fit into a box that would still be small enough to fit on a supermarket shelf or carried home with ease. For parents, that meant more trips to the store at a stage in life when they already had more than enough to do. It also made a regular cotton-diaper delivery service seem pretty attractive, since the whole point of disposables was to make the diapering experience more convenient.

If you traced a bulky paper diaper's trail back to the manufacturer, the inconvenience problem created for the consumer became magnified. Since diaper makers were basically selling bulky, lightweight boxes of fluff, they had serious problems with shelving, stocking, warehousing, transporting, and even running the appropriate number of production plants needed to produce those big, fat paper diapers. For example, supermarkets, which allot only so much space to each product category, could not afford to dedicate an entire aisle to display low-profit, low-density disposable diapers. That meant the few boxes they could display sold out quickly, which meant that a parent dispatched to solve a leakage crisis at home often found the shelves empty.

That, in turn, meant that diaper makers had to have more warehouse space to maintain large inventories so they could keep diapers flowing constantly from the distribution centers to the stores. But the bulky fluff problem was the same for truckers as for supermarket managers. While the diaper boxes weren't very heavy, they took up a lot of room on the trucks that delivered them to retailers. The trucks left full, but nowhere near their weight limit. That meant the manufacturers either needed more drivers and fume-spewing tractor-trailers to deliver the diapers to supermarkets, or needed to make more trips in those trucks. That meant that diaper makers had to maintain more manufacturing facilities around the country, and have more employees, so they wouldn't have to truck the fluff boxes far. All of that made diapers inefficient to produce and expensive to buy—a concern when, according to the *Journal of Pediatrics*, the typical child uses ten thousand diapers before becoming toilet trained.

Enter our heroes, Harmon and Harper, whose 1966 innovation eventually led to mass-produced diapers that were only half as bulky as the old paper-fluff models, but could contain roughly twice the leakage. (How far ahead of their time were the two scientists? The commercial production of superabsorbent polymers didn't begin until 1978, when Japanese companies began making the stuff for use in sanitary napkins, and the big American diaper makers didn't begin producing superabsorbent diapers until the mid-1980s.) Not only did the phrase "diaper rash" virtually disappear from a parent's list of anxieties—a fear artfully implanted by companies trying to sell diaper-rash treatments—but the high-tech diapers boasted a 1 percent leakage rate compared to the 20 percent rate for plastic-covered cloth diapers and 10 percent for the early generation disposables. Like the computer chip in the 1980s, diapers had the rare distinction of getting smaller and better at the same time. And, of course, toddlers stopped looking like waddling little pears.

Smaller, less bulky diapers also had a domino effect on the process of making, distributing, and selling disposable diapers. Thinner diapers meant more diapers in a box and more boxes on supermarket shelves, less warehouse space, fewer delivery truck trips, and fewer manufacturing plants.

"We cut the cost of trucking in half," former Procter & Gamble logistics manager Ralph Drayer told the *New Yorker*'s Gladwell in 2001. "We cut the cost of storage in half. We cut handling in half, and we cut the cost of store shelf in half, which is probably the most expensive space in the whole chain."

Thinner, superabsorbent diapers also muted, somewhat, the rising outcry over the impact that disposable diapers were having on the environment. In the early 1980s, just before the diaper makers shifted from bulky paper to the Harmon-Harper superabsorbent diaper formula, environmental activists were raising the alarm that American landfills were filling up with diapers that would not degrade for five hundred years and which contained intestinal bacteria and other unpleasant human byproducts that before disposables stayed pretty much in the sewage system. In 1990 alone—the year in which the world celebrated the twentieth anniversary of Earth Day—more than eighteen billion disposable diapers were thrown into U.S. landfills and made up about 1.5 percent of America's solid waste stream. By then, according to one researcher, at least twenty U.S. states had considered bans or taxes on disposable diapers, and sales in the cotton diaper service industry reached a high of $200 million.

That may have been the last gasp of the cotton diaper, though. While the public still perceives disposable diapers as an environmental problem, the superabsorbent revolution (along with some savvy marketing by the diaper makers, which put convenient disposables into maternity wards as free samples for new parents) went a long way toward muting the concerns. There was undeniable logic to the argument that a diaper that was half as bulky took up only half as much space in landfills, and that a more absorbent diaper meant that parents had to change their leaky charges less often. Plus, the disposable diaper companies fought back rather than let their market share erode. They launched advertising campaigns that raised doubts about whether reusable cotton diapers were any better for the environment than disposables.

Not all of their claims were true. According to one report published in an environmental magazine, Procter & Gamble produced and aired a commercial that showed tree roots in rich compost as a narrator explained that "ninety days ago, this was a disposable diaper"—even though subsequent lawsuits revealed that there were, in fact, no composting facilities for disposables at the time. By the time the truth was revealed, though, the ads had worked magic on a public just looking for an excuse to use the more convenient disposables. Seventy-five percent of the nation's reusable diaper services were out of business by 1997, and even some environmentalists were waving the white flag. The debate continues, but the national conversation, like the modern disposable diaper, has changed.

"We've come to appreciate that downstream solid waste is only one of many public health and resource-use issues associated with diaper technology," said Natural Resources Defense Council senior scientist Allen Hershkowitz in 1998. He conceded that competing social and ecological concerns made it harder to condemn disposables. Parents, hospitals, and others began to weigh their reusable-versus-disposable diapering decision not on the single issue of the environment, but on the "Four Cs": cost, convenience, comfort, and conscience. Was it more expensive to employ a diaper service, or buy disposables? Was it practical to expect millions of working mothers and out-of-home child-care facilities to forego the undeniable convenience of disposables? Was it fair to condemn babies to dreaded diaper rash and incontinent adults to embarrassing accidents when a product existed that virtually eliminated those problems? Was it worse to divert diapers into landfills, or use the vast amounts of water required to launder reusable cotton diapers?

While disposable diaper makers continue their search for the industry's Holy Grail—the biodegradable, flushable, and commercially successful superabsorbent diaper—it's already clear that the generation of superabsorbent diapers spawned by Harmon's and Harper's innovation has forever tilted the scale toward disposables. The reason is simple: Babies still leak, but their diapers no longer do.

THE OPERATIVE NUMBER: 500

Number of milliliters of fluid (about two cups) that a modern diaper with superabsorbent polymers can hold without leaking. A much bulkier early generation disposable paper diaper could hold only about 275 milliliters. A baby's typical "insult" might unleash a total of 70 milliliters of fluid.

The Rash of Diaper Disinformation

Disposable diaper makers have never hesitated to bend the truth in their marketing, whether by demonizing diaper rash, falsely suggesting that a dirty diaper will decompose into rich compost within ninety days, or commissioning studies that "proved" that disposables were no less damaging to the environment than reusable cotton diapers.

But the disposable diaper doomsayers haven't always taken the high road either. They have consistently multiplied the actual percentage of disposable diapers thought to be in landfills and in the solid-waste stream, and at times have stoked unfounded fears about the harmless—but mysterious—chemical polymers that have been a hallmark of disposable diaper design since the mid-1980s.

For example, a web site billed as an "online guide for expecting parents" advocates the use of cloth diapers and unsubtly suggests that despite the lack of any evidence of harm, "there are two chemical substances that many health advocates feel just shouldn't be in a baby's diaper at all: sodium polyacrylate and dioxin."

Sodium polyacrylate is the polymer that makes modern disposables so absorbent and revolutionized the diaper industry. Dioxin sometimes is found in trace amounts in chlorine-bleached paper goods, claims the web site, and "no one knows the exact amount of dioxins it would take to damage our health." Theresa Rodriguez Farrisi echoed that alarm in her 1997 book *Diaper Changes: The Complete Diapering Book and Resource Guide*. She linked the minute possibility of dioxin in diapers to their use in Agent Orange during the Vietnam War and the gruesome specter of "birth defects, miscarriage, cancer, and genetic damage."

You Want *More*?

- *Diaper Changes: The Complete Diapering Book and Resource Guide*, by Theresa Rodriguez Farrisi, Homekeepers Publishing, Richland, Pa., 1997.
- "Smaller," by Malcolm Gladwell, *The New Yorker*, Nov. 26, 2001.
- "How 'Tactical Research' Muddied Diaper Debate," by Cynthia Crossen, *Wall Street Journal*, May 17, 1994.
- *Shared Values: A History of Kimberley-Clark*, by Robert Spector, Greenwich Publishing Group, Lyme, Connecticut, 1997.

15

When Mayhem Went Postmodern

In 1968, Night of the Living Dead—*the* Citizen Kane *of low-budget, cannibalistic, zombie thrillers—spawned a new cinematic genre and helped reshape cultural sensibilities.*

AT ITS DEBUT ON OCTOBER 1, 1968, the film *Night of the Living Dead* was a bit of a shock for moviegoers whose idea of horror was yet another musty remake of *Frankenstein* or *Dracula*.

The setting wasn't some suitably spooky medieval castle, gadget-laden laboratory, or fog-shrouded London street, but rather the bland rural Pennsylvania countryside. The cast of characters didn't include any brilliant scientists, noblemen in ruffles and flowing cloaks, or hauntingly beautiful damsels in distress. Instead, they were a bunch of thoroughly ordinary-looking middle-class folks—the sort you could imagine lingering indecisively in a super-market aisle, trying to decide whether to buy the large or family-size box of laundry detergent. When confronted with the threat of impending doom, their response was to bicker among themselves about whether it was safer to hide in the living room or in the basement. The flesh-eating monsters they were attempting to flee were even more unremarkable—no fangs, fur, scales, bolts in the neck, or outlandishly developed physiques. In fact, they were almost indistinguishable in appearance from their would-be victims, except for their glassy gazes and lurching, unsteady gaits. Lacking any superhuman physical prowess, the zombies simply overwhelmed victims with their sheer numbers, like a horde of shoppers swarming after a "blue light special" at Kmart. But the violence, when it finally came, wasn't the elegant neck nibble of a Transylvanian count, but something truly nauseating. These ghouls gnawed upon severed hands, played tug-of-war with unraveled strands of bowel, and sucked upon still glistening internal organs with ravenous slurps.

From there, it got even *more* disconcerting. The hero of the piece, the one man with toughness, courage, and moral certainty, eschewed the usual romantic interest in the heroine (who shrieked hysterically and babbled nonsense, when she wasn't sleeping or staring catatonically at the walls). When faced with doom, the hero jettisoned his altruistic principles and committed grisly acts of his own in the mad scramble for survival. The denouement was the ultimate downer: In the end, good failed to triumph, and the hero was killed, just like everyone else. There simply was no escape from the menace—or rather, from fate.

At the time, nobody was quite sure what to make of *Night of the Living Dead.* It came not from Hollywood, but from Pittsburgh, Pennsylvania, a midwestern city known for the smoke spewed by its steel mills. The director was George A. Romero, at the time an obscure local maker of commercials and industrial films, who made the movie with a bunch of college friends, by various accounts, for just $114,000. *Night of the Living Dead* was shot on cheap black-and-white stock and featured a cast of mostly amateur actors and special effects created with materials one might buy from the corner grocery—the blood that drenched the most horrific scenes, for example, was actually chocolate syrup. When Romero somehow convinced a distributor to put it in theaters, the film was derided by critics not just for its technical shortcomings, but also for its unrelenting gore and nihilistic ending. *Variety* dismissed it as "an unrelieved orgy of sadism" and the *New York Times* called it "a grainy little movie made by some people in Pittsburgh."

But those detractors turned out to be as sadly mistaken as the film's protagonist, who decamped a bit too soon from his refuge in the basement. In the first twenty years after its release, *Night of the Living Dead* grossed somewhere in the vicinity of $100 million, according to one published estimate. Today, the low-budget horror flick is included in the prestigious National Film Registry and merits a spot on the American Film Institute's list of the one hundred greatest thrillers of the twentieth century (a select group that includes Alfred Hitchcock's *Psycho* and *North by Northwest*, Steven Spielberg's *Raiders of the Lost Ark*, and Roman Polanski's *Chinatown*.) *Entertainment Weekly* picked it as the thirteenth scariest film of all time, higher on the list than Hollywood efforts with big-name casts such as *Carrie* and *The Omen*.

Indeed, *Night of the Living Dead* is the veritable *Citizen Kane* of cannibalistic zombie thrillers. It was the first truly modern horror film to supplant the elegant, mannered Gothic style of its tamer predecessors with a darker, more disturbing vision. By hacking to bits many of the rules and conventions of the classic Hollywood monster movie, it created a whole new way to scare people for entertainment's sake. It was the first "splatter" flick, a genre in which fantastically horrific mayhem is used to depict a world in which evil is not a malevolent monster or warped scientific genius but an overwhelming force of nature, beyond reason or explanation. The conventional struggle between right and wrong no longer matters; the only choice is to flee—and hope that you escape. Romero's humble, low-budget thriller paved the way for a slew of big-budget successors—films such as *Friday the 13th, A Nightmare on Elm Street, Scream, I Know What You*

Did Last Summer—that would draw vastly bigger box office by emulating and expanding upon Romero's gory formula, though often without his clever irony and social commentary. Arguably, the ninety-six-minute film's grisly ambiance also has indirectly influenced everything from video games and comic books to rap music.

The roots of *Night of the Living Dead*, in a sense, go back to the French Théâtre du Grand Guignol of the 1890s, which featured horrifically violent plays filled with gory special effects designed to shock audiences. The American horror films that first became popular in the 1930s and 1940s, in contrast, presented a safe, sanitized version of fright, in which a monster's menacing rampage ultimately was thwarted in the interests of right and good. In the 1950s, Frankenstein, Dracula, and the Wolfman had become too familiar to frighten, and gradually gave way to B movies filled with space creatures and flying saucers. The scares became silliness.

As a child of the 1950s, director Romero's vision of the world was shaped by a multitude of other influences—the nuclear air-raid drills he had to perform as a child in Catholic school in the Bronx, and EC Comics, whose pages, filled with gruesome-looking monsters and macabre violence, actually prompted a congressional investigation of its effect upon impressionable youth. As a teen, he borrowed his uncle's eight-millimeter home-movie camera and started trying to make his own films. At fourteen, police arrested him after he threw a burning dummy off a roof—a stunt, as it turned out, for one of his early efforts, *The Man From the Meteor*. After high school Romero moved to Pittsburgh to enroll at Carnegie Institute of Technology (now Carnegie Mellon University), supposedly to train to become a commercial artist. But movies were still on his mind. "In art class, there would be a nude and everybody would be drawing her except for George," a fellow student who went on to work with him in the movie business once recalled. "He would be drawing this epic with people dragging cannons or a huge rock with BEN HUR carved into it."

Romero eventually gave up on college and left without a degree. Instead, he and a few college friends set up a small company, Latent Image, with plans of making commercials and industrial films and using the proceeds to make a feature movie. (At one point they came up with another ingenious gambit to raise capital—selling home-makers giant "paintings" of their houses, created by projecting slide photos onto sheets and painting between the lines.) With the help of some local investors, Romero and his friends eventually raised the seed money to start a film.

Just as Virgil built upon Homer, Romero was inspired by a book, Richard Matheson's *I Am Legend*, about the last human in a world taken over by vampires. He wrote his own short novel, which became the basis for a screenplay by Romero and collaborator John A. Russo. The plot centered on a mysterious contagion that turns people into zombies with a craving for human flesh. Those attacked and killed by the ghouls become zombies themselves. Cannibalism is one of the creepiest taboos and had been used for shock effect on the screen before—the 1963 low-budget horror film *Blood Feast*, for example, centers around the crimes of a depraved caterer. Romero's premise was even more disturbing because his film had no tangible villain. Instead, the menace came from ordinary folks who'd been stripped of their humanity and transformed into ghastly, degraded shells of themselves. An assortment of people fleeing the mysterious outbreak of zombification are thrown together in a remote farmhouse, cornered by the ghouls. The survivors include a woman whose brother has been murdered, an affectionate but naïve young couple, two bickering middle-aged parents and their sick young daughter, and a resourceful young man named Ben who becomes their de facto leader.

Inside the boarded-up house, they gather around the radio and TV, taking in news bulletins about the government's ineffectual attempts to cope with an outbreak of murderous violence across the nation, and gradually piece together the truly dire nature of their predicament. The official explanation—some vague nonsense about radiation from a space probe from Venus—matters about as much as Gregor Samsa's discovery that he has become a giant insect in Franz Kafka's story *The Metamorphosis*. There's really no time to ponder why the world has suddenly changed into a terrifying place. The only thing that matters is survival.

But what should they do? Hide in the basement? Make a desperate run for one of the distant shelters that civil-defense forces are setting up? The characters' biggest struggle becomes one against their fear, selfishness, and inability to cooperate. It's a premise vaguely reminiscent of Albert Camus's classic 1948 existentialist novel, *The Plague*, and the lead character, Ben, is an existential hero: the only character who retains his dignity and refuses to give up either the fight or his moral values, even in the face of what seems like certain doom. In the end, he alone manages to escape—only to be slaughtered, accidentally, by rescuers who carelessly mistake him for one of the cannibalistic monsters when he emerges from his basement hiding place.

Romero reportedly shot in black-and-white to save money, and he and his collaborators used a house scheduled for demolition as the main set. Without money to spend on elaborate special effects or monster costumes, they were forced to be inventive in finding ways to make the movie scary. One of the investors owned a chain of meat markets, which became a convenient source for the intestines, livers, hearts, and other organs that the zombies munched on as they feigned devouring their human victims. An apparently half-eaten head happened upon by one of the survivors was fashioned from a plastic store-bought skull, which was then outfitted with Ping-Pong balls for eyes. To stage a scene in which a zombie is taken out by a Molotov cocktail, Russo reportedly volunteered to be set afire—without the elaborate protective gear that a professional stuntman might require. ("The flames would race up my back and I'd stagger as far as I could until it singed my hair," he later explained to the London *Daily Telegraph*. "Then I'd fall over this hill where people had blankets ready to smother me.")

As film writer Paul R. Gagne's recounts in his 1987 book on Romero, *The Zombies That Ate Pittsburgh*, the director had difficulty getting the completed film into movie theaters. One studio turned down a chance to distribute it because it was in black-and-white, and another because it didn't have an upbeat ending. Finally, a small distributor took a flyer on it, in hopes that it might make a few bucks on the drive-in circuit. When *Night of the Living Dead* premiered in 1968, American film reviewers generally were as repulsed as if they'd been served a bucket of offal for lunch. Chicago *Sun-Times* critic Roger Ebert wrote an article describing how young children at a Saturday matinee wept and screamed in genuine terror at the grisly thriller. (Later, he would explain that his intention was to warn parents to be more careful in selecting what films their kids were allowed to see, and that he actually admired Romero's work.)

Nevertheless, *Night of the Living Dead* eventually became a surprising commercial success—one that paved the way for other independently made low-budget horror films, ranging from 1974's *The Texas Chainsaw Massacre* to the 1999 megahit *The Blair Witch Project*. To his misfortune, Romero himself reportedly lost out on much of the film's revenues, thanks to a long legal battle over accounting of the film's grosses and a copyright snafu that resulted in numerous unauthorized video releases of the film. Ultimately, according to Romero biographer Gagne, he regained rights to the film in 1978.

Beyond the shock entertainment value, as critics eventually noticed, there was something about Romero's gritty little film that resonated with audiences. It may be because *Night of the Living Dead* accomplishes the rare trick of working on two seemingly incompatible levels. It comes off as both a grisly exploitation film *and* a work of social commentary. The film reached theaters at a time when America's nerves were frayed from turmoil over the Vietnam War, the assassinations of Robert Kennedy and Martin Luther King, and race riots that threatened to destroy American cities. *Night of the Living Dead* glommed onto moviegoers' real-life fears like some depraved fairy tale embroidered with black humor. The mock news broadcasts that fill in the story also depict a government dumbfounded by the crisis, bogged down in fruitless Cabinet meetings, civil defense warnings, and other laughably bureaucratic attempts to shove the monstrous menace into a desk drawer. In the opening scene one of the characters mocks another character's anxiety by doing a sort of Boris Karloff imitation—"They're coming for you, Barbara!"—moments before he is attacked by a ravenous ghoul. The quarreling middle-aged couple spouts dialogue that's a deliberate parody of 1950s melodrama. ("We may not enjoy living together, but dying together isn't going to solve anything!") And like the cheery bombardier in *Dr. Strangelove*, the cigar-chomping sheriff who leads the zombie-eradicating rifle squad is ludicrously nonchalant about the mind-bending horror he is confronting. His explanation of the mysterious murder-inducing, flesh-craving infection that afflicts the zombies is that "they're all messed up." Some people interpreted the zombies themselves as a satiric symbolic equivalent of the "silent majority" that the Nixon administration would later claim supported its policies (undoubtedly a bit of a reach, since the film was completed before Nixon took office).

In what was a daring move in 1968, Romero cast an African-American actor, Duane Jones, in the role of Ben, the resourceful but doomed protagonist. The film doesn't make any references to his race, and Romero has said he chose Jones simply because he was the most skilled actor available. All the same, it's impossible not to notice that Ben spends much of the film arguing with ineffectual white characters and trying to prod them into action. Ultimately, he's slaughtered by a rifle-wielding white member of the antizombie militia, which then handles his corpse almost like a hunting trophy—an eerie parallel to the atmosphere of a southern lynching or hate-crime murder. (The sharpshooter was played—reluctantly—by a kindhearted roller-rink owner who was one of Romero's investors.)

"I think it was a reflection of the times," Romero once told the *Hollywood Reporter*. "It was the whole zeitgeist. Those of us who were making films tended to be part of that liberal gang—hippies who didn't want to grow up—and I think we were generally more active in those days. We were using film as a format to voice our own opinions. I know at least speaking for myself, I've always tried to do that."

Romero's social commentary was more evident in a sequel, *Dawn of the Dead*, which was released in 1979 and enjoyed even more box office success. *Dawn* is more blatantly satirical than *Night*. The army of zombies subtly pokes fun at various cultural stereotypes (one ghoul, for example, is a former Hare Krishna devotee). And the horde, after being turned into mindless cannibals, instinctively converges upon an abandoned suburban shopping mall, where a group of survivors have been holed up, greedily consuming the stores' luxury goods—a deliciously sarcastic send-up of society's oft-mindless materialism. The film featured even more graphic carnage, thanks to the skills of local low-budget special effects whiz Tom Savini, to the extent that the Motion Picture Association of America threatened to give *Dawn* an X rating unless some of it was cut. (Instead, it became one of the first mainstream films to be released without a rating.) Romero followed with a third *Dead* film, *Day of the Dead*, in 1985.

Romero drew a distinction between the comic book–like, fantastical gore of his films and the realistic brutality in movies such as *Taxi Driver*. Audiences, after all, weren't likely to be confronted by cannibalistic zombies on the street outside the theater. Nor were his zombies dispatched to third world countries to fight secret wars to further U.S. foreign policy objectives. "My stuff is pure fantasy," he once explained to the *Washington Post*. "I strongly feel that fantasy violence is not as dangerous as the violence in movies like *Rambo*, movies that imitate life more closely, that paint a moral character who uses violence as a way of solving life's problems."

Nevertheless, just as Bob Dylan was the unintentional progenitor for scores of singers who copied his adenoidal wail but neglected the poetry, Romero's gory successes inadvertently opened the way for a generation of horror filmmakers who mostly succeeded in outdoing his visceral splatter but neglected to give their movies much message beyond the pursuit of grisly thrills. In the early 1980s, the sort of bloody tongue-in-cheek allegories he liked to make were overwhelmed by another evolutionary stage, the slasher film, which had an equally violent but far more simplistic premise—a succession of adolescents, just as they were on the verge of engaging in sex, were set upon by some sort of grisly supernatural killer who wore a hockey mask or was armed with stilettolike metal fingernails. With Hollywood's liking for slick, stylized, marketable clichés, the teen terror genre came to dominate the multiplexes of America so totally that by the late 1990s films such as *Scream* began to poke self-referential fun at their own kind.

Meanwhile, the business's blockbuster mentality—in which a disproportionate share of the nation's movie screens at any given time were filled with a few heavily hyped projects—made life difficult for small-time iconoclasts like Romero. As he told the *Hollywood Reporter* in 2000, the horror film genre has become "just a race for the bucks. I don't think anybody's thinking very deeply about it." His 2001 film, *Bruiser,* is about a man who awakes one day, realizes that his face has been replaced by a mask (inspired by the French classic *Eyes Without a Face*) and begins taking revenge upon people who've bullied him. It was released theatrically in Japan, Italy, and France, but went straight to video in the United States.

But even as he struggled commercially, the Pittsburgh filmmaker who once was denounced by critics increasingly received belated highbrow recognition for his work. The zombie auteur is now considered sufficiently arty to be the subject of a retrospective at the American Museum of the Moving Image, and the National Film Registry now preserves an archival print of *Night of the Living Dead* alongside *The Ten Commandments* and *A Streetcar Named Desire*. And rightly so. "Before *Night of the Living Dead*, horror films were about rubber monsters or hands groping in the dark," John Carpenter, director of the horror hit *Halloween* and other films, once explained to a British newspaper. "George Romero revolutionized all that. He made the horror films something to contend with."

THE OPERATIVE NUMBER: 250

Number of extras that portrayed zombies in the film, according to film writer Paul R. Gagne. They included clients and employees of Romero's commercial-making company and local residents from the Evans City area. One ringer was an artist's model who wanders around in the nude, portraying a "morgue zombie."

Variations on a Grisly Theme

I Am Legend, the 1954 novel by Richard Matheson that inspired *Night of the Living Dead*, was adapted to make two other films: *The Last Man on Earth* in 1964 and *The Omega Man* in 1971. Matheson also worked as a scriptwriter for numerous TV series, from *The Twilight Zone* to *Star Trek*, and is a favorite of writers such as Stephen King.

You Want *More*?

- *The Zombies That Ate Pittsburgh: The Films of George A. Romero*, by Paul R. Gagne, Dodd Mead, New York, 1987.
- *The Naked and the Undead: Evil and the Appeal of Horror*, by Cynthia A. Freeland, Westview Press, Boulder, Colo., 2000.
- *Stephen King's Danse Macabre*, by Stephen King, Everest House, New York, 1981.
- "Chill Factor: They Don't Make Horror Films the Way They Used To," by Gina McIntyre, *Hollywood Reporter*, November 1, 2000.

Dawn of the Point-Click Culture

*On December 9, 1968, a visionary computer geek showed the
world how man and his machines eventually would interact.
And he did it when Steve Jobs and Bill Gates
were still struggling with puberty.*

THERE WAS A TIME WHEN the relationship between man and his machines was a one-sided affair, back before touch-screen voting and personal digital assistants and electronic airline ticket-counter check-ins and the "Internet refrigerator," which, according to one recent magazine ad, connects you "to the vast matrix of information and entertainment available through advanced multimedia technology." In those days, we plugged in our toasters and refrigerators and televisions, and they either worked or they didn't. We didn't particularly care to *interact* with them, for heaven's sake, beyond getting warm toast, cold butter, and a steady supply of *Gilligan's Island* reruns.

That all changed with the proliferation of something most people now take for granted—the graphical user interface, or GUI. It's a fancy term for something even cavemen understood: When you want something, just point. Whether you realize it or not, each command you give your computer, your Palm Pilot, or your cell-phone Web browser begins an impossibly complex series of algorithmic computations performed at light speed along a vast miniature landscape of silicon. The GUI reduced all that to the electronic equivalent of a grunted gesture, and in doing so helped transform computers from the inscrutable playthings of cloistered academics into user-friendly tools for everyday living.

Some people credit Microsoft's Bill Gates with pioneering the graphical user interface because of the ubiquity of the company's Windows software, which since 1985 has been the way most people communicate with dominant IBM-based PCs. Others trace it back to the day in December 1979 when Steve Jobs, the cofounder and enfant terrible of fledgling Apple Computer, first saw a ninety-minute product demonstration of a graphical user interface at Xerox Corporation's Palo Alto Research Center, or PARC, and walked away with a plan to graft the same basic concept into a personal computer.

But the oft-told tale of Jobs's PARC revelation obscures a far more momentous ninety-minute product demonstration that occurred more than a decade before, on December 9, 1968, during an engineering conference in San Francisco. The protagonist of that little drama was no less compelling a character than Jobs—"a prophet of biblical proportions," according to one admirer—and what he did that day is, in retrospect, the epicenter of personal computing as we know it.

His name was Douglas C. Engelbart, and his story, like Jobs's, is now woven into computer-industry mythology. It begins in the Philippines, in a Red Cross library. Engelbart had completed his military service and was waiting to go home when he read an article in the July 1945 issue of the *Atlantic Monthly* that, for him, was no less an epiphany than Jobs's visit to PARC more than three decades later. The article, "As We May Think," was written by MIT engineering dean Vannevar Bush, a science adviser to Franklin D. Roosevelt. After surveying the astounding scientific advances produced during the war years, Bush suggested ways that some technology could be put to peacetime use. He correctly predicted that people soon would be adrift in a sea of information and envisioned the sort of rudder we would need to navigate—an easy-to-use machine capable of creating order out of chaos. He described that technology as a "memex" and imagined "a device in which an individual stores all his books, records, and communications, and which is mechanized so that it may be consulted with exceeding speed and flexibility."

Engelbart may as well have been reading a Jules Verne novel. He saw the future in an unforgettable flash. Remember, this was 1945, nearly a decade *before* the electric typewriter became America's hottest new office technology. Inspired, Engelbart spent the years that followed trying to bring Bush's vision to life. He pursued a doctorate degree in engineering at the University of California at Berkeley and began developing his ideas while working at a small government-funded think tank, the Stanford Research Institute in Palo Alto. There he developed a reputation as a brilliant—if commercially oblivious—iconoclast. "Tall and craggy, with deep-set eyes and a hawklike nose, he might have been carved from a slab of antediluvian granite," wrote Michael Hiltzik, author of *Dealers of Lightning: Xerox PARC and the Dawn of the Computer Age*. "Soft-spoken but intransigent, his years of battling unbelievers had convinced him that he was fated to remain the solitary leader of a devoted cadre" of engineers. By all accounts, Engelbart wasn't particularly interested in building something to sell; he wanted to change the fundamental relationship between man and his machines.

It's hard to imagine today, but the early mainframe computers didn't even have video screens. They were oversized, boorish, and surly to their most ardent fans—imagine Barry Bonds's attitude in a baseball player only capable of bunts—and if they communicated at all with their users, they did so using flashing lights and crude teletypes. Engelbart and his protégés were among the first people to wire a monitor to a computer, giving the user a visual way to communicate with the machine. They also invented an electronic pointing device by rigging a hollowed-out block of wood with two small wheels and wiring it into the computer, making it easy to move the cursor around the screen without touching the keyboard—to simply point and click. Dozens of other stunning innovations followed, but the advances of Engelbart's team took place far from the public eye, known only to government grant makers and pointy-headed computer theorists. Had they been the kind of attention grabbers who celebrated major breakthroughs by dancing naked, the world might have noticed their work much sooner. But no, these were pocket-protector people.

By the fall of 1968, though, Engelbart was ready for a little show-and-tell. With two leading engineering societies planning a joint computer conference in San Francisco in December, he asked for ninety minutes of stage time to demonstrate what he and sixteen fellow researchers at his think tank called the NLS, for oNLine System. They had been working on the system since 1962, and spent months preparing for the demo. Using a patchwork of existing and homemade technology—including leased microwave lines, a borrowed dynamic projector and a large video screen, and eight antennas hoisted between a 192-kilobyte mainframe computer at their Stanford Research Institute and the conference about thirty miles away—they intended to turn Vannevar Bush's visionary ideas into reality in what since has been dubbed "the mother of all demos."

They were, it turns out, a decade ahead of their time. As Engelbart took the stage, Bill Gates and Steve Jobs—the men who usually get credit for bridging the gap between man and computer—were just then dealing with puberty.

As the estimated one thousand conferees gathered before the video screen, they had no idea that they were about to see, live on stage and projected twenty feet tall, ideas that until then had been only vague utopian theories to many in the engineering community. An interactive system of videoconferencing? Multimedia displays? Split-screen technology? Hypertext?

Wearing a headset microphone, seated before his keyboard command center, Engelbart looked like a modern-day telemarketer. He asked the audience members to imagine "if you had a workstation at your disposal all day that was perfectly . . . responsive" to commands issued from the collection of devices arrayed before him: a standard keyboard in the center; a homemade five-key "chord set" on his left; and a now familiar pointing device on the right that Engelbart called a "mouse," which was making its public debut. To show how a user of such a machine might type a letter or other document, he conjured a "blank piece of paper" on the projected computer screen. Using the mouse for cursor placement, he typed the word "word." He copied it, then pasted it again and again to form a short paragraph, much like the copy and paste function of modern word-processing programs.

To show how the computer could organize information, Engelbart prepared a text file based on a fictional thirty-four-item shopping list from his wife. With a few keystrokes, he identified and labeled the fruits and vegetables on the list as "produce," then with a few more, he showed how to rearrange the shopping list by category. To show how the mouse worked, he transmitted live the split-screen images of, on the right, an assistant's hand rolling a mouse around a desk at his lab in Menlo Park, and on the left, a dutiful cursor tracing the same path on the computer's projected screen. He demonstrated key-word searching and revealed plans to "network" twenty different computer sites around the country within the next year. He audaciously suggested that with such a network and improving technology, he might be able to stage the same networking demonstration when the group met the following year—in distant Boston.

"The pièce de résistance was Engelbart's implementation of the memex," Hiltzik wrote. "The screen showed how a user could select a single word in a text document and be instantly transported to the relevant portion of a second document—the essence of hypertext, found today . . . on every World Wide Web page and countless word-processed documents."

What followed the ninety-minute demo, after the standing ovation, was a slow-motion sequence of events that reshaped everything about the man-machine relationship. On July 1, 1970, Xerox, the office-copier giant, officially opened its Palo Alto Research Center to pursue research in computing. The man hired to help staff its now legendary Computer Science Lab was Bob Taylor, who in the early 1960s had helped fund Engelbart's research from his budget at a Defense Department agency and had helped him scrounge the money he needed to stage his 1968 demo. Taylor began hiring away the best engineers from Engelbart's cutting-edge lab, using Xerox's substantial budget to build a peerless team of the most creative minds in computer research. The Engelbart refugees were eager to move into what they thought was an environment that would bring their electronic marvels more quickly to market.

They were, it turns out, wrong. During the 1970s, the PARC team produced an extraordinary number of breakthroughs in computer technology, including significant refinements to Engelbart's GUI: overlapping windows, variable type, the laser printer, the list seems endless. They stood at the flashpoint of the revolution and helped transform sluggish calculators into electronic helpmates.

But tiny, precocious PARC existed within Xerox like a misunderstood prodigy, as if Mozart had been born into a family of deafmutes. The giant copier company simply didn't understand or appreciate the commercial possibilities these new technologies represented. By the time Jobs showed up for his private show-and-tell with the PARC staff in December 1979, Vannevar Bush's 1945 vision of an easy-to-use personal computer was in full flower, if corporately unappreciated, behind the solid walls of Xerox's California research lab. What Jobs saw there that day during a ninety-minute product demonstration—a personal computer commanded by a point-and-click GUI that featured overlapping screen windows, smoothly scrolling text, and other PARC innovations—triggered an epiphany. Jobs already was considered the P. T. Barnum of the computer age, not particularly skilled on the tech side (he left that to his friend and Apple cofounder Steve Wozniak) but a man who had demonstrated his ability to connect emerging technology to the vast nation of potential computer users. He became, in a sense, a flesh-and-blood missing link between computers and the people they were increasingly designed to serve.

Published accounts vary, and usually are skewed toward Jobs's version of events, but Jobs and the engineers who accompanied him that day clearly were impressed with PARC's version of the graphical user interface. Apple already was developing its graphically oriented Lisa computer when the Apple team got the 1979 PARC demo, but they weren't even sure if they wanted to include a mouse in the design. However, by the time the Lisa hit the market in 1983, it included not only a mouse but an interface clearly based on principles refined by Engelbart's progeny at PARC.

The Lisa failed, due in no small part to its ten-thousand-dollar price tag, and a great many of them eventually ended up in a Utah landfill. The following year, though, in 1984, Apple introduced its Macintosh, the beatific happy face of personal computers whose development Jobs had overseen personally. The Mac, advertised as "the computer for the rest of us," debuted in a landmark Super Bowl ad that promised relief to all those frazzled computer users struggling with how to proceed from the "C" prompt of Microsoft's rudimentary MS-DOS, the operating system for rival IBM-based personal computers that required users to type in dizzying strings of command code to coax even the simplest tasks from their computers.

The Mac, costing about twenty-five hundred dollars, was a sensation, and its commercial success proved to the world, and in particular to Microsoft's Bill Gates, that the growing nation of fledgling computer users hungered for simplicity. In 1985, with PCs already outpacing Apples in the world's homes and offices, Microsoft introduced the first of many versions of its own GUI, Windows, which without apology used many of the same metaphors and icons as the Macintosh. (For example, Microsoft's Windows continued the "desktop" concept of the popular Mac, and it thinly disguised the Mac's "Trash Can" function, where unwanted files could be dragged and dumped, as the politically correct "Recycle Bin.")

After Microsoft worked out the many bugs in various Windows incarnations, it introduced Windows 95, which quickly became the most familiar graphical user interface in the world. With it, the GUI entered popular culture with a speed that alarmed even Microsoft. Summing up that sequence of events in 1988 after Jobs and Apple accused Microsoft of filching the idea for Windows, Microsoft founder Bill Gates is said to have defended himself thus: "No, Steve, I think it's more like we both have a rich neighbor named Xerox, and you broke in to steal the TV set, and you found out I'd been there first, and you said, 'Hey, that's no fair! I wanted to steal the TV set!' "

Let's leave aside the question of whether there's honor among thieves because, by then, the vast majority of the world's personal computers had been transformed from intimidating and dense to friendly and helpful. The hard road of advanced technology suddenly looked more like Sesame Street. But that was just one of the immediate aftershocks of the transition to a point-and-click culture.

Computers quickly became as ubiquitous in American homes as telephones and threatened to topple the television as the electronic king of the household. Because the same basic concepts are found in most GUIs, operating a computer—any computer—has become as familiar as steering a car with a wheel. As more people embraced the technology, the exclusive and sometimes peculiar subcultures that had grown up with the personal computer began to fade. Where once only "wizards" could tread, kids and former technophobes could now command these powerful machines to do their bidding.

Even the Internet remained a mystifying place to most people until 1993, when the first GUI-based commercial World Wide Web browsers enabled users to hyperlink their way to computers and web sites around the globe. In all its manifestations, the GUI threw open the doors of a once exclusive club. Longtime computer cultists were reduced to defending the moral purity of *their* arcane way of computing. By mid decade, they were whining about how America Online (the graphically groundbreaking Internet service) was so simple that it was strictly for online amateurs and spewing complaints on web sites such as the "Interface Hall of Shame," an irreverent and ever-changing forum for picking nits over boneheaded GUI design mistakes.

Since then, the graphical user interface has become the standard way for people to communicate with machines of all kinds, including Web TVs, PCs capable of downloading and playing DVD video, "vision-enabled" cell phones, personal digital assistants whose data can be synched to a PC with a few deft clicks, and automotive global-positioning systems with read-while-you-drive graphics. After the 2000 presidential election vote-count debacle, touch-screen voting was heralded as a permanent cure for hanging chads, and by the mid-term 2002 election one state, Georgia, had gone totally GUI at the polls. That same year, a respected South Korean company called LG Electronics—founded about the time the visionary Douglas Engelbart was starting his first postgraduate job at the Stanford Research Institute—began marketing the "Internet Refrigerator," a convergent technology if ever there was one.

"Not simply a computer mounted onto a refrigerator door, the LG Internet Refrigerator acts as a residential gateway to the home," reads the company news release announcing its debut. "The touch-screen display acts as an easy-to-use interface, allowing anyone in the home the ability to access the Internet, check their e-mail, download digital music, or even watch TV"— all with commands from its remote control.

As for Engelbart, he never left the Bay Area and he continued working well past the age when most people retire. He continued to nurture organizations developing cutting-edge technology, and on December 1, 2000, President Clinton acknowledged his contributions with the National Medal of Technology, the highest award for technological achievement the United States has to offer. He holds twenty patents, including the patent for the mouse, and for years kept an office in the operational headquarters of Logitech, the world's largest supplier of computer mice.

But nothing says more about how far we've come—or how far Engelbart was ahead of the curve—than the accessibility of the original black-and-white video of Engelbart's astounding 1968 demonstration. Just type his name into one of the many Web search engines, find the appropriate link, and within seconds you'll be transported to http://sloan.stanford.edu/mousesite/1968Demo.html, a special collections site at Stanford University. The original video has been edited into thirty-five segments and reformatted as RealVideo streaming clips. Just point, click, and see history for yourself.

THE OPERATIVE NUMBER: 532,876,000

Apple Computer's revenue increase, in dollars,
between the $983 million it generated in fiscal year 1983 and
the $1,515,876,000 it generated in 1984, the year it introduced
the GUI-based Apple Macintosh.

Why the GUI Isn't For Everybody

One subset of the world's computer users greeted the advent of the graphical user interface with an extreme lack of enthusiasm—the visually impaired.

Around the middle of 1994, as Microsoft was gearing up to release Windows 95, organizations that dealt with disability issues began getting concerned calls from blind or partially sighted workers who pointed out an overlooked aspect of visually oriented computers: If the vast majority of the world's computers were about to become graphically based, where would that leave all of the visually impaired people who'd made careers for themselves using text-based personal computers (equipped with screen readers) as their primary tool?

"It wasn't huge numbers, but . . . it was very alarming," wrote the authors of a 1996 report by the National Council on Disability. "Here were people who were very skilled computer users, and they were getting bounced out of what had been a phenomenally good technology to use: the combination of [Microsoft's] DOS and [audible] screen readers. As the release date for Windows 95 drew near, advocates feared that blind computer users were about to face vocational extinction."

Advocacy groups had done little to address the issue, and in retrospect the national council interpreted their inaction as similar to the denial stage among people diagnosed with a terminal illness. Some even suggested the possibility of picketing the corporate headquarters of Microsoft, which wasn't opposed to the idea of making Windows accessible to the visually impaired but wasn't actually doing much about it.

Finally, advocates hit upon the idea of spurring Microsoft by using federal legislation that required state governments to guarantee accessible technology in their operations. They argued that states installing Microsoft's Windows 95 might be violating the law unless Microsoft designed the program to include "hooks," or programming aids for screen readers, embedded in the operating system.

With multimillion-dollar government contracts suddenly hanging in the balance, the media—and Microsoft—finally got interested. In January 1995, Microsoft agreed to modify its Windows program to include hooks, and to allow other software companies to develop products that could help visually impaired users interact with Windows-based computers.

You Want *More*?

- *Dealers of Lightning: Xerox PARC and the Dawn of the Computer Age*, by Michael Hiltzik, HarperCollins, New York, 1999.
- *The Big Score: The Billion-Dollar Story of Silicon Valley*, by Michael S. Malone, Doubleday, New York, 1985.

The Righteous Stuff

In 1976, with one flamboyant feat of athleticism,
Julius "Dr. J." Erving introduced America to the slam dunk—
and professional sports suddenly got funky.

FROM THE FREE-THROW LINE, Julius "Dr. J" Erving clutched a red, white, and blue basketball in his right hand, and gazed down court at the far basket, deep in concentration.

The scene was Denver's McNichols Arena on January 27, 1976, and the occasion was the annual all-star game put on by the American Basketball Association, an upstart professional league that had arisen to challenge the established National Basketball Association. Unlike its counterpart, the ABA lacked well-heeled owners and a lucrative network TV deal to broadcast its games, and the seven-team league found itself struggling for financial survival. Desperate to attract some attention, league officials had dreamed up a then novel halftime attraction—a contest, featuring five of the league's highest jumping players, to see who could perform the most spectacular slam dunk.

For the ABA, the dunk contest was a bid for brand recognition as well. At the time, the NBA was the staid, respectable league with a brown ball, where the players were neatly groomed and play was precise and efficient, sometimes to the point of being dull. The ABA, in contrast, resembled the way basketball was played on glass-strewn asphalt courts with bent, rusty rims in the African-American ghettos of urban America, where sport afforded a rare opportunity for self-expression and a measure of respect. It wasn't enough just to win—you had to do it with style. ABA players sported headbands and improbably flamboyant hairstyles, talked trash to opponents, and fired off wild shots from twenty-five feet out (the ABA gave them an extra point if the ball went in). When NBA players—with the exception of a few seven-foot centers—got close-in shots, they tended simply to lay the ball against the backboard and let it drop with businesslike efficiency into the hoop.

For ABA players, driving to the hoop was a chance to get funky, to wow the crowd with flashy aerial maneuvers. They reveled in the opportunity to soar above the rim and jam the ball into the hoop. As author Nelson George wrote in *Elevating the Game*, a history of African-American influence on the sport, "It was airborne brothers who defined ABA ball."

Among the contestants that day was Erving, a twenty-five-year-old, six-feet-seven-inch forward for the New York Nets who was not only the league's finest all-around player but its most magnificently creative dunker as well. Erving thought of himself as sort of a jazz musician in sneakers and shorts—"when it's my turn to solo," he once told the *New York Times*, "I'm not about to play the same old riff." He watched as his competitors did their best slam dunks. Artis Gilmore, the seven-feet-two-inch center for the Kentucky Colonels, put on a display of force, stuffing the ball through the hoop so violently that the backboard shook. Denver Nuggets guard David

Thompson, in contrast, opted to display balletlike agility, leaping and pirouetting 360 degrees in midair on his way to the rim. It was up to Erving to top them with something even more astounding.

Before the contest, he'd chatted with a friend, Denver assistant coach Doug Moe, about a legendary New York playground player, Jackie Jackson, who supposedly had been able to take off from the free-throw line and dunk. The feat was the basketball equivalent of Bigfoot, something that ballplayers talked about, though none seemed to actually have witnessed it. Erving said he could do it. Moe bet him that he couldn't.

Now, in front of fifteen thousand people, Erving was about to give it a try. As he later recalled in an interview with the Houston *Chronicle*, he knew he was taking a big chance, and not just one of possible embarrassment. Today, rims have a spring-back design that allows them to absorb the force of a dunk, but in 1976, the basket was still bolted securely to the backboard. "If you didn't get above it, and dunk the ball through the right way, the rim would throw you to the ground. Not only that, but it would throw your shot back to half court or throw it out of bounds," Erving said. "With that rigid rim . . . you had to bring the truth in. That made a difference. There were a lot of guys who didn't even attempt to dunk because they had been thrown, like getting thrown off a wild stallion."

The arena was deadly silent as Erving took off in long, gazelle-like steps, his luxuriant Afro bouncing in synch. Rather than dribbling, he ran clutching the ball in his palm, so that he wouldn't lose any momentum. (The fact that he could hold the ball that way spoke to his myriad physical gifts, which included hands that from palm to fingertip measured about an inch bigger than a typical baseball fielder's mitt.) He reached the free-throw line and left the hardwood, sailing through the air for close to a full second. At the apex of his leap, Erving straightened his right arm, raising the ball and bringing it back almost behind his head. He was already descending as he brought his arm down, and with perfect timing, cleared the rim and rammed the ball though.

His friend Moe insisted that Erving hadn't quite duplicated the apocryphal playground feat, pointing to the spot where Erving's Converse sneakers had touched slightly past the line. "Look, I'm not doing that again," Erving responded, with a laugh. It didn't matter. The crowd was going wild. He'd won the humble grand prize: one thousand dollars and a new stereo. And although he didn't realize it, Erving had not only revolutionized the sport of basketball, but also altered the very course of American culture.

A quarter century after Erving's astonishing feat, the shock waves it created still resonate, conspicuous as that resounding cash-register noise that a basketball rim makes after being bent back by the force of a monster jam. Call it "Above the Rim America," or "Slam-Dunk Nation," but today we live in a high-flying, spine-tingling, 360-degree-spinning, rim-bending, in-your-face society, a culture fascinated—or rather, obsessed—with the slam dunk. Although the slam-happy ABA wasn't able to overcome its money woes and went out of business after the 1976 season, today's NBA has come to resemble it; in a league where dunking was once an outré rarity, it's now so ubiquitous that the game highlight footage on ESPN SportsCenter often consists mostly of one ferocious dunk after another. Chicago Bulls and Washington Wizards guard Michael Jordan, who in the 1980s and 1990s emulated and surpassed Erving's high-altitude acrobatics, has become the most famous athlete on the planet, a product endorser capable of generating an astonishing $700 million in annual sales for wares ranging from shoes to underwear. A select cadre of NBA players such as Steve Francis, Tracy McGrady, and Vince Carter receive eight-figure salaries based, in large part, upon their ability to astonish fans with their spectacular dunks.

And it's not just pro players who dunk. Slams have become relatively commonplace in college competition and even in high school games—places where, for a time in the 1960s and 1970s, the shot actually was against the rules. Today, even some tall and/or particularly springy women basketball players have begun to dunk.

Of course, the ability to jump high enough to slam a ball into a regulation ten-foot hoop still remains rare among the general population. For the average five-feet-ten-inch man to reach up and stuff a nine-and-a-half-inch diameter ball down into the hoop, he'd need to make a vertical leap—that is, the space between the bottom of his sneakers and the floor—in excess of thirty inches. Even for an athlete considerably taller—the average pro basketball player is slightly under Erving's height of six-feet-seven-inches—attaining that sort of elevation requires an abundance of fast-twitch muscle fibers in the gluteus muscles, quadriceps, and calves. Researchers have discovered that an adept leaper's muscles generate an average force of about two to three times his weight as he pushes off from the court surface. "People think, mistakenly in most cases, that they could hit a baseball," sports announcer Bob Costas once explained in a *Los Angeles Times* interview. "They think they could track down what the announcer calls a routine fly ball. They couldn't, of course, because those things are so much harder than they look. But with a leaper, everybody instantly knows they couldn't do it, that only the tiniest fraction of humans can jump that high."

But that may be what makes it all the more appealing as a fantasy. Preschoolers cram foam rubber balls into three-feet-high baskets. Just as comic books once peddled pimple remedies and Charles Atlas bodybuilding courses, the Internet now features scores of Web pages touting products—jump-improving regimens and special tendon-stretching shoes—that promise to have teenage purchasers dunking on the hoops in their driveways in just a few weeks' time. Those who don't dare to attempt the feat themselves can enjoy Sony's popular NBA Shootout video game, which has a "Create Dunk" mode that makes animated versions of their favorite players hover like alien spacecraft before throwing down other-worldly dunks.

Beyond that, however, as a symbol for flamboyant dominance, the slam dunk has spread beyond the game of basketball and come to pervade popular culture, even for those who think of Shaquille O'Neal merely as that hefty fellow in the Burger King commercials. *Newsweek* may have been the first to use the term metaphorically in 1979, when it asked whether then president Jimmy Carter might try to "slam dunk" an economic program. Today, a query for the term "slam-dunk" on the Google search engine will yield 166,000 hits, many of which, on closer examination, have nothing to do with basketball. Car dealers and realtors boast of slam-dunk financing deals. A newspaper restaurant critic in San Diego writes of a gourmet pizza parlor whose cuisine is a slam dunk. A piece of educational computer software is named "Slam-dunk Typing." A Christian web site even extols the slam dunk of bringing sinners to Jesus.

Most of the storied aerialists in hoops history have been African Americans, a fact that some have mistakenly attributed to some sort of inherent, racially-based physical gift. (To expose the flaw in that theory, one need only look to the six-feet-six-inch Argentine guard Emanuel Ginobili's spectacular slam over the Detroit Pistons's high-leaping forward, Ben Wallace, in the 2002 World Basketball Championships.) And in fact, the progenitor of the slam dunk was a six-feet-ten-inch Caucasian from Oklahoma named Bob Kurland, who led Oklahoma A&M (today known as Oklahoma State) to the national collegiate championship in 1945 and 1946. During a game against Temple University in Kurland's sophomore year, by one account, he grabbed a loose ball under his team's basket, tried to put up a quick shot, and because of his height found himself throwing the ball down into the hoop. The astonished referee promptly disavowed the two points, saying that Kurland committed a violation by reaching into the space over the basket. As it turned out, the "duffer" shot, as Kurland and his compatriots called it at the time (perhaps because it looked so easy for a big man), wasn't actually against the rules, and tall players began dunking occasionally in college games.

But it was a different story in the NBA, whose forerunner, the Basketball Association of America, began play in 1947. In photos from the 1940s and 1950s, pro players, with their knee pads and crew cuts and pale, nonbuff bodies, seemed like earthbound, graceless clods for whom playing above the rim would have been an impossible dream. The truth is that there were players, even then, who were capable of dunking. Six-feet-five-inch Minneapolis Lakers forward Jim Pollard, known as the Kangaroo Kid, is said to have entertained teammates in practice by performing the free-throw-line slam that Dr. J. would later make famous. But he and other early aerialists never even thought of showing off their ability in a game. The old NBA was filled with plenty of rough, dirty players, and embarrassing an opponent with flashy moves wasn't the way to stay healthy. "If you dunked on someone, you expected to end up on your butt later in the game," former Philadelphia Warriors player and coach Al Attles recalled in an interview with *Sporting News*. Into the 1960s, even superlative leapers such as the Los Angeles Lakers's Elgin Baylor still usually laid the ball in when they got to the rim.

The conspicuous exception was seven-feet-one-inch nonconformist Wilt Chamberlain, who as a rookie with the Philadelphia Warriors in 1959 became the first NBA player to dunk regularly—and savagely. Chamberlain, who also played for the Philadelphia 76ers and the Lakers during his fourteen-year career, was far too physically powerful to be deterred by rough stuff. "The Big Dipper," as he liked to be called, may have been the highest jumping player ever; he could dunk without much difficulty on a special rim raised two feet higher than usual, and claimed to be able to reach the top of a regulation backboard, thirteen feet up, and place coins on it. The only thing that could stop Wilt from dunking was his own vanity. He knew that his dunks, which were more frighteningly forceful than acrobatic, didn't seem as impressive because of his size, and instead tried to demonstrate his gracefulness with fade-away jumpers and finger-rolls. (Indeed, the perception that dunking gave seven-footers too much of an advantage led National Intercollegiate Athletic Association officials to prohibit it altogether for nine years, starting in 1967.)

Largely deprived of a showcase in big arenas, dunking became an underground art, practiced on inner-city recreation centers and playgrounds. New York City spawned a lost generation of high-altitude virtuosos with nicknames such as Helicopter and Dr. Blackheart, who never made it to the NBA but regularly embarrassed big name pros on Harlem's asphalt courts. The most renowned was Earl "The Goat" Manigault, who despite being only slightly over six feet tall reportedly could elevate high enough to dunk a ball, catch it as it came through the net, and dunk a second time before returning to the earth. The ravages of poverty and drug addiction cost the Goat a chance to play major college or NBA ball, a sad story that would be repeated many times by other players. Another playground superstar, six-feet-eight-inch Connie Hawkins, was the prototype for Dr J. and Michael Jordan, the first to palm the ball and wave it around in midair to dodge hapless defenders on the way to the rim. After starring at Boys High in Brooklyn—where being able to dunk was a requirement for making the team—Hawkins's career was marred by the fates. Unjustly implicated in a gambling scandal while at the University of Iowa, "The Hawk" was banned from college and NBA competition. After a decade, he finally managed to clear his name and signed with the Phoenix Suns, but by then he'd developed knee problems that robbed him of much of his explosive grace.

Instead, it was left to Julius Erving, who first learned to dunk on the eight-foot rims at his elementary school in Long Island, to introduce America to the joy of slamming. A basketball autodidact,

Erving synthesized his game from bits and pieces of other players' repertoire—Baylor's fakes, Chamberlain's dunking, the unorthodox palming maneuvers of Hawkins, who like Erving was blessed with huge hands. Although he didn't even start on his high school team until he was a senior, Erving managed to earn a scholarship from the University of Massachusetts. There he averaged a breathtaking twenty-six points and twenty rebounds a game before leaving school a year early in 1971 to sign with the Virginia Squires of the ABA. Freed from the college game's then prohibition on dunking, Erving started displaying his true gifts. In a preseason rookie workout, Erving rose up out of a pack of five players to catch a rebound with one hand and, in one motion, slam it into the hoop. "The gym went silent," Johnny Kerr recalled in Terry Pluto's book, *Loose Balls.* The Squires's coaches quickly ushered Erving off the court, not wanting to take a chance on him possibly being injured before the season.

But as a player for the Squires and later the New York Nets, Erving couldn't help but display his aerial creativity. Once, in pregame warmups, for example, he threw the ball off the backboard, turned his back, jumped up to catch the ball, and reverse dunked. He told another player that he'd seen himself do it in a dream. In actual competition, his moves were even more jaw dropping. Not content merely to put on a show when he had an uncontested path to the hoop, Erving often startled crowds by slamming over the outstretched hands of seven-foot centers such as Gilmore, the sort of power move that today is known as "posterizing" an opponent. (It's particularly galling to become the backdrop for someone else's moment of triumph, depicted in full color on the bedroom walls of countless preadolescent boys.) Erving also is credited with inventing the alley-oop, a stock maneuver in today's NBA, in which a player catches a lob pass with one hand and dunks in one dramatic swoop. Hubie Brown, who coached in both the ABA and NBA, described to author Terry Pluto an even more astonishing feat: He once saw Dr. J. drive to the hoop, rise up for a two-handed dunk, and at the apex of his leap actually touch the ball against the painted square on the backboard before slamming it down through the rim. "Do you realize how high you have to jump, and how long you have to stay up, to do something like that?" he asked.

"Players dunked before the Doctor," longtime pro basketball executive Rod Thorn told Pluto, in an interview for the *Sporting News*, "but no one ever dunked like Doc. It was as if Julius invented the dunk."

Since few ABA games were ever televised nationally—in those days, sports cable channels didn't yet exist—the nation only got a chance to see Erving's incredible aerial stunts in still photographs from newspapers and *Sports Illustrated*. Even his signature feat in the 1976 slam-dunk contest was seen live only by the crowd in Denver and scattered hard-core basketball junkies who stayed up to watch a late-night syndicated replay. Nevertheless, the video footage of Erving's free-throw-line slam was simply too remarkable to remain a secret. "The reason it had that kind of impact was the next morning on the news shows like the *Today Show*, [when] everybody showed it," Jim Bukata, former director or marketing and public relations for the ABA, recalled for the Houston *Chronicle* in 1996. "That was really the start. More people saw those [video clips] than saw the game."

The excitement of the dunk contest and Dr. J.'s dramatic finale helped the NBA to see clearly what it lacked. At the time it was stagnating from mediocre TV ratings and lackluster play. When the ABA folded after the 1976 season, the older league absorbed four of its more successful franchises and most of the ABA players. Erving moved over to the Philadelphia 76ers, where he continued his midair magnificence. But now, when he made a spectacular move, it was witnessed by crowds in the nation's biggest cities, and often by millions more who watched on national TV. His most memorable moment may have been in the deciding game of the 1983 NBA finals, when he stole a pass from Kareem Abdul-Jabbar, raced up court, and soared to the hoop. Lakers guard Michael Cooper, who was in his flight path, froze for a split-second, and then simply ducked out of the way ("as if a brick wall was collapsing on him," as the *Sporting News* would later put it). Erving threw down a high-velocity jam that—in a play on his "Dr. J." nickname—became known in the annals of dunking as "the House Call."

Just as important, other players began to emulate Erving's high-altitude flamboyance. For example, another Sixers player, forward-center Darryl Dawkins, even came up with colorful names for his dunks—the Rim Wrecker, the Look out Below, the In-Your-Face Disgrace, the Yo-Momma, the Sexophonic, and the Spine Chiller Supreme. The NBA began to promote the dunk as the ABA had, even adding a slam-dunk competition to its all-star-game weekend. By the time Erving was ready to call it quits in the late 1980s, a new generation of leapers—the Atlanta Hawks's Dominique ("the Human Highlight Film") Wilkins, the Portland Trailblazers's Clyde "The Glide" Drexler, and the 76ers's Charles Barkley—had NBA fans expecting to see spectacular dunks every game. One of the most sensational dunkers was Hawks guard Spud Webb, who, despite standing just five-feet-seven-inches, actually won the 1986 dunk competition.

But Erving's obvious successor was the Chicago Bulls's Michael Jordan, who came into the league in 1984. Just as Dr. J. had copied Connie Hawkins and Wilt, Jordan none too subtly mimicked Dr. J., down to replicating his free-throw-line stunt on his final attempt in the 1988 slam-dunk competition. "I looked up into the box seats and came across the guy who started it all, Dr. J.," Jordan later told the press. "He told me to go back all the way, go the length of the floor, then take off from the free-throw line. And I did it." Jordan, who went on to win six NBA championships with the Bulls, ultimately would eclipse Erving's feats and become vastly more famous—and far richer. Today, yet another generation of dunkers is striving to surpass them both.

THE OPERATIVE NUMBER: 1

Maximum number of seconds of "hang time" that even the most astonishing leapers achieve, even though it may seem as if they float through the air for an eternity on the way to the basket. Brooklyn College professor Peter Brancazio, who analyzed the physics of dunking, devised a formula to calculate hang time: $V=48T^2$. V stands for vertical leap in inches; T equals hang time in seconds.

The Proto-Jordan

Julius Erving did more than just turn the slam dunk into an art form. Bursting upon the scene in the early 1970s, a time of tremendous racial tumult, he also became the first black basketball star to emerge as a truly major marketing phenomenon.

In many ways, Erving had the attributes to be a "crossover" personality who could make the inner-city playground style both appealing and accessible to suburban white America. His stylish skills enabled him to dominate games without appearing threateningly powerful, as Wilt Chamberlain had seemed. And while he looked the part of an urban hipster, with his towering Afro and goatee, Erving's public manner was soft-spoken and friendly. Converse made him one of the first ballplayers to have a signature shoe in 1976, and he eventually did TV commercials for Nabisco cookies, ChapStick, and other products.

In addition to jumping ability, Erving also was gifted with a head for business; after retirement, he set up an empire of companies to oversee his diverse ventures, which ranged from an interest in a Coca-Cola bottling plant to a stock-car racing team. He also became an executive with the parent company of the NBA's Orlando Magic.

"Dr. J. was ahead of everybody in bringing business to pro basketball," Michael Jordan told *Fortune* in 1998. Just as Erving's popularizing of the dunk opened the way for Jordan on the basketball court, however, Jordan followed in Dr. J.'s footsteps as a marketing phenom.

Jordan, it turned out, was even more charismatic and broadly appealing to the audience that advertisers wanted to capture, and he has used those skills to create wealth on a scale that would have been inconceivable for an African-American athlete—or any athlete—in Erving's heyday. *Fortune* estimated that by the time Jordan retired from the Chicago Bulls in 1998 he had generated some ten billion dollars in revenues during his career, ranging from increased NBA ticket sales to sales of Nike's Air Jordan line of sneakers.

You Want *More*?

- *Loose Balls: The Short, Wild Life of the American Basketball Association, As Told by the Players, Coaches, and Movers and Shakers Who Made It Happen*, by Terry Pluto, Simon & Schuster, New York, 1990.
- *Elevating the Game*, by Nelson George, HarperCollins, New York, 1992.
- http://www.hoophall.com, the Basketball Hall of Fame Web site.
- http://www.geocities.com/fantasyspecs/, an unofficial Julius Erving Web page.

Betty Ford's Intervention

*Personal confessions went from anonymous whispers to
public declarations to a steady roar on the talk-show circuit.
It began April 1, 1978.*

LOOKING AROUND HER LIVING ROOM that spring morning, former first lady Betty Ford, like most hard-drinking junkies, didn't
quite get it.

"My makeup wasn't smeared, I wasn't disheveled, I behaved
politely, and I never finished off a bottle, so how could I be an alcoholic?" she recalled years later in one of her autobiographies. "And
I wasn't on heroin or cocaine; the medicines I took—the sleeping
pills, the pain pills, the relaxer pills, the pills to counteract the side
effects of other pills—had been prescribed by doctors, so how could
I be a drug addict?" One of the medical professionals in the room
that day remembers that Ford "looked small, almost like a doll, lost
in the [sofa] cushions, and as her husband made his opening
remarks, you could see the confusion on her face."

Ford was still in her bathrobe as, one by one, her husband and children told her the truth. Former president Gerald R. Ford lamented the slurring of her speech and the times his wife had fallen asleep in a favorite chair. Son Mike and his wife, Gayle, raised the possibility that she wouldn't live long enough to ever know the children they intended to have. Son Steve recounted the day he and his girlfriend prepared an elaborate dinner for her, only to have her ignore their efforts as she watched TV and slid into an alcoholic haze. Son Jack said he "was always kind of peeking around the corner into the family room to see what kind of shape mother was in." Daughter Susan, the youngest, who had rallied the family to confront its matriarch, broke down as she explained how she had always admired her mother's grace as a Martha Graham–trained dancer and couldn't stand to see her "falling and clumsy." (Not too long before, Ford had fallen in the middle of the night and cracked her ribs and chipped a tooth.)

The Ford family intervention didn't take long that morning of April 1, 1978, but it began a series of events that profoundly changed Betty Ford's life, and much more. Devastated, she agreed to undergo a week of medically supervised detoxification at her brand-new Rancho Mirage, California, home, during which she was weaned from alcohol, Librium, and what she later described as "gourmet medications." Then, the day after her sixtieth birthday, Ford was driven two hours to the Navy hospital in Long Beach to eat a giant serving of humble pie and learn the twelve steps of Alcoholics Anonymous. She was met by clamoring cameramen as she arrived for treatment, and suddenly the term "public drunkenness" took on a whole new meaning.

After settling into a standard room with her three roommates, Ford released a statement to the media that without apology described her "insidious" addictions and her intention to overcome them. To a world that knew only the former first lady's sparkling public image, it was as if Snow White had come out as a lesbian. By making hers a public rather than a private struggle, irrepressible, straight-talking Betty Ford transformed the image of a drug-abusing alcoholic from a nameless, faceless loser into a noble and likable survivor. She helped diminish the stigma long associated with addiction and treatment, especially for women. Confronting personal problems and past traumas stopped being shameful evidence of personal weakness and became, instead, a symbol of personal strength and righteous resolve.

The grim little surprise party that started her down that road also spawned a recovery movement that Ford never could have imagined, a national conversation in which troubled souls seemed willing, even eager, to make a cathartic public confession or act of contrition. In the decades that followed, it became hard to turn on a television talk show without hearing survivors' tales about overcoming everything from incest, gender confusion, compulsive eating disorder and bulimia to sexual addiction, codependence, rape, even alien abduction and satanic possession.

To understand why Betty Ford's intervention had such impact, it's important to understand her unexpected role in what's known as the "modern alcoholism movement," which began in 1935 when two men, a New York stockbroker (Bill W.) and an Akron, Ohio, surgeon (Dr. Bob S.) pioneered a method of dealing quietly and anonymously with addiction by creating Alcoholics Anonymous and preaching the twelve-step gospel that has changed the lives of countless apostles. Back then and into the 1960s, no one knew quite what to do with drunks and junkies. Some steered them into mutual-aid societies such as A.A. and hoped for the best, or simply watched them medicate themselves to death. Others dispatched their substance abusers to sanitariums for rounds of detox. Still others subjected substance abusers to experimental behavior-modification treatments, including hypnosis, electroshock therapy, and methadone treatment.

In 1970, a federal law called the Hughes Act officially recognized drug and alcohol addiction as a disease rather than the bad behavior of degenerates, setting the stage for what eventually became a multibillion-dollar-a-year industry of specialty treatment centers, court-ordered compliance, and sophisticated marketing. Even so, there remained a crushing social stigma that kept most substance abusers hidden deep in society's shadows.

Anonymity wasn't an option for a woman who, as first lady, had spent the previous three years as one of the most visible and influential women in the world. More important, Betty Ford in 1978 didn't fit neatly into any of the public's stereotypes of a drunk or a drug addict, a stereotype enthusiastically promoted for more than a century by various American temperance crusaders. She wasn't a classic loser like Ray Milland's failed writer character in the film *Lost Weekend*. She wasn't a fallen woman or twitching zombie like the druggies in *Reefer Madness*, *Go Ask Alice*, or the government's antidrug public-service flicks. She wasn't even considered a lovable lush like entertainers Dean Martin or Foster Brooks. No, Betty Ford was a very clean, very polite, very successful substance abuser—someone admired rather than reviled.

Even though her husband had lost the 1976 presidential election to Jimmy Carter, Ford left the White House in January 1977 as the most popular first lady since Jackie Kennedy. She had entered the international spotlight in a buttoned-down era when the prototypical Republican wife was a lacquer-haired deaf-mute with the adoring eyes of an acolyte. (Can you describe Pat Nixon's voice? Didn't think so.) Born in Chicago and raised in Grand Rapids, Michigan, Ford brought to Washington a midwesterner's disconcerting tendency to answer any question asked, and to answer it honestly. This is not a local custom in Washington, D.C., where one of Ford's early exchanges with the White House press corps signaled an era of often refreshing honesty in the nation's capital.

"Why didn't you tell us?" a reporter once scolded after learning that Mrs. Gerald Ford had once been Mrs. Bill Warren, between 1942 and 1947.

"You never asked," she replied.

By then, Ford's reputation for sometimes startling candor was already growing. It's hard to imagine in this age of routine political vivisection, where every facet of a politician's life is considered open to question, but one of Ford's first unofficial actions as first lady was to publicly declare her intention to sleep not only in the same White House bedroom as her husband, but in the same bed, thereby raising the possibility, technically, that sex could occur. She certainly wasn't the first presidential spouse to submit to her wifely duty, but she may have been the first to actually *talk* about it—sometimes with a bit too much gusto. She once complained to a Washington columnist that the only question she had not been asked since her husband rose to power was how often she slept with Jerry, so the obliging columnist asked, "Well, how often do you?"

Ford's answer: "As often as possible!"

She'd proudly declared her enthusiastic support for the Equal Rights Amendment for women—a position not shared by her husband or his party—and when her husband was vice president under Richard Nixon she told journalist Barbara Walters how pleased she was by the Supreme Court's 1972 *Roe v. Wade* decision legalizing abortion. After ascending to the White House after Nixon's resignation in 1974, Ford told Morley Safer on *60 Minutes* that she "wouldn't be surprised" to hear that her daughter, then eighteen, was having sex, or that her children were experimenting with drugs. During the furor that followed, the president's press secretary issued a statement declaring that Gerald Ford "long [ago] ceased to be perturbed by his wife's remarks."

It's tempting to speculate what role Betty Ford's long-standing fondness for stiff drinks and growing reliance on painkillers (prescribed to ease the pain of a pinched nerve in her neck) may have played in her preference for living out loud, but her openness was consistent, not erratic. "It never really occurred to me to simply ignore questions I didn't like. No one ever trained me to do that,"

Ford later told the *Los Angeles Times*. "I wish sometimes someone had."

If Ford's openness was at times a liability, she also was well aware of the positive public impact that her personal behavior could have. A month after moving into the White House, her doctors had found a malignant lump and were forced to remove her right breast. Ford immediately went public with the news and began a course of chemotherapy in the full glare of the public spotlight. Supportive mail poured in, and the American Cancer Society saw a spike in donations. Ford's frank confrontation with a disease that was freighted with cultural taboos sent a wave of awareness through the country. "Even before I was able to get up, I lay in bed and watched television and saw on the news shows lines of women queued up to go in for breast examinations because of what had happened to me," she later recalled. One of those women was Happy Rockefeller, wife of then vice president Nelson Rockefeller. Turns out she had a lump, too, and had a similar operation a month after Ford's mastectomy. Her husband credited Ford's frank public disclosure with saving his wife's life by convincing her to go, in time, for a checkup.

After leaving the White House in 1977, Betty Ford hired ghostwriter Chris Chase and, to no one's surprise, set to work on her autobiography, *The Times of My Life*. She and her husband eventually retreated to the new home in Rancho Mirage, a posh desert community outside of Los Angeles, and by the spring of 1978 she was polishing the final chapters of the memoir. Ford devoted its early chapters to her unlikely rise to the very pinnacle of power. In later chapters, she recounted the many moments when, after the cloak-and-dagger secrecy of the Nixon years, her candor had caught official Washington and much of the nation off-guard. You'll find in those chapters an unmistakable whiff of Ford's defiant pride at having survived the fishbowl on her own terms. For better or worse, Betty Ford had always told the truth.

But nothing in Ford's nearly finished manuscript hinted at the most startling truth of all, one that not only would require a rushed final chapter for that book—subtly titled "Long Beach"—but an entirely new autobiography less than a decade later that dealt entirely with her battle against addiction. She had managed to completely ignore her slide into a haze of cocktails and pain pills— apparently the only Ford family member able to do so.

The intervention, back then, had not yet become one of the most controversial features of the recovery culture. The idea is based on the theory that the most effective way to compel someone with a problem to seek treatment is for the people closest to them, family and friends, to confront them with the truth about how the problem has affected their lives. Interventions represent a significant departure from the methods established by the founders of A.A., who favored a voluntary, rather than a confrontational, approach. This also was long before the horror stories of abuse in which well-intentioned parents essentially had their troubled children kidnapped and hauled off to tough-love treatment facilities, a rather unfortunate aberration of the intervention technique lamented by the mid-1980s band Suicidal Tendencies in its song, "Institutionalized."

Ford was no less skeptical that morning as her family gathered from around the country to confront her in a home still filled with moving boxes. But a week later, the former first lady of the United States of America was taking meals in a basement cafeteria at the Navy base and sharing a room with three other women. One was an admiral's wife with a taste for Valium, the other two were young, regular Navy. One had been shipped home from overseas because of her drinking problem. As word spread about Ford's treatment, the media began to portray addiction as a disease with no discernible demographic, the great equalizer.

"After I came into the hospital, it was as though a dam had burst," Ford later recalled. "Newspapers and magazines poured in, filled with articles about women and drugs and alcohol. Bags of mail followed, and flowers, and messages sent by well-wishers." A *Washington Post* editorial praised her courage and determination to overcome her addiction, and for being "unafraid and unembarrassed to say so."

Two years after the intervention and her public disclosure, on October 9, 1981, Betty Ford helped break ground for an addiction treatment center at the Eisenhower Medical Center in Rancho Mirage. She committed her fund- and consciousness-raising efforts to the cause and, reluctantly, lent her name and face to what has become the best known facility of its kind in the world. The Betty Ford Center was dedicated one year later. One of the earliest to step forward for treatment was another of America's most influential women, actress Elizabeth Taylor. She had become quite the substance abuser during her years on screen, on Broadway, and as a serial bride. Her decision to disclose her struggle had nearly as much impact as Ford's in terms of destigmatizing alcohol and drug rehabilitation.

Taylor's treatment also added a touch of glamour to the Betty Ford Center and to treatment in general, paving the way for other celebrity substance abusers to talk about their addictions and treatment. A curious snowballing began. At the time, medical insurance laws made rehabilitation centers a potential profit center for hospitals, and facilities began cropping up fast. According to Stanton Peele, a psychologist, substance-abuse specialist, and frequent critic of the recovery movement, the number of U.S. hospital beds dedicated to treating alcoholics quadrupled between 1978 and 1984.

The language began to soften. "Drunks" and "drug fiends" became "alcoholics" and "substance abusers." The people around them became "enablers" and "codependents." The culture began suspending harsh judgments about an addict's character defects and began looking to family histories and childhood traumas as a way to explain someone's drinking or drug abuse problem. Ford's treatment also was followed by what one addiction specialist calls a "new temperance movement." Mothers Against Drunk Driving (M.A.D.D.) was founded in 1980, the same year Nancy Reagan stepped into the first lady's role after her husband defeated Carter and began a two-term campaign against substance abuse. Her "Just Say No!" slogan became one of the most memorable—and ridiculed—catchphrases of that decade. Warnings began to appear on beer, wine, and liquor labels, and antialcohol and antidrug programs became a staple of secondary and even elementary education.

More than fifty-three thousand patients have sought help at the Betty Ford Center since it opened. They have included housewives, truck drivers, doctors, lawyers, athletes. Some were nearly as famous as Ford and Taylor: baseball legends Mickey Mantle and Darryl Strawberry; football player Todd Marinovich; country music singer Tanya Tucker—the list reads like a who's who of the entertainment and sports worlds, even though celebrities represent only a fraction of the center's clients. Today, Betty Ford's name turns up in a startling number of celebrity biographies and memoirs, often with an expression of gratitude. Ford herself, still sober, was seen straightening artwork and picking up cigarette butts around the center's sparkling campus well into her eighties.

But after all the talk, after decades of often dramatic self-exposure, there remains a bottom line: A government report suggests that of the estimated thirteen million to sixteen million Americans who need treatment for alcohol or drug problems in any given year, only three million actually get it. And something else is happening that Ford could not have foreseen that day in 1978 when she took her first tentative steps toward sobriety. While recovery has doubtless changed many lives for the better, and while Ford's public struggle may have coaxed thousands of closeted addicts into the open and diminished the stigma of treatment, the lasting impact of all those public acts of contrition is hard to pin down. The snowball began to melt.

The Substance Abuse and Mental Health Services Administration (SAMHSA), an arm of the federal Department of Health and Human Services, has designated September as National Alcohol and Drug Addiction Recovery Month partly because of a "restigmatization" of substance abuse and addiction in recent years. That same agency notes the impact of critics who have raised concerns about whether substance abuse is a medical or a behavioral problem. The backlash to the recovery theories and methods espoused by A.A. and Ford is obvious from a search of the Amazon.com online book catalog, which contains titles such as Stanton Peele's *Diseasing of America: How We Allowed Recovery Zealots and the Treatment Industry to Convince Us We Are Out of Control*; and *I'm Dysfunctional, You're Dysfunctional: The Recovery Movement and Other Self-Help Fashions* by Wendy Kaminer.

Spending on substance abuse treatment between 1987 and 1997 shifted heavily from private to public, meaning that fewer alcoholics and drug addicts in this age of managed care can count on insurance companies and other private payers to cover the cost of treatment. Says SAMHSA spokesman Leah Young: "While Betty Ford may have opened the conversation, the economics tell you that the stigma of addiction and treatment is alive and well."

"Three trends are evident since 1990," wrote William L. White, author of *Slaying the Dragon: The History of Addiction Treatment and Recovery in America*. "The first is the re-stigmatization of severe and persistent alcohol and other drug problems. The images of First Ladies, next-door neighbors and our own family members are being replaced with more demonized images that elicit fear and anger rather than compassion." White said that trend, combined with the "demedicalization" of treatment and the "recriminalization" of addiction, now finds people like Betty Ford portrayed as "infectious agent[s] of evil" and recovery as an exception rather than a rule. It's worth noting that the national conversation that Ford began in 1978 now includes a bumper sticker that reads: "Alcoholics go to meetings. I'm just a drunk."

White has called for a "New Recovery Movement" in which "a vanguard of recovering people . . . step forward to offer themselves as living proof of the hope for sustained recovery from addiction"— a seemingly radical departure from the A.A. philosophy. During a speech to a New Jersey recovery group several years ago, White wistfully recalled Ford's long ago public confession as perhaps the best moment in the country's history to be an alcoholic.

THE OPERATIVE NUMBER: 4

Factor by which the number of U.S. hospital beds dedicated to treating alcoholics multiplied between 1978 and 1984.

How Confession Got Cachet

John Schwarzlose, the longtime director of the Betty Ford Center in Rancho Mirage, California, recalls the day during the center's early years when he realized that Ford's name was becoming synonymous with drug and alcohol treatment, and that admitting to addiction and rehabilitation had developed a weird cachet.

He was watching an episode of *Good Morning, America*, and then host David Hartman was interviewing a prominent young actor. When Hartman queried the actor about his reputation for

carousing, the young man identified himself to the national audience as "a Betty Ford kid," putting himself among a pantheon of
celebrities, including Elizabeth Taylor, whose personal journeys
had once brought them to the desert alcohol and drug treatment
center.

"The thing was," Schwarzlose says, "he'd never been here."

You Want *More*?

- *The Times of My Life*, by Betty Ford with Chris Chase, Harper &
  Row, New York, 1978.
- *Betty: A Glad Awakening*, by Betty Ford with Chris Chase, Dou-
  bleday, New York, 1987.
- *Diseasing of America: How We Allowed Recovery Zealots and the
  Treatment Industry to Convince Us We Are Out of Control*, by Stan-
  ton Peele, Jossey-Bass, San Francisco, 1999.
- *I'm Dysfunctional, You're Dysfunctional: The Recovery Movement
  and Other Self-Help Fashions*, by Wendy Kaminer, Vintage
  Books, New York, 1993.
- *Slaying the Dragon: The History of Addiction Treatment and Recov-
  ery in America*, by William L. White, Chestnut Health Systems,
  Bloomington, Ill., 1998.

From E.T. to "Astroturfing"

Most people understood the difference between a sales pitch and real life—at least until 1982 and that adorable alien with a penchant for peanut butter.

ONE LAZY AUGUST AFTERNOON NOT long ago, sightseers began to gather at New York's Empire State Building, Seattle's space needle, and other well-known tourist attractions across America to gawk, marvel, and maybe snap a few souvenir photos. Mingling among them, though, were "tourists" with a more commercial agenda.

The interlopers were sixty trained actors and actresses employed by Sony Ericsson Mobile Communications Ltd., and they were part of a "stealth" marketing campaign that the cell-phone company had dubbed "Fake Tourist." The idea was that the fakes would infiltrate the crowds of actual tourists in teams of two or three. They would ask strangers to take their pictures and, when a stranger agreed, the fake tourists would hand them not a camera but a cell phone—not just any cell phone, mind you, but the T68i model, which had the then startling ability to take digital photos. A conversation would ensue, and when it was over the stranger would walk away not only having been introduced to a whole new concept in technology, but completely unaware that they'd just been given a hands-on product demonstration by an attractive salesman.

Whether you realize it or not, you're bombarded with similar below-the-radar pitches every day, everything from the shoes on basketball star LeBron James's feet to the Omega watch on James Bond's wrist to the unfamiliar but exceedingly friendly Internet chat room "buddy" who really, really likes to shop at the Gap and read *Elle* magazine. Marketers are waging a relentless, pitched battle for the hearts, minds, and disposable income of every citizen of the planet—citizens increasingly barraged by products and services that often have no discernable differences. Coke or Pepsi? Bud or Miller? McDonald's or Burger King? Nike or Adidas? Eventually you'll choose, and often for reasons you never fully understand.

That's where the need for stealth comes in. Advertising used to be as clumsy and obvious as a Burma Shave sign, but today's typical American—barraged by thousands of commercial messages every day—now comes standard with a healthy dose of skepticism that filters paid commercial endorsements from the rest of what they see and hear, and interprets those messages accordingly. Consumers react to advertising in much the way they react to a virus—too much exposure can either make them sick or immune—and have developed lightning-quick channel-change fingers to avoid TV and radio commercials. They've also embraced digital video recording technologies such as TiVo and ReplayTV that enable them to skip commercial interruption of their favorite shows.

That's bad news for anyone with something to sell. Their challenge is to break through that defense and catch the consumer in what psychologist Monroe Friedman calls a "noncritical mindset," planting a seed—a brand name, a "new and improved" feature, a general impression that Mountain Dew is the drink of choice among the young and hip—that will sprout and bloom at the precise moment the consumer makes his or her buying decision. Stealth marketing is based on the principle that consumers are more receptive to a message if they perceive it as part of the passing scenery of everyday life rather than as a paid ad placement.

"It's effective because it comes in under the level of conscious awareness," said Michael Kamins, an associate professor of marketing at the University of Southern California. "It's advertising that doesn't seem like advertising to you. Face it, advertising is not a credible source."

Sneaky salesmanship isn't new. For decades tobacco companies bartered their way into films and other forms of entertainment to create the impression that smoking was glamorous. Sean Connery's James Bond preferred Larks during the 1960s, for example. Joan Crawford drank Jack Daniels whiskey in the 1945 production of *Mildred Pierce*. Clothing designers have always donated expensive eveningwear to Hollywood stars knowing that the stars' "taste" in couture would be noted as they stepped onto the red carpet at a film premiere or an awards show. Psychologist Friedman notes that restaurateurs have been known to pack a new establishment with friends and family pretending to be patrons to make the place look hot and happening, and Kamins recalls a technique begun in East Coast metro areas during the 1950s in which companies sent people into the field to engage in loud, seemingly normal, subway conversations designed to plug a company's products. What does it tell you about credibility that information exchanged by total strangers and overheard on a subway car is considered more trustworthy than paid ads?

Nothing propelled the stealth-marketing phenomenon forward quite like a moment in 1982 when the world's unlikeliest pitchman—a short, green illegal alien with no prior celebrity credentials—demonstrated an apparent fondness for a then unknown product called Reese's Pieces. The celebrity endorser was the title character in film director Steven Spielberg's blockbuster *E.T., the Extra-Terrestrial*. In the movie, an impossibly cute and kindhearted California boy named Elliott discovers a wary but kindhearted alien who has been accidentally left behind by his fellow interplanetary explorers. Screenwriter Melissa Mathison created a scene in which Elliott tries to lure E.T. into his house with food. What kind of food? A choice had to be made, and therein lies a tale whose impact continues to echo in the world of commercial marketing.

The target audience for the film was kids and young adults, so Spielberg's Amblin Entertainment decided to use candy, specifically M&Ms, as the bait. The producers approached the M&M Mars Candy Company with the idea, but according to various accounts, they weren't looking for money, just for the company's blessing and the chance to discuss the possibility of a little mutually beneficial cross-promotion in which the candy company would plug the movie in its advertising. The film's production company was cagey about details, revealing only the film's central concept—a space alien living with an Earth family. Turns out, they were a bit too cagey. M&M Mars decided to pass, not sure it wanted its product associated with a film that might scare children.

Next stop was the Hershey Foods Corporation, which since 1963 had owned the H. B. Reese Candy Company and was preparing to launch a new candy designed to compete directly with ever popular M&Ms. The candy's taste was modeled after Reese's Peanut Butter Cups—a blend of chocolate and peanut butter—but delivered in a pea-sized, candy-coated nugget that looked almost exactly like an M&M. "They said that if we were interested, there might be promotional opportunities available," Hershey spokesman Natalie Bailey said in a 1991 interview. "But there was no obligation on Hershey's part. They were going to be used anyway whether or not we chose to follow through in promotional opportunities."

At first reluctant to associate its product with a "monster" movie, Hershey eventually decided to take a chance. The only money that changed hands was the small licensing fee the company paid to use the E.T. character on T-shirts, posters, and in-store promotional material for Reese's Pieces. When Spielberg's movie hit theaters—and quickly became one of the most popular films of all time—E.T. followed a trail of Reese's Pieces into Elliott's house and into marketing history.

The lesson was dramatic and unforgettable—"the grand slam of product placement," according to one Amblin executive. Sales of Reese's Pieces skyrocketed, swamping Hershey's with back orders and forcing the company to put two plants on twenty-four-hour production schedules to meet demand. An unknown brand of candy had burst into the marketplace with such force that advertisers immediately understood the untapped potential of "product placements" in films, television, and other forms of entertainment— and began to explore other ways in which to integrate sales pitches into nonadvertising formats that would catch consumers with their guard down.

Hershey's Bailey said many people have mistaken the E.T.–Reese's Pieces arrangement for a paid product placement because, by today's standards, to have been otherwise seems impossible. That particular type of stealth marketing has since become big business as movie producers began looking for creative ways to offset ridiculous production costs. Multimillion-dollar placements now are brokered by scores of marketing companies represented by their own trade organization, the Entertainment Resources & Marketing Association. Its efforts explain why Pierce Brosnan's James Bond wears an Omega wristwatch and ditched his trusty Aston Martin for a BMW Z3 roadster in *Goldeneye*; why the characters in the *Men in Black* films wear Ray-Ban sunglasses; and why the movie *Castaway*, in addition to being fine entertainment, also was a 143-minute commercial for the FedEx overnight delivery service and featured a Wilson-brand volleyball as a character that got nearly as much screen time as Tom Hanks. Spielberg is still at it as well, with the protagonist of his *Minority Report*—set in 2054—surrounded by talking billboards touting Lexus cars and, at one point in the story, shopping briefly at the Gap. Where was Jack Nicholson's character when his wife died in the 2002 film *About Schmidt*? At Dairy Queen, and for no apparent reason.

It's not always a matter of filmmakers looking to make a buck, either. In one hall-of-mirrors moment in 2001, Chrysler actually reversed the creative flow by sponsoring the "Chrysler Million Dollar Film Festival." That competition provided the cash to enable a handful of independent filmmakers to pursue their dreams—provided that at least one Chrysler vehicle made it into their films.

The ripple effects of E.T.'s appetite for peanut butter spread quickly from the world of feature films into almost every realm of culture. From film, it was a short hop into television, where during one recent season, for example, Revlon paid between $3 million and $7 million to be featured as a regular story element in ABC's long-running daytime drama *All My Children*, and the teen cast of *Dawson's Creek*—a hit show at the turn of the millennium—dressed in clothing from the J. Crew catalog. (Subtle efforts like those were downright invisible compared to less sophisticated product-plugging TV game shows such as *The Price Is Right*, where contestants competed to guess the prices of lovingly described brand-name products.) The integration of subtle sales pitches into television recently took a giant step forward when Princeton Video—the same New Jersey company that developed the technology to enable football broadcasters to insert a virtual yellow first-down marker on your TV screen—figured out how to insert brand-name products into television scenes that weren't in the original version. They've even figured out how to customize the syndicated scenes for specific markets so that, for example, the cereal boxes in Jerry Seinfeld's cupboard are the ones the cereal maker wants to pitch to buyers in, say, Chicago. The questions that once guided entertainment—Is it dramatic? Is it funny?—now compete with questions of a different sort, including, "Who'll pay the most to have their product plugged?"

The notion of integrating sales pitches into unexpected situations and locations also spilled over into sports, with chosen athletes proclaiming "I'm going to Disneyland!" while in the throes of a World Series or Super Bowl victory celebration and downhill racers not-so-casually holding their brand-name-emblazoned skis next to their faces during postrace TV interviews. Sometimes the marketing was mutually beneficial. For example, the National Basketball Association worked hand-in-hand with 20th Century Fox to produce the 2002 film *Like Mike*, which on one level was the story of a boy propelled into the NBA by a pair of magic hand-me-down sneakers presumably from NBA icon Michael Jordan. On another level, though, the film was an elaborate $20-million effort to promote the pro basketball league and its biggest stars, including *Like Mike* costars Jason Kidd, Chris Webber, and Vince Carter. The noun "brand" has become a verb as retinal impressions and chanted mantras burn logos and messages into our brains. If you ever doubt it just ask the recreational golfers who sometimes find a printed ad in the bottom of the cup after sinking a putt, or try to find a photo of pro golfer Tiger Woods in which Nike's familiar swoosh is not visible on his hat, his shirt, his shoes, or the bottom of his driver.

Not all post-E.T. efforts at stealth marketing are so subtle. ATM machines now dispense commercials along with cash, ads appear in public toilets, and at one point a Los Angeles traffic correspondent was broadcasting his updates from "the Mercedes-Benz of the South Bay helicopter." A recent report in the *Washington Post* noted that during the popular TV talent show *American Idol*, it was "nearly impossible to judge where the show ended and the ads for corporate sponsors Ford and Coca-Cola began. Coke cups were found in every shot involving the judges during auditions for the show; during the show itself, contestants were shown riding in a Ford Focus and the Coke logo was omnipresent."

As stealth marketing saturated popular culture, it seeped into the wider culture as well. For example, novelist Bill Fitzhugh became one of the first known authors to incorporate a product placement into a work of fiction. He'd sold the film rights to his 2000 book *Cross Dressing* to Universal Studios, which at the time was owned by distilling giant Seagrams. He struck a deal to replace generic references to liquor in a bar scene with flattering references to Seagrams spirits, and says he was rewarded with an ample supply of liquor. But here's the twist: Fitzhugh wasn't really interested in helping Seagrams sell liquor. He struck the deal because he knew that when his book came out, he could market its product-placement deal as a unique, if lamentable, literary landmark. In other words, by generating hand-wringing stories in *Brill's Content*, *Publishers Weekly*, *Time*, and *Entertainment Weekly*, Fitzhugh wasn't selling liquor so much as selling books.

Now that's stealth.

Cartoonist Garry Trudeau recently lampooned the whole phenomenon by creating a full-color Sunday *Doonesbury* strip in which characters Mike Doonesbury and Zonker Harris celebrate the fine character of "Denny Klatz," a fictional recent college grad who Doonesbury explains paid fifty thousand dollars to have his name inserted into the strip but could not yet afford to have Trudeau draw his likeness as one of the strip's characters, and therefore was presented as a headless body with no spoken lines.

Film studios continue to lead the rest of the culture into brave new worlds of stealth marketing. In early 2002, the people who run web sites featuring forums for discussing new movies noticed a curious phenomenon. Some of the postings from supposed film buffs began reading a lot like outright publicity plugs, or "plants." They featured the poor punctuation and net slang typical of online communication and were intended to seem like authentic enthusiasm, but they always included a hyperlink to the studio trailer for the lionized film. Patrick Goldstein, an entertainment reporter for the *Los Angeles Times*, described several typically effusive reviews, including one from "filmfreak234" that read: "Lemme just say that I really can't wait to see undercover brother . . . am I alone here? For one it looks hella funny, and two its got denise richards. You just can't get better than that combo!!!!" Some enterprising web site operators traced the Internet protocol address from those postings back to studio marketing departments and exposed the postings as the studios' stealthy attempts to generate buzz.

Such efforts seem ham-fisted when compared to sophisticated Web software applications known as "bots" that are designed to simulate online conversations with real people as a way of plugging rock bands, movies, magazines, TV shows, and other goods and services. The virtual Web "buddies" seek out chat rooms and navigate instant messaging systems in search of opportunities to interject themselves like boors at a cocktail party. Taking cues from human acquaintance questions, the bots are designed to mimic the slang and interests of the people they're trying to reach, then slip in product plugs. Their creators imbue them with likable features, and according to one account, the bots' attempts at online conversation aren't much different than an Al Gore stump speech—"formulaic and stilted [but also] witty, provocative and startlingly lifelike." For example, according to a story in the *Los Angeles Times*, "ELLEgirl-Buddy," the Internet bot of teen magazine *Ellegirl*, describes itself as a redheaded sixteen-year-old who says, "I looove making my own clothes. I use gap tees a lot. You just shrink em and add ribbons. Insta-chic! I like kickboxing (major crush on gabe, my kickboxing instructor!:-*)"

The techniques pioneered by commercial marketers inevitably found their way into noncommercial use in a stealth-marketing strategy known as "astroturfing"—a term derived from the fake grass. Generally, astroturfing involves a special-interest group trying to push its political or social agenda by hiring a public relations firm to pose as concerned citizens. The firm writes letters to the editors of local newspapers pushing its client's point of view, submits opinion pieces to the paper's op-ed pages, and may even form "grassroots" lobbying groups to advance the cause. The most notable case involved software giant Microsoft, which in 1998 allegedly employed astroturfing to create the impression that the preponderance of public opinion was against the U.S. Department of Justice's antitrust case against the company.

Because it's done so often, and at such great expense, it's easy to assume that stealth marketing is very effective. There is, alas, a bottom line to all of this, and the question remains: How effective are the various forms of stealth marketing? Perhaps the best answer is this: Not as effective as advertisers and wild-eyed subliminal-advertising conspiracy theorists would like to believe.

Kamins, the USC marketing professor, said advertising involves a "hierarchy of effects," beginning with cognition, followed by affect, followed by behavior. "Basically," he said, "you have to know about something before you can like it, and you have to like it before you will buy it." A product placement in a film or some other form of stealth marketing can make the public aware of a product, or can reinforce a product's existing image. But Kamins said, "To ask a product placement to get you all the way to behavior is kind of silly. People say, 'What about Reese's Pieces?' I say, 'Yeah, but what about the nine million other placements you didn't mention?'"

THE OPERATIVE NUMBER: 65

Percentage jump in sales for Reese's Pieces following the opening of the film E.T., the Extra-Terrestrial, *in which a young boy lures a lovable space alien into his house by leaving a trail of the peanut butter–chocolate candy.*

The Inspirational Alien

⁊

A staggering amount of money changed hands because of the success of Steven Spielberg's 1982 film *E.T., the Extra-Terrestrial*. The film grossed an estimated $704.8 million worldwide during its initial release on 1,100 screens, and that doesn't include the money it made in 2002 during its twentieth anniversary re-release on 2,500 screens.

But lost among those staggering figures is a number that speaks volumes about the odd synergy between Hollywood and product sales. According to *Entertainment Weekly* magazine, singer Neil Diamond, after seeing an early screening of the film, paid twenty-five thousand dollars for the rights to be "inspired by" E.T. to write, with collaborators Burt Bacharach and Carole Bayer Sager, the cloying tribute "Heartlight."

The song in turn generated its own impressive sales numbers, reaching number 5 on the *Billboard* singles chart.

You Want *More*?

- http://www.erma.org, the Entertainment Resources & Marketing Association's Web site, for an eye-opening education about how product placement works in the film industry.
- *A "Brand" New Language: Commercial Influences in Literature and Culture*, by Monroe Friedman, Greenwood Press, New York, 1991.
- *Age of Propaganda: The Everyday Use and Abuse of Persuasion*, by Anthony Pratkanis and Elliot Aronson, W. H. Freeman and Company, New York, 1992.
- *Advertising and the Mind of the Consumer*, by Max Sutherland and Alice K. Sylvester, Allen & Unwin, Australia, 1993.

The Toink! Heard Round the World

In 1991, an obscure Southern California golf-club maker
introduced a revolutionary new driver, the Big Bertha.
Rather than lower scores, it raised self-respect.

GOLF HAS THE REMARKABLE ABILITY to reduce even the most accomplished and mature people—okay, usually men—to profane, gibbering, club throwers. And those players are never more vulnerable than when they step into a golf course tee box. Their playing partners gather around and fall into hushed silence. The golfer stands alone to be judged, required to demonstrate in a controlled burst of motion a lifetime of accumulated skill and power—or lack of it. Failures can be spectacular. Duffed drives have sent even genial Tiger Woods into volcanic televised tantrums. After an errant drive in the 1992 Los Angeles Open, pro Mark Calcavecchia slammed his driver so hard on a cart path that the head broke off and nearly struck a spectator. The term "golf rage" has crept into the sport's lexicon because, in their solitary moment of truth, even the world's best golfers sometimes crash and burn.

For most of the game's five-hundred-year history, hitting a long, straight drive was especially difficult for the average golfer to do. To strike a golf ball well—to hear the satisfying "tick!" off the sweet spot of a traditional persimmon driver and see the tiny ball soaring toward the horizon—a ridiculous series of improbable events has to take place in proper sequence so that, for the 450-millionths of a second when the speeding club head finally meets the stationary ball, every joint in the human body is correctly aligned and every imaginable physical law is harnessed to a single purpose.

Golfers traditionally employ liquor to that end, but it usually doesn't help.

But in 1991, in the tiny seaside town of Carlsbad, California, an obscure golf-equipment maker, Callaway Golf, began producing a big-headed metal thing called the Big Bertha driver—"A ham on a stick," observed one convert. Its generous "sweet spot" usually rewarded even an imperfect swing with a reasonably long, reasonably straight tee shot. During the decade that followed, the Big Bertha and its more evolved cousins—the Great Big Bertha Titanium Driver and the Biggest Bertha Titanium Driver—turned Callaway into one of the most astounding success stories of the century-ending boom years. The Big Bertha came along just as aging baby boomers were turning to a pastime second only to bowling in fostering the delusion that overweight, aerobically challenged middle-agers can be elite athletes. They helped Callaway Golf grow from $5 million in annual sales in 1988 to $842.9 million in 1997. In the process, they transformed the quasi-masochistic sport from a predictable exercise in futility into a game that even dilettantes could enjoy.

By the time Tiger Woods became the sport's Pied Piper in the late 1990s, the United States had 26.4 million golfers—almost two million more than it had in 1991, according to the National Golf Foundation. By June 2002, the country also had 4,812 more golf courses than the 13,004 it had when the Big Bertha was introduced eleven years earlier. *Golf Magazine* senior editor Mike Purkey calls the Big Bertha "the defining product for this generation of golfers."

"Thanks to the Big Bertha—and to all the innovations that came before and after—we don't have to worry about that uncharted territory in the middle of the clubface any more," Purkey wrote in May 1998. "We can hit it on the heel [of the club head] and the ball will go straight. We can hit it on the toe and it'll go straight. The game is easier and more pleasurable for all of us who don't play golf for a living."

That's only part of the story. The truth is—bad jokes notwithstanding—golf really *is* a lot like sex. It's not simply a matter of a powerful start. It's about finesse and good judgment, about pacing and self-control at critical moments. What counts, ultimately, is the finish. While men, in particular, have always been susceptible to the bigger-is-better argument, the success of the Big Bertha demonstrated how golfers crave self-respect as much as they crave a consistent fairway lie and a few extra yards off the tee. Even though golfers now know that these clubs are nowhere near the technological leap that the one-piece rubber-core ball was when it was introduced in 1900—a leap that practically guaranteed an extra twenty yards off the tee—they're still paying five hundred dollars or more for a Big Bertha or one of its many big-headed rivals. That's what golfers might have paid for an entire *set* of high-end clubs in the pre-Bertha era.

What once seemed like Viagra turned out to be Prozac, though. While an oversized metal driver can make a golfer feel more virile off the tee—and drives are, in fact, getting longer—the club and its many imitators haven't had much impact where it counts. According to the National Golf Foundation, the average score for all golfers playing a full-size, eighteen-hole course still hovers around one hundred, the same as it has been for generations. The old golf axiom "Drive for show, putt for dough" still holds. But thanks to the new breed of wonder drivers, which can make a few of those one hundred shots a bit less humiliating, shooting a crappy score just doesn't *feel* as terrible as it used to. And along the way, the Big Bertha and the countless imitators it inspired have created vast fortunes, transformed an industry, and forced the stuffy high priests of golf—some of them still struggling with this whole equality thing forty years after the civil-rights movement—to confront the collision of the game's grand traditions with new technology that helped open the game to newcomers who aren't necessarily, you know, Our Type.

There's no way to separate the Big Bertha phenomenon from the man who created it. Ely Callaway, who died in 2001 at age eighty-two, was a maverick with a televangelist's knack for converting skeptics into believers. His business philosophy, according to one obituary, was simple: "Develop a product that's pleasing and demonstrably different, and then merchandise the hell out of it." (It's worth noting that Callaway did not claim, in person or in advertising, that the Big Bertha could make one a *better* golfer. Its initial ad campaign promised only "the world's friendliest driver," a claim so vague it could not be challenged on any level.) He'd pursued that philosophy in two vastly different trades before conquering the golf industry, leaving textile giant Burlington Industries as its president and CEO in 1973, and then, against the odds, creating the successful Callaway vineyard in arid Temecula, California, outside San Diego, hundreds of miles south of the state's wine center in the Napa Valley. Skeptics predicted disaster, as if Callaway had announced plans to grow cantaloupes on the moon. But when Callaway sold his unlikely wine company in 1981, he pocketed about nine million dollars in profit—and went looking for something else to do.

In 1984 he paid four hundred thousand dollars for a small California golf company called Hickory Stick, which was marketing a line of clubs distinguished by their hickory-wrapped steel shafts. The clubs were a nostalgic nod to an earlier generation of golf clubs, which began in the early 1500s with expensive, hand-carved wooden heads and shafts of various hardwoods. (A typical golfer of the time broke a club or two during each round, cementing the sport's reputation as a pastime for the moneyed classes.) Specific woods proved better for specific purposes, and during the nineteenth century hickory became the preferred wood for club shafts and persimmon became the choice for club heads.

Among the cast steel and aluminum equipment of the 1980s, Callaway's Hickory Sticks stood out like vintage Cadillacs at the Indy 500. They were quite heavy. Even Callaway—"a natural huckster" according to *Forbes* magazine—couldn't convince high-profile golfers to try the clubs, much less use them on the professional tour. The problem was that he was trying to sell nostalgia in an era of innovation.

Leading club makers at the time were experimenting with the metals, metal alloys, and graphite composite materials emerging from Southern California's troubled aerospace industry. Displaced aerospace workers were taking innovative ideas and featherweight materials into the private sector, making everything from tennis racquets to wheelchairs stronger *and* lighter—a revolutionary combination in the sports equipment industry.

The metal golf driver was not a new idea. Driving ranges had been renting them for years because they were more difficult for the game's desperately hacking neophytes to break. In the late 1970s an innovator named Gary Adams noticed that a new breed of golf balls seemed to fly farther when struck by a metal clubface, and in 1979 he founded the Taylor Made Golf Company to make high-end "metalwoods" from what he jokingly called "Pittsburgh persimmon," after the nation's one-time steel capital. Those club heads were relatively small: a "standard" 148 cubic centimeters in volume. Adams set up shop in Carlsbad, where land was cheap, workers were plentiful, and the climate was sea-cooled and golf-perfect twelve months a year.

Ely Callaway eventually located his company there as well. He also convinced the General Electric Pension Fund to invest $10 million in it, and used that money to develop a competing line of irons and drivers. Those clubs hit the market in the late 1980s. By the end of 1990, Callaway's $400,000 company was generating nearly $22 million in annual sales. But the big leap came when Callaway convinced Dick Helmstetter, his chief club designer, that increasingly lightweight graphite shafts and metal club heads gave them an opportunity to increase the striking surface of a golf driver and reduce the club's weight at the same time. With velocity being the critical factor in distance, wouldn't the lighter weight mean the club head would be traveling faster when it struck the ball? With an inflated club head, wouldn't a typical golfer have a better chance to hit the ball longer and straighter? Wouldn't a club like that make the game more satisfying to those long-suffering hookers and slicers? Wouldn't it entice more people to try the once exclusive sport (and thereby expand the market)?

Callaway wasn't afraid of commitment. In his personal life, that translated into four marriages. In business, it meant the kind of take-no-prisoners risk taking that can lead to disaster. Callaway believed so strongly in his idea that after judging Helmstetter's third design ready for market, he ordered sixty thousand club heads from the foundry at twenty dollars each—twice the cost of his company's best driver. He also named that oversized 198–cubic centimeter club head the Big Bertha after a fabled long-range World War I artillery piece, ignoring the warnings of everyone from Helmstetter's wife to former General Electric CEO Jack Welch that the name was misguided. His final gamble was to price the club at $250, nearly twice the price of a smaller headed metalwood club from industry leader Taylor Made.

The risk paid off. Callaway's sales force sold 150,000 Big Bertha drivers the first year, and probably could have sold twice that many. Here, finally, was something to excite golf snobs and wannabes alike. The Big Bertha was both expensive *and* effective—a club that not only worked but also screamed "status" each time it stuck its fat head out of a golfer's bag. Golf researchers also began to understand *why* some metal drivers were so effective in driving a golf ball. Unlike solid wood drivers, the metal ones are hollow. The PGA now allows them to be up to 460 cubic centimeters. As the new metals got lighter and stronger, the face of the club heads got wider and thinner. This created a "spring-like effect," with the clubface acting as a miniature trampoline to give the ball a little extra push during the fraction of a second when they meet. That's recently become a matter of grave concern to golf's governing powers, but let's not get ahead of ourselves.

As the Bertha's reputation spread, mostly by word of mouth, buyers began waiting weeks and sometimes months for their Big Berthas to arrive. Because demand far outpaced supply, Callaway began doing something that previously would have been unthinkable in the generally genteel world of golf-equipment sales: The company began rationing clubs to golf course pro shops and favoring off-course retailers. This cheeky decision essentially cut out the middlemen of PGA professionals and sold clubs more directly to the public. It was a shot across the bow of the golf establishment, which could only whimper in protest as Callaway and his intensely popular golf club changed the traditional dynamics of golf-equipment sales. Today, the vast majority of golf equipment is not sold through golf course pro shops, but rather through off-course retailers.

Callaway began lining up endorsement deals, some of them traditional (retired 1973 U.S. Open champion-turned-broadcaster Johnny Miller and motor oil—plugging golf god Arnold Palmer, who called oversized drivers "one of the most important things that ever happened to the game") and some of them not (boa-constrictor-toting rock ghoul Alice Cooper, jazz sax somnambulist Kenny G, comedic provocateur Tommy Smothers, impish boxer Sugar Ray Leonard, even Microsoft cofounder Bill Gates appeared in a commercial for the Big Bertha). The club's reputation was enhanced in 1994 when Miller, whose best years were two decades behind him, won the AT&T Pebble Beach National Pro-Am on television using Callaway equipment—his first victory in seven years.

By then the Big Bertha driver already was the number 1 driver on the PGA Tour, the LPGA Tour, and the PGA Senior Tour, though not entirely by general acclaim. Callaway was paying some pros generously to use his equipment, certain that the masses would follow their lead. He was right. By 1997, Callaway was boasting that 69.1 percent of all professional golfers played a Callaway driver, with the last two persimmon-playing holdouts having switched to metal drivers the year before. Callaway's annual revenue peaked at nearly $843 million that year before a tough economy in Japan, a critical golf market, triggered a downturn that lasted into the new millennium.

Still, the Big Bertha's impact continues. It's most apparent in Carlsbad, which today is known as "Titanium Valley." Along with Taylor Made and Callaway, Cobra Golf set up shop there. By the late 1990s, the flowers, avocados, and strawberries that once covered Carlsbad's hillsides were dotted with facilities bearing the logos of other companies whose names became part of the golf-equipment revolution: Odyssey, Lynx, even apparel maker Ashworth and the venerable Titleist.

Big Bertha's phenomenal success also began a golden era of growth and innovation in the golf-equipment industry. Club sales boomed from $1.3 billion in 1993 to $2.5 billion in 2001 even though the number of golfers rose only slightly during that time, according to the National Sporting Goods Association. Every equipment maker began promising the Next Big Thing, including Wilson, one of the oldest brands in golf equipment, which at one point was offering something called "Fat Shaft Hyper Carbon .535 Irons." Golf bags got lighter and easier to carry. Spikes went from metal to plastic. In the mid-1990s, the classic wound-core golf balls gave way to balls featuring solid cores and more responsive covers that practically explode off of metal clubfaces. In the fall of 2000, Titleist introduced its Pro V1 that by simply spinning less than other balls is thought to further increase the distance of some drives.

During those years, the complexion of golf began to change. As Tiger Woods began rewriting golf's record books, he focused a harsh spotlight on the golf establishment's mostly unspoken but long-standing distaste for nonwhite and female players. Woods, whose father is African-American, even established a foundation to entice disadvantaged kids into the game, and a messy public debate erupted about the exclusive rules at certain clubs. In May 2003, Annika Sorenstam, then the reigning queen of the Ladies Professional Golf Association tour, accepted a sponsor's exemption to play in a men's pro tournament and became the first woman in fifty-eight years to compete in a PGA Tour event.

Along with social change, technological innovation continued uninterrupted until 2001, when Callaway introduced a new driver called the ERC II. The United States Golf Association, the governing body for golf gear, put the thin-faced metal wood through a battery of tests and flunked it, saying the ERC II didn't conform to rules limiting the "spring-like effect" of drivers. Callaway decided to fight the ban, and continued to claim the USGA was stifling innovation right up until the day in July 2001when he died from pancreatic cancer.

Still, the question remains: Are Callaway and golf's other innovators selling more sizzle than steak?

Despite all these technological advances, the average handicap for the typical golfer nationwide has not dropped, wrote Al Barkow in his 2000 book, *The Golden Era of Golf: How America Rose to Domi-*

nate the Old Scots Game. It remains about a sixteen, and even the tour pro's average score per round on the year has remained steady. The average drive of leading PGA ball-crusher John Daly increased from 288.9 yards to 306.8 between 1991 and 2002, but PGA Tour stroke totals also have stayed pretty much the same. Barkow notes that in 1950 Sam Snead won the Vardon Trophy for low-stroke average with 69.23, and that in 1999 Tiger Woods—with better athletic training and playing with state-of-the-art equipment on courses that were far better groomed—had the lowest stroke average on the pro tour at 68.43, less than a one-stroke improvement.

"The real difference," Barkow wrote, "is that today's golfer enjoys his mishits more. The clubs are lighter to swing, get the ball airborne more readily and a little farther down the road. The game is no easier than it ever has been, it just *seems* like it."

As the Big Bertha so convincingly demonstrated, that's apparently enough.

THE OPERATIVE NUMBER: 500

Displacement, in cubic centimeters, of the Ball Launcher driver sold by a Canadian golf-equipment maker Jazz Golf. It exceeds the 460cc PGA size limit and is 302 cubic centimeters larger than the original oversized metal driver, Callaway's 198cc Big Bertha.

Driving Toward Perfection

℘

If you had won thirty-four PGA tournaments by the time you were twenty-six, including the 1997, 2001, and 2002 Masters Tournaments, the 1999 and 2000 PGA Championships, the 2000 and 2002 U.S. Open Championships, and the 2000 British Open, you'd probably keep using the clubs that already had helped you put an indelible stamp on golf history.

But you are not Tiger Woods.

For most of 2002—a year when he ranked sixth in driving distance with an average tee shot of 293.3 yards—Woods worked with engineers at Nike, his primary sponsor, to find the perfect combination of shaft length and club head size that would raise his game to an even higher level and establish Nike as a force in driver design, a business that Ely Callaway's Big Bertha proved could be extremely lucrative.

During what *Los Angeles Times* golf writer Thomas Bonk described as "an unusually long and intricate campaign to test drivers and find the one he wants to play," Woods sampled at least 173 different prototypes during 2002. Graphite shaft, or steel? His favorite 43.5-inch shaft length, or a longer shaft that might produce more distance? A larger forged titanium club head for distance, or a slightly smaller one to better control ball spin when trying to draw or fade his tee shot?

After testing nearly fifteen dozen drivers, Woods concluded, "We're pretty close."

Golf's Big-Bang Theory

℘

The sweet "tick" of an old persimmon driver squarely striking a golf ball was one of the most satisfying sounds in the game, and the designers of metal golf clubs well understood how critical sound could be in a golfer's perception of performance. Callaway's original Big Bertha drivers, in fact, were filled with foam to make them sound more like a wooden driver.

But in late 1992, according to Scott Kramer, a senior editor of *Golf* magazine, Callaway removed the foam from the hollow Big Bertha and slightly thickened the club head walls. The resulting sound was far different from other drivers on the market, a ringing "toink!" that Big Bertha designer Richard Helmstetter said initially "freaked everybody out." As sales of the driver took off, though, Kramer said, golfers began to conclude that "a big drive should make a big bang, and many golfers think they've crushed one only when the metal head rings like a church bell."

Tests have shown that louder drives don't necessarily go farther, but as with so many other things in golf, perception can become reality. In a story in the December 2001 issue of *Golf* magazine, Kramer quoted one club-company executive who claimed that sound had become "more important than actual performance" and noted that Callaway even acquired a patent to put "sound-enhancing" devices inside a composite club head then under development.

You Want *More?*

- *The Golden Era of Golf: How America Rose to Dominate the Old Scots Game*, by Al Barkow, St. Martin's Press, New York, 2000.
- "Great Big Empire," by *Golf* senior editor Mike Purkey, May 1998, http://sportsillustrated.cnn.com/golfonline/equipment/features/callawaymay98.html
- www.ngf.org, the National Golf Foundation web site.
- http://www.callawaygolf.com, the corporate Web site of Callaway Golf.

Think We Blew It?

● ● ● ● ● ● ● ● ●

IF WE OVERLOOKED AN UNLIKELY PERSON, invention, or event that reshaped American life, which you feel has never been fully appreciated, please let us know about it. Just visit our web site, www.poplorica.com, and drop us an e-mail explaining the idea and how you feel it influenced the world in which we now live.

Chapter Notes

● ● ● ● ● ● ● ● ●

DESCRIBING THE DIFFERENCES between writing fiction and nonfiction, writer Tom Wolfe once said: "The problem with fiction, it has to be plausible. That's not true with nonfiction."

He's right. We couldn't have made this stuff up, especially the part about the jet-powered lawn mower. But we also couldn't expect you to take us at our word, so we've compiled the following list that identifies, chapter by chapter, all the material we used to research and write this book, or at least all of it we can remember. It includes information we culled from the books, newspaper and magazine articles, and Web sites listed on the following pages, as well as information we developed by doing our own reporting and interviews.

Rather than bog down the chapters with footnotes, endnotes, or cumbersome attribution—the sausage-making part of what writers do—we stuffed all that into this easily avoidable section and hid it way back in the book. The information is here if you need it, but really, you probably have better things to do. And if you don't, that's just sad.

Chapter 1: Frank J. Scott's Great Green Manifesto

"About Dixie Chopper." http://www.dixiechopper.com/about.htm (Dec. 10, 2002)

Bellis, Mary. "Greener Pastures." http://inventors.about.com/library/inventors/bllawns.htm (Dec. 12, 2002)

Birnbaum, Charles A.; Karson, Robin S. *Pioneers of American Landscape Design*, New York: McGraw-Hill Professional, 2000.

"Dixie Chopper: The World's Fastest Lawnmower." http://www.dixiechopper.com/about.htm (Dec. 10, 2002)

Graham, Wade. "The Grassman." *The New Yorker*, Aug. 19, 1996.

"History of Mowing." http://www.opei.org/guide/history.htm (Dec. 3, 2002)

Jenkins, Virginia Scott. *The Lawn: History of an American Obsession*, Washington, D.C.: Smithsonian Institution Press, 1994.

Kilborn, Peter T. "Gentlemen, Start Your Lawn Mower Engines." *New York Times*, June 12, 2000.

"Longest Lawn-Mower Ride." http://guinnessworldrecords.com (July 14, 2003)

Pollan, Michael. "Beyond Wilderness and Lawn." *Harvard Design Magazine*, Winter/Spring 1998.

Pollan, Michael. *Second Nature: A Gardener's Education*, New York: Dell, 1991.

"Reel Lawn Mower." http://users.crocker.com/~jricci /history.html (Dec. 3, 2002)

Schultz, Warren. *A Man's Turf: The Perfect Lawn*, New York: Clarkson Potter, 1999.

Schuyler, David. Introduction to the 1982 edition of *The Art of Beautifying Suburban Home Grounds*, Watkins Glen, N.Y.: Library of Victorian Culture, American Life Foundation, 1982.

Scott, Frank J. *The Art of Beautifying Suburban Home Grounds*, Watkins Glen, N.Y.: Library of Victorian Culture, American Life Foundation, 1982.

Simo, Melanie. Interview by Martin J. Smith, Sept. 18, 2002.

Stilgoe, John R. *Borderland: Origins of the American Suburb, 1820–1939*, New Haven, Conn.: Yale University Press, 1988.

Teyssot, Georges. ed: "Surface of Everyday Life." *The American Lawn*, Princeton: Princeton Architectural Press, 1999.

Thompson, Bill. Interview by Martin J. Smith, Sept. 4, 2002.

Virag, Irene. "What's Happening to Lawn Island?" *Newsday*, Sept. 15, 1996.

Wigley, Mark. "The Electric Lawn." *The American Lawn*, New York: Princeton Architectural Press, 1999.

Wilson, Craig. "Gentlemen, Start Your Mowers." *USA Today*, Aug. 8, 2002.

Chapter 2: The Birth of Cool

Ackermann, Marsha. *Cool Comfort: America's Romance with Air Conditioning*. Washington, D.C.: Smithsonian Institution Press, 2002.

"Bank One Ballpark: A Unique Baseball Experience." http://arizona. diamondbacks.mlb.com/NASApp/mlb/ari/ballpark/ari_ballpark _history.jsp (Oct. 30, 2002)

Caniglia, Julie. "The Big Chilly." http://archive.salon.com/21st/feature /1998/07/02featurea.html (Oct. 7, 2002)

Cart, Julie. "Rapidly Growing Phoenix Finds Dust Unsettling." *Los Angeles Times*, Sept. 7, 1999.

Cobb, Jim. "The Air Conditioning of the South: Mr. Carrier's Cooling Machine Stopped Out-Migration and Helped Create the Sunbelt." *Georgia Magazine*, September 2002.

Cooper, Gail Ann. *Air-Conditioning America: Engineers and the Controlled Environment, 1900–1960,* Baltimore, Md.: Johns Hopkins University Press, 1998.

Craven, Scott. "Refrigeration 'Real Godsend' for Valley." *Arizona Republic*, July 24, 2002.

Friedricks, William B. "Phoenix: History of an Urban Metropolis." Book review. *Business History Review*, June 22, 1991.

"The George H. N. Luhrs Family in Phoenix and Arizona, 1847–1984." http://www.asu.edu/lib/archives/luhrs/page500.htm (Oct. 30, 2002)

"Gilder-Lehrman History Online." http://www.gliah.uh.edu/database/article_display.cfm?HHID503 (Oct. 29, 2002)

Hall, John R. "1930s Bring A/C into the Mainstream." *Air Conditioning, Heating & Refrigeration News*, April 30, 2001.

Ingels, Margaret. *Willis Haviland Carrier, Father of Air Conditioning*, Garden City, N.Y.: Country Life Press, 1952.

Ivins, Molly. "TIME 100: King of Cool." *Time*, Dec. 7, 1998.

Killian, Michael. "Cool and Collected: Museum Assembles Chilling Evidence of Air Conditioning's Effect on American Culture." *Chicago Tribune*, July 5, 1999.

Kurtz, Howard. "Not from the South or West? Better Not Run for President." *The Record* (Bergen County, N.J.), July 25, 1999.

Lang, Robert E.; Renger, Kristopher M. "The Hot and Cold Sunbelts: Comparing State Growth Rates, 1950–2000." *Fannie Mae Foundation*, April 2001.

"Letter from America: Air Conditioning and Changes in Society." BBC News, July 14, 1999. http://news.bbc.co.uk/1/hi/world/letter_from_america/392328.stm (Oct. 12, 2002)

Lightman, David. "Barry Goldwater—1909–1998: A Rock of the

Right, Out of the West, Goldwater Shaped U.S. Conservatism."
Hartford Courant, May 30, 1998.

Luckingham, Bradford. *Phoenix: The History of a Southwestern Metropolis*, Tucson, Ariz.: University of Arizona Press, 1989.

Mitchell, John G. "Urban Sprawl." *National Geographic*, July 1, 2001.

Padgett, Mike. " 'Sick' Buildings in Valley Examined by L.A. Engineer." *Business Journal-Phoenix & the Valley of the Sun*, April 30, 1999.

Proby, Nelson W. "How Congress Evolves: Work in Progress." Presentation at American Enterprise Institute, May 9, 2002. http://www.aei.org/ra/rawatt010103.htm (Oct. 15, 2002)

Rodriguez, Patricia. "Scottsdale Becomes a Mecca of Tony Spas." *Charlotte Observer*, Sept. 8, 2002.

"The Sonoran Desert." http://www.desertusa.com/du_sonoran. html (Oct. 31, 2002)

"Stay Cool! Air Conditioning America." National Building Museum exhibitions. http://www.nbm.org/Exhibits/past/2000-1996/ Stay_Cool!.html (Oct. 1, 2002)

"Time Machine: Air Conditioning and the Cinema." *Air Conditioning, Heating & Refrigeration News*, June 12, 2000.

de Uriarte, Richard. "Bob Goldwater Looks Back to Phoenix's Roots." *Arizona Republic*, April 28, 2002.

Wattenberg, Ben J. "America by the Numbers." *Wall Street Journal*, Jan. 3, 2001.

Chapter 3: How Thin Became In

"America's Top 6 Fad Diets." http://magazines.ivillage.com/ goodhousekeeping/diet/plans/articles/0,12873,284559_290212- 6,00.html (Feb. 18, 2003)

Burke, John. *Duet in Diamonds: The Flamboyant Saga of Lillian Russell and Diamond Jim Brady in America's Gilded Age*, New York: Putnam, 1972.

Dietrich, Bill. "Medicine Reruns." *Seattle Times*, April 16, 1992.

"Early Diet Book Holds Up Thin Ideal." Associated Press, Sept. 20, 1990.

"Excess Weight Her Specialty." *Los Angeles Times*, May 13, 1923.

Flanigan, Kathy. "Now and Thin; Stars Need a Healthy Portion of State Fair's Fare." *Milwaukee Journal Sentinel*, Aug. 7, 2001.

Fumento, Michael. "Living Off the Fat of the Land." *Washington Monthly*, January–February 1998.

"Harvey Banting Diet." Low Carb Diet Plans, http://www.low-carb-diet-plans.com/harvey_banting_diet.htm (Feb. 25, 2003)

"Health Food Pioneer Dies at 89." Associated Press, Dec. 28, 1984.

"History of Dieting." The Community Foundation for Blood Type Living, http://www.er4yt.org/Education/Food/Dieting_History.html (Feb. 20, 2003)

Jackson, Donald Dale. "The Art of Wishful Shrinking Has Made a Lot of People Rich." *Smithsonian*, November 1994.

Lelwica, Michelle. "Fulfilling Femininity and Transcending the Flesh: Traditional Religious Beliefs and Gender Ideals in Popular Women's Magazines." *Journal of Religion and Society*, 1999.

"Lulu H. Peters Dies." Associated Press, June 28, 1930.

National Eating Disorders Association web site, http://www.nationaleatingdisorders.org/ (March 1, 2003)

Peters, Lulu Hunt. *Diet and Health, With Key to the Calories*, Chicago: Reilly and Lee Co., 1939.

Schwartz, Hillel. *Never Satisfied: A Cultural History of Diets, Fantasies, and Fat*, New York: Free Press, 1986.

Seid, Roberta Pollack. *Never Too Thin: Why Women Are at War with Their Bodies*, New York: Prentice Hall, 1989.

Stearns, Peter N. *Fat History: Bodies and Beauty in the Modern West*, New York: New York University Press, 1997.

Sugarman, Carole, "The History of Thinking Thin." *Washington Post*, June 16, 1987.

Timmerman, Tom. "Ephedra Is Popular Supplement—and Can Be Dangerous." *St. Louis Post Dispatch*, Feb. 23, 2003.

Who Was Who Among North American Authors, 1921–1939, Detroit: Gale Press, 1976.

Chapter 4: Alfred Kinsey's Honeymoon

"Art and Artifacts." http://www.indiana.edu/~kinsey/library/kiart.html (Aug. 21, 2002)

"Data from Alfred Kinsey's Studies." http://www.indiana.edu/~kinsey/research/ak-data.html (July 8, 2002)

"Dr. Kinsey Is Dead; Sex Researcher, 62." The Associated Press. *New York Times*, Aug. 26, 1956.

"Frequently Asked Sexuality Questions to the Kinsey Institute." http://www.kinseyinstitute.org/resources/FAQ.html (Sept. 3, 2002)

Gathorne-Hardy, Jonathan. *Sex, the Measure of All Things: A Life of Alfred C. Kinsey*, Bloomington, Ind., Indiana University Press, 1998.

Greene, John. "What Was The Kinsey Report? How a Revolutionary 1948 Book Revealed That Most Sex Happens When People Are Alone." http://www.jackinworld.com/library/articles/kinsey.html (July 8, 2002)

Harris, Daniel. "America's Greatest Sexologist: A New Biography of Alfred C. Kinsey Shows He Not Only Studied Many Forms of Sexual Behavior But Experimented with Them as Well." http://www.salon.com/health/sex/urge/2000/04/15/kinsey/print.html (July 8, 2002)

"The Hef Files." http://tlc.discovery.com/convergence/sex/article/hefner_2_print.html (July 8, 2002)

Johnson, Catherine A. (Curator of art, artifacts, and photographs for The Kinsey Institute for Research in Sex, Gender, and Reproduction.) Interview by Martin J. Smith, Aug. 28, 2002.

Jones, James H. *Alfred C. Kinsey: A Public/Private Life*, New York, W.W. Norton, 1997.

"The Kinsey Report." http://fsweb.wm.edu/amst370/2001/sp1/Kinsey.html (July 8, 2002)

"Kinsey's Heterosexual-Homosexual Rating Scale." http://www.indiana.edu/~kinsey/resources/ak-hhscale.html (Sept. 3, 2002)

McLemee, Scott. "The Man Who Took Sex Out of the Closet: Alfred Kinsey Outed America's Sexual Secrets—While Keeping a Few of His Own." http://www.salon.com/books/feature/1997/11/cov_05kinsey.html (July 8, 2002)

"Photography." http://www.indiana.edu/~kinsey/library/photog.html (Aug. 21, 2002)

Reinisch, June M. *The Kinsey Institute New Report on Sex*, Jupiter, Fla.: Pharos Books, 1990.

Chapter 5: The Rise of Tacky Chic

Allen, Henry. "Oil or Nothing; Mass-Produced Paintings Fill Demand for, Um, Original Art." *Washington Post*, Feb. 2, 2000.

Cobb, Nathan. "Black Velvet: The Art." *Chicago Tribune*, Sept. 7, 1987.

Conrad, Eric Von Fossen. "Latin Phrases Used in English," http://www.math.ohio-state.edu/~econrad/lang/lphrase.html (Jan. 20, 2003)

Davis, Phil. "Va Va Velvet." *Los Angeles Times*, Aug. 19, 1998.

"Elvis Presley Estate Aggressive in Removing Some Icons." National Public Radio *All Things Considered* (transcript of radio broadcast), Dec. 21, 1995.

Geiberger, Peter. "The Black Velvet Underground." *Scram*, No. 10, undated. Available online at http://www.insound.com/Zinestand/Scram/feature.cfm?aid=3476

Groer, Annie. "Elvis on Velvet: The King Lives On." *Washington Post*, Aug. 15, 2002.

Harris, Moira F. "It's a Dog's World, According to Coolidge." *Antiques & Collectibles*, March 1997.

"Introduction to American Paintings and Sculpture." Metropolitan Museum of Art, http://www.metmuseum.org/collections/department.asp?dep=2 (Jan. 5, 2003)

"John Everett Millais—Biography," http://www.pre-raphaelites.co.uk/a-millais.htm (Jan. 12, 2003)

Michener, James A.; Day, A. Grove. *Rascals in Paradise*, New York: Random House, 1957.

"Nuts to Art!" *Barracuda*, No. 6, undated. http://www.barracuda-magazine.com/leeteg.htm (Jan. 12, 2003)

Price, Jennifer. "The Plastic Pink Flamingo." *American Scholar*, Spring 1999.

Rose, Cynthia. "Voluptuous Visions in Velvet." *Seattle Times*, Dec. 14, 1998.

Sime, Tom. "Bath House Black-Velvet Show: Kitsch as kitsch Can." *Dallas Morning News*, Sept. 10, 1999.

"Stone Age Governs Our Minds, Says Scientist Author." *Providence Journal*, Jan. 25, 1998.

Thomas, Cynthia. "Velvet Visions." *Houston Chronicle*, Dec. 11, 1994.

"Velvet Elvis Art." http://www.velvetelvisart.com/pageone.html (Jan. 17, 2003)

Ward, Peter. *Kitsch in Sync: A Consumer's Guide to Bad Taste*, London: Plexus, 1991.

Yankovic, Al. "Velvet Elvis." *Even Worse* LP, Santa Monica: Scotti Bros., 1991. Compact Disc.

You, Brenda. "The Soft Sell." *Chicago Tribune*, June 12, 1994.

Chapter 6: Les Paul's "Log"

Bacon, Tony. *50 Years of the Gibson Les Paul: Half a Century of the Greatest Electric Guitars*, San Francisco, Calif.: Backbeat Books, excerpted in *Guitar Player*, July 2002.

Bacon, Tony; Day, Paul. *Gibson Les Paul Book: A Complete History of Les Paul Guitars*, San Francisco, Calif.: Miller Freeman Books, 1993.

Beckerman, Jim. "Les Is More." *The Record* (Bergen County, N.J.), Aug. 13, 2001.

Carter, Walter. Interview by Martin J. Smith, Oct. 29, 2002.

Dale, Dick. Interview by Martin J. Smith, Aug. 1, 2002.

Duchossoir, A.R. *Gibson Electrics: The Classic Years*, Milwaukee, Wis.: Hal Leonard, 1994.

"History of Fender." http://www.americanvintageguitar.com/Fender%20History.htm (June 27, 2002)

"A History of the Guitar." http://www.guitarsite.com/history.htm/ (June 27, 2002)

Houston, Frank. "Father of Invention." http://www.salon.com/people/feature/1999/07/08/paul/ (June 27, 2002)

Shaughnessy, Mary Alice. *Les Paul: An American Original*, New York: William Morrow, 1993.

Waksman, Steve. *Instruments of Desire: The Electric Guitar and the Shaping of Musical Experience*, Cambridge, Mass.: Harvard University Press, 1999.

Chapter 7: Wrestling with a Contradiction

Assael, Shaun; Mooneyman, Mike. *Sex, Lies, and Headlocks: The Real Story of Vince McMahon and the World Wrestling Federation*, New York: Crown, 2002.

Ball, Michael R. *Professional Wrestling as Ritual Drama in American Popular Culture*, Lewiston, Me: Edwin Mellen Press, 1990.

Boal, Sam. "Big Boom in the Grunt and Groan Business." *New York Times Magazine*, Nov. 20, 1949.

Bolchunos, Brad. "Life with Gorgeous George—His Former Wife Remembers." *Daily Astorian*, June 22, 2001.

Brioux, Bill. "When Rasslin' Was TV's King." *Edmonton Sun*, March 17, 2001.

Eck, Kevin. "The Fabulous Fifty." *Wrestling Digest*, April 2002.

"The Early Years of Televised Wrestling." http://www.solie.org/oldays.html (Feb. 2, 2003)

Frey, Phil. "Violent Friday Night." *Sunday Oklahoman*, April 1, 1973.

"The Golden Age of Wrestling: The 1950s." http://www.classic-wrestling.com/ (Feb. 10, 2003)

"Gorgeous George (Arena) Dead at 84." United Press International, July 19, 1992.

"Gorgeous Georgeous." *Newsweek*, Sept. 13, 1948.

"Guaranteed Entertainment." *Time*, May 31, 1948.

Halley, Peter; Nickas, Bob. "John Waters." *Index* magazine. http://www.indexmagazine.com/interviews/john_waters.shtml (March 2, 2003)

Harvey, Steve. "Mussel or Muscle." *Los Angeles Times*, March 30, 1986.

Hicks, Tony. "A Kiss Goodbye." *Contra Costa Times*, March 25, 2000.

Hirshey, Gerri. "Tooty, Fruity." *Rolling Stone*, July 1984.

Lano, Mike. "Gorgeous George's Widow Passes Away." Solie's Tuesday Morning Report, http://members.aol.com/solie3/svwn606.html (Feb. 10, 2003)

McLure, Laura. "Lecture 26: Male and Female Rites of Passage in Ancient Greece." From *Gender and Sexuality in the Classical World*, a class at the University of Wisconsin-Madison, Fall 2000. http://polyglot.lss.wisc.edu/classics/CLAS_351/lecture26.html (Feb. 14, 2003.)

Meyers, Jeff. "Wrestling: The Art on Canvas." *Los Angeles Times*, Feb. 18, 1990.

Mills, Bart. "Oddest Character of All Adjusting to Life after NBA." *Chicago Tribune*, Dec. 4, 1999.

Murray, Jim. "Wrestling Fans—Why Tell 'Em?" *Los Angeles Times*, March 19, 1985.

Ostler, Scott. "Only in This Group Could Lord Blears Be a Guest of Honor." *Los Angeles Times*, Aug. 22, 1985.

The Professional Wrestling Online Museum, http://www.wrestling-museum.com/ (Dec. 31, 2002)

Rasmussen, Cecilia. "Then and Now: A Gorgeous Era in Wrestling." *Los Angeles Times*, Dec. 14, 1997.

Remnick, David. *King of the World: Muhammad Ali and the Rise of an American Hero*, New York: Random House, 1998.

Schuyler, Ed Jr. "Boorish Behavior Is Big Business for Dennis Rodman." Associated Press, May 8, 1997.

Vontz, Andrew. "Rocker Androgyny Has Pride of Place in the Designs of Ryan Heffington." *Los Angeles Times*, Sept. 8, 2002.

The Unreal Story of Pro Wrestling, a documentary by A & E Entertainment, 1998.

Wolf, Buck. "Gorgeous George Advises Mike Tyson & Madonna Goes Classical." http://abcnews.go.com/sections/us/DailyNews/wolffiles38.html (March 1, 2003)

Chapter 8: The War Against Wrinkles

Abend, Jules. "Wrinkle Resistant: Ironing out the Process." *Bobbin*, July 1994.

"Answers to Frequently Asked Cotton Questions." http://www.cottoninc.com/MediaServices/homepage.cfm?page113-faq11 (Jan. 18, 2003)

Bellis, Mary. "The History of Irons." http://inventors.about.com/library/inventors/blirons.htm (Jan. 24, 2003)

Bellis, Mary. "Polyester PET." http://inventors.about.com/library/inventors/blpolyester.htm (Jan. 24, 2003)

"The Big Three." *Daily News Record*, July 1, 1986.

"Is Britain Becoming a Nation of Scruffs?" http://www.bold2in1.com/en_UK/special/shtml (Jan. 28, 2003)

"Edgar Degas." The Collection—National Gallery of Art, http://www.nga.gov/collection/gallery/gg89/gg89-53248.0-exhibit.html (Feb. 27, 2003)

"Fabric History: Natural Fibers." http://www.fabriclink.com/ (Feb. 1, 2003)

"Get Your Grip on History." Living History Farms, http://www.lhf.org/cgi-bin/gygactivity.pl?26 (Feb. 20, 2003)

Greene, Jan. "OSHA Delays Formaldehyde Ruling." *Women's Wear Daily*, Oct. 3, 1985.

Handley, Susannah. *Nylon: The Story of a Fashion Revolution,* Baltimore, Md.: Johns Hopkins University Press, 1999.

"The History of Ironing." http://www.cinet-online.net/english/news/historyironing.htm (Feb. 10, 2003)

Lloyd, Brenda. "You Gotta Have a Gimmick." *Daily News Record,* Aug. 6, 2001.

Maycumber, S. Gray. "1945–1995: 50 Years of Textile and Fiber Innovations That Outstripped the Previous 5,000 Years." *Daily News Record,* Dec. 7, 1995.

Mink, Michael. "Ruth Benerito Gave to Society Power of Focus: Diligence Helped Her Invent Easy-Care Cotton." *Investors Business Daily,* April 30, 2002.

Motta, Katie, "Permanent Press—Corpo Nove designs a 'smart shirt.' " *Industry Standard,* Aug. 20, 2001.

"Nylon Threads Through Fiber History." *Journal of Commerce,* Sept. 29, 1987.

Orecklin, Michele. "Look Ma, No Stains." *Time,* Dec. 9, 2002.

Rahner, Mark. "Slob Couture: Survey Ranks Seattle as One of the Most Casual Cities." *Seattle Times,* Sept. 16, 2002.

Ross, Rachel. "Extreme Ironing: Danger, Action, Steam and Starch." *Toronto Star,* Nov. 22, 2002.

Rudie, Raye. "Permanent Press Makes a Smooth Comeback." *Bobbin,* May 1993.

"Save Us From Ironing." *Cleveland Plain Dealer,* June 24, 1993.

Schurnberger, Lynn. *Let There Be Clothes: 40,000 Years of Fashion*, New York: Workman Publishing, 1991.

Spomar, John Jr. "Cleaning Through the Millennia." *American Drycleaner*, Dec. 1999.

Sussman, Richard J. "Permanent Press Takes on the '90s." *Bobbin*, May 1993.

Sustendal, Diane. "Men's Style: Wash It, Wear it." *New York Times*, April 28, 1985.

Walsh, Peter. "Outside Forces That Influenced Fashion." *Daily News Record*, May 22, 1992.

"Wonderfully Wrinkle-Free: The Wrinkle-Resistant Cotton Phenomenon." http://www.touchofcotton.com/WrinkleFree/homepage.cfm? PageID=122&SectionID=1 (Feb. 8, 2003)

Chapter 9: The King of Leer

Arluke, Arnold; Levin, Jack. *Gossip: The Inside Scoop*, New York: Plenum Press, 1997.

Bird, S. Elizabeth. *For Enquiring Minds: A Cultural Study of Supermarket Tabloids*, Knoxville: University of Tennessee Press, 1992.

Boccella, Kathy. "Springing a Tabloid Trap on a Superstar Spouse." *Philadelphia Inquirer*, May 21, 1997.

"Brief of Appellant, State of Utah v. Ian Michael Lake, Supreme Court for the State of Utah." http://www.acluutah.org/lakeappeal.htm (Jan. 29, 2003)

Fleischman, Joan. "Woman Sues Tabloid Over Gifford Scandal." *Miami Herald*, July 23, 1999.

Gabler, Neal. *Winchell: Gossip, Power, and the Culture of Celebrity*, New York: Knopf, 1994.

Hill, Gladwin. "Police Here Cited at Scandal Trial." *New York Times*, Aug. 13, 1957.

Hill, Gladwin. "Film Colony Fidgets in Confidential Case." *New York Times*, Aug. 18, 1957.

Hill, Gladwin. "Counsel Appears for Confidential." *New York Times*, Aug. 20, 1957.

Hill, Gladwin. "Jury Told Family Ran Confidential." *New York Times*, Sept. 11, 1957.

Hill, Gladwin. "Accord Approved for Confidential." *New York Times*, Nov. 13, 1957.

Kashner, Sam; MacNair, Jennifer. *The Bad and the Beautiful: Hollywood in the Fifties*, New York: W.W. Norton, 2002.

"Liberace Biography Says Intended Bride's Father Prevented Marriage." Associated Press, Dec. 22, 1987.

Maeder, Jay. "Turncoat: The Estrangements of Howard Rushmore." *New York Daily News*, Feb. 26, 2001.

Maeder, Jay. "From 'Five Star Final': Joseph Randall." *New York Daily News*, Sept. 10, 2002.

"Magazine Fights Post Office Ban." United Press, Sept. 9, 1955.

"Mistrial Verdict for Confidential." Associated Press, Oct. 21, 1957.

The Motion Picture Production Code." http://wings.buffalo.edu/courses/faoo/eng/256mar/documents/MPPDA.html (Jan. 16, 2003)

Nelson, John. "Vintage Smear." Undated. http://www.themediadrome.com/content/articles/film_articles/vintage_smear.htm (Jan. 16, 2003)

Nordheimer, Jon. "Mild-Mannered Buyers Tame Wild Tabloids!" *New York Times*, Feb. 4, 1988.

"Putting the Papers to Bed." *Time*, Aug. 26, 1957.

Sisk, John P. "Worm's Eye View: The Expose Magazines." *Commonweal*, June 1, 1956.

Stone, Rosalinda. "Porn Yesterday: True Confessions of a Celebrity Skin Editor." *Village Voice*, July 28, 1999.

Streete, Horton. "Why Liberace's Theme Song Should Be 'Mad About

the Boy,'" *Confidential*, July 1957. http://www.bobsliberace.
com/decades/1950s/1950s.9.html (Jan. 20, 2003)

"Success in the Sewer." *Time*, July 11, 1955.

"Tape Recorder Advertisements," http://history.acusd.edu/gen/
recording/tapeads.html (Jan. 10, 2003)

"U.S. Court Eases Curb on Magazine." United Press, Oct. 7, 1955.

Wilkinson, Joseph. "Look at Me." *Smithsonian*, December 1997.

Wilson, Theo. "Courtroom Confidential." *Los Angeles Times*, Feb. 12,
1995.

Wolfe, Tom. "Public Lives." *Esquire*, April 1964.

Chapter 10: The Wonder Garment

Alsop, Ronald; Abrams, Bill. *The Wall Street Journal on Marketing*,
Burr Ridge, Ill.: Richard D. Irwin, 1986.

Blackwood, Francy. "Alaska Volcano Eruption Not a Major Disrup-
tion." *Supermarket News*, Aug. 31, 1992.

Bober, Joanna. "Execs Mull Donahue's Blast." *Women's Wear Daily*,
March 4, 1993.

Bober, Joanna. "NAHM Tells of 'Sheer Facts'." *Women's Wear Daily*,
April 28, 1994.

Bosanko, Deborah. "The Pantyhose Market Is in a Bind." *American
Demographics*, April 1994.

Forster, Rebecca. Interview by Martin J. Smith, Feb. 4, 2003.

Hall, June. "A Primer on Pantyhose." *Fort Lauderdale Sun-Sentinel*,
May 23, 1996.

Handley, Susannah. *Nylon: The Story of a Fashion Revolution*, Baltimore, Md.: St. Johns University Press, 1999.

Helliker, Kevin. "Kingsize, Not Queen: Some Men Have Taken to
Wearing Pantyhose." *Wall Street Journal*, Feb. 19, 2002.

"The Hosiery Association." http://www.nahm.com/newhome.html
(Jan. 16, 2003)

Hughs, Ina. "Pantyhose Was Biggest Fashion News of the '60s." *Knoxville News-Sentinel*, Sept. 30, 1996.

Johnson, Judy. "Historic Stride Celebrating a Giant Step into Pantyhose." World Press Network, *Chicago Tribune*, Dec. 11, 1988.

McEnroe, Colin. "Pantyhose Keep Leg up on Stockings." *Hartford Courant*, July 13, 1995.

Mechling, Lauren. "Multi-Tasking Pantyhose." *National Post* (Canada), Oct. 7, 2000.

Miles, Janelle. "Swimmers Trial Pantyhose." *AAP General News* (Australia), June 4, 2002.

Moody, Lori. "How Sally Rand Helped Pantyhose Become an Idea with (Great) Legs." *Los Angeles Daily News*, Feb. 24, 1995.

Namath, Joe. "Voices of the Century: Sports." *Newsweek*, Nov. 25, 1999.

Phillips, Jeanne; Phillips, Pauline. "Dear Abby." *Newsday*, July 10, 2002.

Smith, Sid. "The History of Hosiery." http://bluechipsocks.com/reserves/history/hist.html (Jan. 15, 2003)

"Tights vs. Stockings: The Great Debate." http://winnie-cooper.com/articles/dress/tightsvsst.html (Jan. 14, 2003)

Van Savage, L.C. "Pantyhose? Fuggedabowdit." http://www.vansavage.com/2000/pantyhose.shtml (Jan. 14, 2003)

Wells, Jennifer. "Footless, Bulge-free, and Rich to Boot." *Toronto Star*, May 25, 2002.

Wicker, Jim. "Handful of North Carolina Innovators Revolutionized Hosiery in 1950s." *Times-News* (Burlington, N.C.), Feb. 17, 2002.

Chapter 11: Thaws and Effect

"About Birdseye Foods." http://www.birdseyefoods.com/corp/about/ (May 29, 2003)

American Frozen Food Institute, http://www.affi.org (Sept. 4, 2002)

Arnold, Gary. "Family Life Goes Wrong in 'Avalon.'" *Washington Times*, Oct. 5, 1990.

Banker, Steven. "The Early Ice Age: How Frozen Potatoes Led to Couch Potatoes." *FSB*, Feb. 1, 2000.

Barker, Leslie. "Four Decades' Worth of TV Dinners." *St. Louis Post Dispatch*, April 26, 1993.

Bartlett, Kay. "At 40, TV Dinners Are Hotter Than Ever." Associated Press, June 26, 1994.

Berry, Walter. "Ariz. Man Invented T.V. Dinner." Associated Press, Nov. 11, 1999.

"Betty Crocker." http://www.adage.com/century/icono4.html (Sept. 2, 2002)

Bundy, Beverly. "Postwar Affluence Expands American Palates and Launches the Age of Convenience Foods." *Fort Worth Star-Telegram*, Aug. 4, 1999.

Collingwood, H. "What's 35 Years Old and in Your Freezer?" *Business Week*, Aug. 7, 1989.

"Comics Started a Century Ago, Banana Seeds Are Sterile." *The Record* (Bergen, N.J.), Feb. 28, 1993.

Csikszentmihalyi, Mihaly; Kubey, Robert. "Television Addiction Is No Mere Metaphor." *Scientific American*, February 2002.

Curry, Dale. "TV Dinner Inventor Inspired by Meals During WW II." *New Orleans Times-Picayune*, June 29, 2000.

Davenport, Rex. "Saving Swanson: Yearlong Crash Program Reinvents Brand and Sets Table for a Return to Dominance." *Refrigerated & Frozen Foods*, August 2002.

"Feasting on Fame." *San Jose Mercury News*, March 31, 1999.

Friedan, Betty. *The Feminine Mystique*, New York: Norton, 1963.

"Frozen Foods." *The Columbia Encyclopedia*, New York: Columbia University Press, 2000.

Gladstone, Jim. "TV Dinners Are Frozen in Our History." *Chicago Tribune*, Dec. 6, 1989.

Grimes, William. "Comfort Food Is Just for Babies." *Contra Costa Times*, Jan. 17, 2001.

"Help in the Kitchen." *Time*, Dec. 20, 1954.

Higgins, Kevin T. "Packaged for Your Convenience." *Food Engineering*, March 1, 2000.

Hirsch, Arthur. "Fifty Years Ago Swanson Introduced the TV Dinner. Folks Have Been Eating and Watching Ever Since." *Baltimore Sun*, Feb. 5, 2003.

"The History of Frozen Foods—Clarence Birdseye." http://inventors.about.com/library/inventors/blfrfood.htm (June 12, 2002)

"History of the Refrigerator." http://www.historychannel.com/exhibits/modern/fridge.html (Sept. 1, 2002)

Keene, Linda. "Fame for the Inventor of the TV Dinner Is Frozen in Time." *Seattle Times*, Sept. 24, 1999.

Marcus, Erica. "Food Without the Fuss." *Newsday*, March 26, 2003.

Norris, Jan. "TV Dinners—a 40 Year Love Affair." *Palm Beach Post*, May 9, 1994.

"One Hundred Great Things: In a Century When the Consumer Became King, Product Innovation Reached Unprecedented Heights." *Time*, Dec. 7, 1998.

Phipps, Robert G. *The Swanson Story: When the Chicken Flew the Coop*, Omaha, Neb: Carl and Caroline Swanson Foundation, 1977.

"Pre-Cooked Meals Raise Sales Hopes." *New York Times*, Feb. 3, 1954.

Riell, Howard. "What's for Dinner?" *Frozen Food Age*, September 2002.

Roberts, Paul. "The New Food Anxiety." *Psychology Today*, March 1998.

Rubenstein, Steve. "A Taste of Nostalgia in Front of the TV." San Francisco *Chronicle*, Sept. 28, 1990.

Shales, Tom. "It Came, It Thawed, It Conquered." *Washington Post*, April 16, 1987.

Shephard, Sue. *Pickled, Potted, and Canned: How the Art and Science of Food Preserving Changed the World*, New York: Simon & Schuster, 2001.

Shrieves, Linda. "TV Dinner Still Hot at 40." *Orlando Sentinel*, May 14, 1994.

Snow, Jane. "The Refrigerator Changed Our Lives, Getting Us out of the Kitchen." *Knight Ridder/Tribune News Service*, April 26, 1999.

Stern, Seth. "Clever Inventions That Came out of the Cold." *Christian Science Monitor*, Jan. 8, 2002.

Stratton, Lee. "Dining Together, Once a Family Mainstay, Now Is Fading Practice," *Columbus Dispatch*, Nov. 21, 1999.

Strauss, Robert. "Savor: The TV Dinner Is Middle-Aged, But Who Cares?" *Newark Star-Ledger*, May 15, 1999.

"Swanson 50th Anniversary Celebration." http://www.swansonmeals.com/50th/ (May 27, 2003)

Tuhy, Carrie. "The Big Thaw." *Money*, March 1986.

"TV Dinner Marks 45th Birthday with Flair." *Frozen Food Age*, May 1999.

"The TV Dinner Turns 45 as Its Inventor Becomes a Celebrity." *Nation's Restaurant News*, Nov. 29, 1999.

"TV JARGON (Definitions to TV Industry Terminology)," http://www.tvacres.com/jargon.htm (Sept. 2, 2002)

"A Visit with Betty Cronin, 'The Mother of TV Dinners.'" *Frozen Food Age*, March 1994.

Waldman, Deborah J. "Life Without Television." http://familyfun.go.com/raisingkids/child/skills/feature/dony57notv/dony57notv.html (Sept. 30, 2002)

Chapter 12: Hell on Wheels

Abadi, Michael Cyrus, "Advertising as Behavioral Science." http://www.targetmarket.org/targe_3.htm (Oct. 13, 2002)

Barron, James. "The Edsel, With All Its Quirks, Is Hailed as It Turns 40." *New York Times*, July 22, 1997.

Bonsall, Thomas E. *Disaster in Dearborn: The Story of the Edsel*, Palo Alto, Calif.: Stanford University Press, 2002.

Brooks, John. *The Fate of the Edsel, and Other Business Adventures*, New York: Harper & Row, 1963.

Byrne, John A. *The Whiz Kids: The Founding Fathers of American Business—And the Legacy They Left Us*, New York: Doubleday, 1993.

"Centennial Journal: 100 Years in Business; They Should Have Picked Mustang, 1957." *Wall Street Journal*, Aug. 15, 1989.

"Ford Facts . . . The Naming of the Edsel." Ford Parts Managers Association web site, http://www.fmanet.com/blart/edsel.htm (Oct. 15, 2002)

Horton, Cleveland. "100 years of Auto Ads." *Advertising Age*, Jan. 8, 1996.

Hunt, Morton. *The Story of Psychology*, New York: Doubleday, 1993.

Miner, Tom. "Customer-Focused Menu Marketing." *Cornell Hotel & Restaurant Administration Quarterly*, June 1996.

Packard, Vance. *The Status Seekers*, New York: David McKay Company, 1959.

Schneider, Greg. "Ford Invents the Model Two." *Washington Post*, Oct. 27, 2002.

Seller, Patricia. "The Fortune 500: Winning Ideas in Marketing to Avoid a Trampling, Get Ahead of the Mass." *Fortune*, May 15, 1995.

Serafin, Raymond. "The Saturn Story: How Saturn Became One of the Most Successful New Brands in Marketing History." *Advertising Age*, Nov. 16, 1992.

"Smith Motor Company." http://www.edsel.net (Oct. 24, 2002)

Standish, Frederick. "Car Symbolizing Auto Failure is Gone, But Not Forgotten." Associated Press, Nov. 20, 1989.

Warnock, C. Gayle. *The Edsel Affair*, Paradise Valley, Ariz.: Pro West, 1980.

Young, Anthony. "The Rise and Fall of the Edsel." *The Freeman*, September 1989.

Chapter 13: The First Angry Mike Man

"As Seen on TV: Jerry Springer Videos Uncensored." http://www.tv-showroom.com/html/JerrySpringer.htm (Dec. 31, 2002)

Baldrige, Letitia. From the video documentary *It's Only Talk—The Real Story of America's Talk Shows*. A&E Home Video, 2000.

Barrett, Don. "Los Angeles Radio People: Where Are They Now?" http://www.laradio.com/about.htm (Jan. 8, 2003)

Benton, Joshua; Sallah, Michael D. "On Air, Nothing Succeeds Like Excess." *Toledo Blade*, Dec. 30, 1999.

Carney, Steve. "22% of Americans Get News from Talk Shows." *Los Angeles Times*, Jan. 10, 2003.

Carroll, Jerry. "What's So Good About Being Bad?" San Francisco *Chronicle*, Jan. 19, 1994.

Downey, Morton Jr. From the video documentary *It's Only Talk—The Real Story of America's Talk Shows*. A&E Home Video, 2000.

Goldstein, Patrick. "Yakity Yak, Please Talk Back." *Los Angeles Times*, July 16, 1995.

James, Meg. "CBS in Negotiations for Clinton Talk Show." *Los Angeles Times*, Aug. 22, 2002.

Kiger, Patrick J. "Snorkeling in the Cesspool." *Los Angeles Times Magazine*, Aug. 20, 2000.

Kurtz, Howard. From the video documentary *It's Only Talk—The Real Story of America's Talk Shows*. A&E Home Video, 2000.

Laufer, Peter. *Inside Talk Radio*, Secaucus, N.J.: Carol Publishing Group, 1995.

Lynch, Stephen. "Morton Downey Jr. Was a Broadcasting Pioneer—Unfortunately." *The Orange County (Calif.) Register*, March 14, 2001.

"The Official Morton Downey Jr. Web Site Dedicated to Television's Ultimate Loudmouth." http://www.mortondowneyjr.com/mortondowney.html (Jan. 8, 2003)

Philbin, Regis. From the video documentary *It's Only Talk—The Real Story of America's Talk Shows*. A&E Home Video, 2000.

Pyne, Joe. From the video documentary *It's Only Talk—The Real Story of America's Talk Shows*. A&E Home Video, 2000.

Scott, Gini Graham. *Can We Talk? The Power and Influence of Talk Shows*, New York: Insight Books, 1999.

Starr, Michael. "Jesse Pumped Up to Be the New Donahue." *New York Post*, Jan. 9, 2003.

Upham, Steadman. "Wooden Leg or Table? The Landscape of Graduate Education." Remarks delivered at the Jonathan Club in Los Angeles to the Financial Executives Institute, March 18, 1999.

Wallace, Mike. From the video documentary *It's Only Talk—The Real Story of America's Talk Shows*. A&E Home Video, 2000.

Wilkinson, Gerry. "Broadcast Pioneers of Philadelphia." http://broadcastpioneers.50g.com/pyne.html (Jan. 6, 2003)

Williams, Montel. From the video documentary *It's Only Talk—The Real Story of America's Talk Shows*. A&E Home Video, 2000.

Chapter 14: The Supertanker Diaper

Baker, Linda. "Bottoming Out: Why Are Diaper Services Disappearing?" *E Magazine*, Sept. 19, 1998.

Boiko, Susan. "Diapers and Diaper Rashes." *Dermatology*, Feb. 1, 1997.

Crossen, Cynthia. "How 'Tactical Research' Muddied Diaper Debate." *Wall Street Journal*, May 17, 1994.

"Diapering Dilemma." *Journal of Pediatrics*, June 1994.

Dodson, Paul. "Mother of Disposable Diapers Born, Raised in South Bend." *South Bend Tribune*, Nov. 22, 1998.

"Dow/NSTA Summer Workshop Lesson Plans." http://thechalkboard.com/Corporations/Dow/Programs/NSTA_Lessons/Diapers.html (Jan. 28, 2003)

Farrisi, Theresa Rodriguez. *Diaper Changes: The Complete Diapering Book and Resource Guide*, Richland, Pa.: Homekeepers Publishing, 1997.

Gladwell, Malcolm. "Smaller." *The New Yorker*, Nov. 26, 2001.

Harrington, Jeff. "Disposable Diaper Inventor Dies." *Cincinnati Enquirer*, Nov. 7, 1997.

"The History of the Diaper." From Diapers Unlimited, a Kalamazoo, Mich., cotton diaper service. http://webhome.idirect.com/~born2luv/history.htm (June 28, 2002)

Pytlik, Erin, et al. "Superabsorbent Polymers." http://www.eng.buffalo.edu/Courses/ce435/Diapers/Diapers.html (Jan. 28, 2003)

Spector, Robert. *Shared Values: A History of Kimberly-Clark*, Lyme, Conn.: Greenwich Publishing, 1997.

Thomas, Robert Jr. "Marion Donovan, 81, Solver of Damp-Diaper Problem." *New York Times*, Nov. 18, 1998.

"What Is the Crystaline Substance Found in Disposable Diapers?" http://www.howstuffworks.com/question207.htm (July 5, 2002)

Chapter 15: When Mayhem Went Postmodern

Ascher-Walsh, Rebecca; et al. "25 Scariest Movies of All Time." *Entertainment Weekly*, July 23, 1999.

Beifuss, John. " 'Dead' Will Live Forever, Thanks to Me and Uncle Sam." *Memphis Commercial Appeal*, Nov. 19, 1999.

Canby, Vincent. "Night of Living Dead." *New York Times*, Dec. 5, 1968.

Collis, Clark. "Back from the Dead," *London Daily Telegraph*, Jan. 23, 1999.

Ebert, Roger. " 'Living Dead' Is Resurrected, Minus Its Ancestor's Horrifying Originality." *The Orange County Register*, Oct. 13, 1990.

Freeland, Cynthia A. *The Naked and the Undead: Evil and the Appeal of Horror*, Boulder, Colo.: Westview Press, 2000.

Gagne, Paul R. *The Zombies That Ate Pittsburgh: The Films of George A. Romero*, New York: Dodd Mead, 1987.

King, Stephen. *Stephen King's Danse Macabre*, New York: Dodd Mead, 1983.

Leavy, Jane. "Grave New World; Filmmaker George Romero Hits 'Dead' Center With His Zombies." *Washington Post*, June 30, 1985.

Lester, Gideon. "Reign of Terror: The Peculiar Charms of the Grand Guignol." http://www.amrep.org/past/caligari/caligari1.html (Jan. 20, 2003)

Lion, Ed. "George A. Romero, Movie's Master Shockmeister." United Press International, Aug. 5, 1988.

"The Living Dead: Dedicated to Romero's Dead Trilogy." (Unofficial fan page). http://www.angelfire.com/film/deadtrilogy/index.html (Jan. 14, 2003)

McIntyre, Gina. "Chill Factor: They Don't Make Horror Films the Way They Used To." *Hollywood Reporter*, Nov. 1, 2000.

"Night of the Living Dead." (Review) http://www.pulpmovies.com/Reviews/Horror/notld.html (Jan. 12, 2003)

The Official Home Page of Tom Savini, http://www.savini.com/ (Jan. 28, 2003)

"Plot Summary." http://www.terrortrap.com/living.htm (Jan. 10, 2003)

Seymour, Gene. "The Dawn of Romero." *Newsday*, Jan. 5, 2003.

"That Living Dead Girl." *Horror-Wood Webzine*, http://www.horror-wood.com/livingdead.htm (Feb. 20, 2003)

Tomsho, Robert D. "George Romero Is Happy Here in His Horror Heaven." *Pittsburgh*, October 1981.

Van Wyngarden, Bruce. "George Romero: Pittsburgher of the Year." *Pittsburgh*, January 1991.

Walker, Gregory (editor). *American Horrors: Essays on the Modern American Horror Film*, Urbana, Ill. and Chicago: University of Illinois Press, 1987.

Weiskind, Ron. "Hitchcock Films Rated the Most Thrilling." *Pittsburgh Post-Gazette*, June 13, 2001.

Weiskind, Ron. "Director Romero Wants to Break Out of Horror." *Pittsburgh Post-Gazette*, Feb. 14, 2002.

Chapter 16: Dawn of the Point-Click Culture

Ad text for the LG Internet Refrigerator, LG Home Appliances, *Gourmet* magazine, October 2002.

"Apple Lisa." http://fortunecity.com/marina/reach/435/lisa.htm (July 3, 2002)

Bellis, Mary. "Inventors of the Modern Computer: History of the Graphical User Interface, or GUI." http://inventors.about.com/library/weekly/aa043099.htm (July 17, 2002)

"Douglas Carl Engelbart." http://bootstrap.org/engelbart/index.jsp (Nov. 6, 2002)

"Douglas Engelbart 1968 Demo." http://sloan.stanford.edu/mouse-site/1968Demo.html (Nov. 6, 2002)

"Douglas Engelbart and 'The Mother of All Demos.'" http://cs.brown.edu/stc/resea/telecollaboration/engelbart.htm (Nov. 6, 2002)

"From Carbons to Computers: The Changing American Office." http://educate.si.edu/scitech/carbons/typewriters.html (Nov. 6, 2002)

Gladden, Jonathan. "Xerox PARC and the GUI." http://www.accad.ohio-state.edu/~jgladden/GradCourses/ComputerGraphicsHistory/ResearchPaper/parcg ui01.html (Nov. 5, 2002)

Hiltzik, Michael. *Dealers of Lightning: Xerox PARC and the Dawn of the Computer Age*, New York: HarperCollins, 1999.

"Interface Hall of Shame." http://iarchitect.com/shame.htm (Nov. 5, 2002)

Knight, Dan. "Macintosh History: 1984" http://lowendmac.com/history/1984dk.shtml (July 17, 2002)

Malone, Michael S. *The Big Score: The Billion Dollar Story of Silicon Valley*, New York: Doubleday, 1985.

National Council on Disability. *Guidance From the Graphical User Interface Experience: What GUI Teaches About Technology Access*, Washington, D.C.: National Council on Disability, March 28, 1996.

"Windows Operating Systems Family History." http://www.microsoft.com/windows/WinHistoryIntro.mspx (Nov. 8, 2002)

"World's First Internet Refrigerator Arrives at Retail Locations on October 1, 2002." http://lgappliances.com/cgi-bin/pr.cgi?idPressRelease=17 (Nov. 4, 2004)

Chapter 17: The Righteous Stuff

Basketball Hall of Fame, http://www.hoophall.com (Dec. 27, 2002)

"Doctor of Dunk Finds Hoops Version of E=MC Squared." *Milwaukee Journal*, Sept. 16, 1991.

George, Nelson. *Elevating the Game: Black Men and Basketball*, New York: HarperCollins, 1992.

"How Does Michael Fly?" *Chicago Tribune*, Feb. 27, 1990.

"Julius Erving, Basketball Legend." (Interview) http://www.achievement.org/autodoc/page/ervopro-1 (Dec. 27, 2002)

Hayes, Tracy Achor. "Today's Hot-Trend Sneaker Is the Sole of Nostalgia." *The Orange County Register*, April 1, 1994.

Herzog, Bob. "100 Years of Hoopla." *Newsday*, Jan. 5, 1992.

Hoenig, Gary. "Dr J.'s Toughest Case." *New York Times Magazine*, Feb. 13, 1977.

Jacobson, Steve. "NCAA Tournament; Tall Tale From Past." *Newsday*, March 31, 1995.

Johnson, Roy S. "The Jordan Effect," *Fortune*, June 22, 1998.

"Julius Erving, Ex-Basketball Star." *CBS This Morning* (transcript), Feb. 23, 1990.

Krentzman, Jackie. "JAMboree." *Sporting News*, Feb. 12, 1996.

Lazenby, Roland. "Of legends and rings: The Elgin Baylor story." http://archive.sportserver.com/newsroom/sports/PressBox/feb96/0207lazenby.html (Dec. 27, 2002)

Murphy, Michael. "The ABA Way: For Pure Entertainment, American Basketball Association Was a Slam Dunk." *Houston Chronicle*, Feb. 4, 1996.

Murphy, Michael. "Martin Loses Possessions in Fire, But Not Memories." *Houston Chronicle*, Sept. 19, 1999.

"NBA's Greatest Moments: Jordan and Wilkins Battle for Dunk Title." http://www.nba.com/history/1988slamdunk_moments.html (Dec. 27, 2002)

Ostler, Scott. "The Leaping Legends of Basketball." *Los Angeles Times*, Feb. 12, 1989.

Ostler, Scott. "Wilt: The Ultimate All-Star." http://www.nba.com/warriors/history/Ostler_chamberlain.html (Dec. 27, 2002)

Pluto, Terry. *Loose Balls: The Short, Wild Life of the American Basketball Association, As Told by the Players, Coaches, and Movers and Shakers Who Made It Happen*, New York: Simon & Schuster, 1990.

Pluto, Terry. "Out of Their League." *Sporting News*, Jan. 8, 1996.

Skolnick, Ethan J. "10 Who Changed the Game." *Palm Beach Post*, Nov. 1, 1996.

"Without DOC, the NBA Will *Never* Be the Same!" http://www.geocities.com/fantasyspecs/ (Dec. 27, 2002)

Wolf, David. *Foul: The Connie Hawkins Story*, New York: Holt, Reinhart and Winston, 1972.

Chapter 18: Betty Ford's Intervention

"The Birth of A.A. and Its Growth in U.S./Canada." http://www.alcoholics-anonymous.org/english/E_factFile/m=24_d14.html (Sept. 7, 2002)

Boop, John M. Interview by Martin J. Smith, Rancho Mirage, Calif., Aug. 29, 2002.

"A Call to Action: An Initiative of the Center for Substance Abuse Treatment." http://www.recoverymonth.gov/2002 (Sept. 7, 2002)

"Changing the Conversation: A National Plan to Improve Substance Abuse Treatment." Substance Abuse and Mental Health Administration, U.S. Department of Health and Human Services, 2000.

Ford, Betty (with Chris Chase). *The Times of My Life*, New York: Harper & Row, 1978.

Ford, Betty (with Chris Chase). *Betty: A Glad Awakening*, New York: Doubleday, 1987.

"Lyrics," as compiled on alt.suicide.holiday ("a.s.h."), an unmoderated Usenet newsgroup. http://ash.xanthia.com/lyrics.htm# suicidal-tendencies (Sept. 10, 2002)

"National Recovery Month Helps Reduce Stigma of Addiction." http://www.hazelden.org/newsletter_detail.dbm?ID=1487 (Sept. 10, 2002)

Peele, Stanton. "Getting Wetter?" http://reason.com/9604/col. PEELE.text.shtml (June 27, 2002)

Peele, Stanton. "A Moral Vision of Addiction." http://peele.net/ lib/vision.html (June 27, 2002)

Peele, Stanton, et al. *Resisting 12-Step Coercion: How to Fight Forced Participation in AA, NA, or 12-Step Treatment*, Tucson, Arizona: See Sharp Press, 2001.

"Recentering Recovery." http://www.lanstat.com/recentering.html (Sept. 17, 2002)

Schwarzlose, John. Interview by Martin J. Smith, Rancho Mirage, Calif., Aug. 29, 2002.

Warrick, Pamela. "Living Out Loud." *Los Angeles Times*, Nov. 12, 1995.

White, William. *Slaying the Dragon: The History of Addiction Treatment and Recovery in America*, Bloomington, Ill.: Chestnut Health Systems, 1998.

White, William. "Stigma." http://www.ncaddillinois.org/White%
20foreword.htm (Sept. 17, 2002)

Young, Leah. Interview by Martin J. Smith, Sept. 12, 2002.

Chapter 19: From *E. T.* to "Astroturfing"

Ahrens, Frank. "The Spy Who Loved Nokia, and Other Next-Stage
Ads." *The Washington Post*, Sept. 28, 2002.

Daly, Steve. "*E.T.* by the Numbers." *Entertainment Weekly*, March 29,
2002.

"E.R.M.A.: Entertainment and Marketing Resources." http://www.
erma.org (July 3, 2002)

Fitzhugh, Bill. "Selling Out Takes a Lot of Bottle." *The Guardian*
(London), Nov. 6, 2000.

Frammolino, Ralph. "NBA and Hollywood Hoping Kids 'Like Mike'
Enough to Become Fans." *Los Angeles Times*, July 3, 2002.

Friedman, Monroe. Interview by Martin J. Smith, Aug. 2, 2002.

Frey, Christine. "Web Friend or Faux." *Los Angeles Times*, July 18,
2002.

Goldstein, Patrick. "Studios' Web 'Plants' Lead to an Ethical
Thicket." *Los Angeles Times*, Oct. 1, 2002.

Hitchon, Jacqueline. "Brand Name Entertainment." *Capital Times*
(Madison, Wis.), June 9, 1997.

Kamins, Michael. Interview by Martin J. Smith, July 30, 2002.

Leith, Scott. "Coke Leads Push to Place Products in Movies, TV."
Atlanta Journal and Constitution, Oct. 29, 2000.

Powell, Betsy. "Licensed to Shill." *Toronto Star*, April 7, 2002.

Roug, Louise. "Lights, Camera, Product Placement." *Los Angeles
Times*, Aug. 19, 2002.

Shaw, David. "A Nation Under Siege . . . by Product Placement."
Los Angeles Times, Nov. 3, 2002.

Smith, Martin J. "Alien's Love of Candy Set the Standard." *The Orange County Register*, July 16, 1991.

Vranica, Suzanne. "Sony Ericsson Campaign Uses Actors to Push Camera-Phone in Real Life." *Wall Street Journal*, Aug. 1, 2002.

"We Ought to Be in Pictures." *St. Louis Post-Dispatch*, April 8, 1995.

Chapter 20: The *Toink!* Heard Round the World

"About Tiger." http://www.tigerwoods.com (Dec. 1, 2002)

Apodaca, Patrice. "Carlsbad, Where Golf Is King." *Los Angeles Times*, Aug. 26, 1998.

"Ball Launcher 500cc." http://www.jazzgolf.com/content/drivers. html (Nov. 30, 2002)

Barkow, Al. *The Golden Era of Golf: How America Rose to Dominate the Old Scots Game*, New York: St. Martin's Press, 2000.

Bonk, Thomas. "Callaway's Passing Marks the Death of a Salesman." *Los Angeles Times*, July 6, 2001.

Bonk, Thomas. "Woods Goes to Great Lengths." *Los Angeles Times*, Nov. 30, 2002.

Bonk, Thomas. "Low Gear." *Los Angeles Times*, Feb. 20, 2003.

Bruscas, Angelo. "Technology Has Spawned Equipment Powerful Enough to Be Banned." *Seattle Post-Intelligencer*, April 11, 2000.

Buckman, Brigid. "Your Golf Club's Changing Face: Technology, Materials Give Game New Spin." http//www.azstarnet.com/ public/startech/archive/040599/main.htm (July 3, 2002)

Christman, David. Interview by Martin J. Smith, May 2, 2002.

"Corporate History." http://www.callawaygolf.com/corporate/history .asp (July 18, 2002)

"Fat Shaft Accuracy Challenge." http://www.wilsonsports.com. au/golf/golfclub_tech.html (Sept. 30, 2002)

"Golf Club Makers in the Rough as Sales Drop and Rules Are Revised." http://www.golfpro-online.com/news/yeartodate/news99/rough.html (July 3, 2002)

"The Growth of U.S. Golf." http://www.ngf.org/faq/growthofgolf.html (July 18, 2002)

"A History of the Golf Club." http://www.golfeurope.com/almanac/history/golf_club1.htm (Nov. 25, 2002)

"A History of Golf Since 1497." http://www.golfeurope.com/almanac/history/history1.htm (Nov. 25, 2002)

Hyman, Mark. "Ely Callaway: He Did It His Way." *Business Week*, July 23, 2001.

"Johnny Miller—Biographical Information." http://www.golfweb.com/players/bios/1815.html (Nov. 29, 2002)

Kramer, Scott. "Playing With Fire." http://sportsillustrated.cnn.com/golfonline/equipment/features/playwfire0399.html (Aug. 1, 2002)

Kupelian, Vartan. "Club makers, USGA Poised for Big Fight: Drivers Keep Getting Larger; No Technology Limits in Sight." http://detnews.com/2002/golf/0201/23/e04-397585.htm (July 3, 2002)

McGrath, Charles. "Clubbing the Opposition." *New York Times Magazine*, May 25, 2003.

"National Golf Foundation Frequently Asked Questions." http://www.ngf.org/faq/ (Nov. 13, 2002)

Nelson, Nik. "The Big Decade—Big Clubs, Big Companies, Big Changes." http://services.golfweb.com/linksmagazine/9711/equipment.html (Aug. 1, 2002)

Peltz, James F. "Ely Callaway, Golf Club Innovator, Vintner, Dies." *Los Angeles Times*, July 6, 2001.

Purkey, Mike. "Great Big Empire." http://sportsillustrated.cnn.com/golfonline/equipment/features/callawaymay98.html/ (Aug. 1, 2002)

Tays, Alan. "When Golf Is All the Rage." *Palm Beach Post*, Jan. 17, 2001.

Index

● ● ● ● ● ● ● ● ●

A

Abdul-Jabbar, Kareem, 199

About Schmidt, 219

Abstract Expressionism, 47

Ackermann, Marsha, 16

Adams, Gary, 229–30

addiction, 202–13

  statistics on, 210, 212

  treatment of, 204–5, 206–9, 210–11

Adventures of Ozzie and Harriet, The, 6

Aerosmith, 78

air-conditioning, 12–22

  Carrier's development of, 15, 19

  early attempts at, 14–15

  environmental hazards of, 19–20

  political impact of, 14, 18–19

  population shifts and, 13–14, 17–19

  postwar boom in, 16–17

  weather wimps and, 20–21

Air Jordan, 201

Alabama, 113, 122

Albert, Prince, 48

Alcoholics Anonymous (AA), 204, 208, 211, 212

Alfred C. Kinsey: A Public/Private Life (Jones), 34

Ali, Muhammad, 70, 72, 77

Allen, Steve, 145–46

Allen, Woody, 41

All My Children, 219

Amblin Entertainment, 217–18

Amedure, Scott, 149

American Basketball Association (ABA), 189–92, 197–99

American Beauty, An, 23

American Broadcasting Company (ABC), 219

American Cancer Society, 207

American Enterprise Institute, 18
American Film Institute, 167
American Idol, 220
American Museum of Natural History, 43
American Museum of the Moving Image, 175
American Society of Landscape Architects, 9
America Online, 185
amplification systems, 60–61
Anchorage, Alaska, 115
anorexia, 24, 30
Antiques & Collectibles, 49
Apollo 11, 113
Applebee's, 140
Apple Computer, 178, 183–84, 186
Arizona, 19, 97, 126
Arizona Republic, 21
Arluke, Arnold, 102–3
Arsenault, Raymond, 19
Artists League of Texas, 56
Art of Beautifying Suburban Home Grounds of Small Extent, The (Scott), 3
Astaire, Fred, 74
astroturfing, 222–23
"As We May Think" (Bush), 178–79
Atkins, Chet, 63
Atkins, Jim, 63
Atlanta Hawks, 199
Atlantic Monthly, 178–79
Atlantic Records, 67
ATM machines, 220
Attles, Al, 195
AT&T Pebble Beach National Pro-Am, 232
Atwater, Wilbur O., 26
Austin Air-Conditioned Village, 21–22
Australia, 115
Austria, 114
Avalon, 125

B
Bacharach, Burt, 224
Bacon, Tony, 68
Bad and the Beautiful, The, 93
bad taste, 45–57

Bailey, Natalie, 217, 218
Baldrige, Letitia, 147–48
Ball, Michael, 73
Bancroft, Anne, 115–16
Bank One Ballpark, 13
Banting, William, 25–26
Barkow, Al, 233–34
basketball, 189–201
Baylor, Elgin, 195, 197
Beach Boys, 67
Beat Generation, 65
Beatles, 67, 110
Beauty Mist, 113
Beauty Parade, 93
Beck, Jeff, 66
"Be My Lover," 78
Benefito, Ruth Rogan, 86–87
Ben-Hur, 168
Berg, Alan, 149
Berry, Chuck, 65
Betty Crocker, 126
Betty Ford Center, 209, 210, 212
Beverly Hills, Calif., 101
Big Bertha, 225–36
    development of, 230
    successful marketing of, 231–33
Biggest Bertha Titanium Driver, 226
Bigsby, Paul, 63
Billboard, 224
Bill Haley and the Comets, 65
"Biological Aspects of Some Social Problems" (Kinsey), 39
Bird, S. Elizabeth, 101
Birdseye, Clarence, 120
Birnbaum, Charles A., 4
birth control, 37, 40
Blackboard Jungle, 65
black velvet paintings, 45–57
    invention and rise of, 50–51
    proliferation of, 53–54
    See also Tacky Chic
Blair Witch Project, The, 171
Blood Feast, 169
Blue Velvet, 7–8
Boal, Sam, 73
Bogosian, Eric, 149
Bold detergent, 89
Bonk, Thomas, 235
Bonsal, Thomas E., 132
bots, 222

Brady, Diamond Jim, 23
Brancazio, Peter, 200
Breech, Ernest, 135
Brill's Content, 221
Broadcaster, 63
Brooks, John, 133, 136
Brooks Brothers, 88
Brosnan, Pierce, 218
Brown, Edmund G. "Pat," 99
Brown, Hubie, 197
Brown & Bigelow, 48–49, 50
Brown v. Board of Education, 65
Bruiser, 174
Buckingham Palace, 112
Buick, 133
Building Research Advisory Board, 21–22
Bukata, Jim, 198
Burlington Industries, 228
Bush, George W., 14, 19
Bush, Vannevar, 178–79, 180–83
Butler, Marion Donovan, 157–58
Byrne, John A., 137

C
Calcavecchia, Mark, 225
Calhoun, Rory, 91, 97
California, 91, 99
California, University of, 18, 84
Callaway, Ely, 228–31
Callaway Golf, 226–36
Callaway vineyard, 228
calories, 26–27, 28, 29, 30
Calypso, 95
Canada, 120
cancer, 87, 207
cannibalism, 169, 170, 173
Capitol, U.S., 18
Capitol Records, 65
Cardin, Pierre, 112
Carlsbad, Calif., 226, 230, 232
Carpenter, John, 175
Carrier, Willis, 12, 13, 14, 15, 16, 19
Carter, Jimmy, 194, 205, 210
Carter, Vince, 192, 220
Carter, Walter, 66
Castaway, 218
"Castro's Sex Invasion of Washington,"
    101
"casual Friday," 114

C. A. Swanson & Sons, 119–28
Catcher in the Rye, The (Salinger), 40
celebrities, private lives of, xvii–xviii,
    90–106
Celebrity Skin, 102
cell phones, 178
Central Intelligence Agency, 101
Chamberlain, Wilt, 195, 197, 200
Chanel No. 10, 75
ChapStick, 200
Chase, Chris, 207
"Cheat with the Ace of Diamonds, The"
    (La Tour), 50
"Chemistry Serves the Realm of Fashion,"
    117–18
Chevrolet, 133
Chicago, Ill., 64, 73, 98, 104
Chicago, University of, 86
Chicago Bulls, 192, 199
Chicago Musical Instruments, 62
Chicago *Sun-Times*, 171
Chicago Tribune, 54
chicken pot pie, 121
China, ancient, 84
Chinese laundry, 86
Chittenden, Russell, 26–27
chlorofluorocarbons (CFCs), 19–20
Christian, Charlie, 59, 61
Christian Science, 29
"Christina's World" (Wyeth), 56
"Chrysler Million Dollar Film Festival,"
    219
Citizen Kane, xviii, 165, 167
civil rights protesters, 147
Clapton, Eric, 66
Clinton, Bill, 102, 152, 186
Cobb, Nathan, 54
Cobra Golf, 232
Coca-Cola, 201, 220
"cock rock," 58
Colliers, 29
Columbia Journalism Review, 97
Columbia University, 133
Comfilon, 114
Commonweal, 96
ConAgra, 126
Condé Nast, 102
Confidential, 90–106
    demise of, 92, 98–101
    influence of, 101–3

Confidential (*continued*)
   launching of, 91, 93–96
   lawsuits against, 92, 95, 98–100, 103
   precursors of, 92–93
   success of, 95–96
Congress, U.S., 35, 65, 93
Connery, Sean, 216
convenience food, xviii, 119–28
   family life and, 123
   food choices and, 125
Converse, 200
Cool Comfort: America's Romance with Air
   Conditioning (Ackermann), 16
Coolidge, Cassius Marcellus, 49–50
Cooper, Alice, 78, 232
Cooper, Michael, 199
Copernicus, Nicolaus, 35
Corpo Nove, 87
cosmograph, 92, 101
Costas, Bob, 193
cotton, 84, 86, 87
Country Music Foundation Museum, 59
Courrèges, André, 112
Craven, Scott, 21
Crawford, Joan, 216
Cronin, Betty, 125
Crosby, Bing, 65, 66, 136
Cross Dressing (Fitzhugh), 221
cultural milestones, introduction to,
   xvii–xix

D
Daily Mail (London), 116
Daily Telegraph (London), 171
Daily Worker, 104
Dairy Queen, 219
Dale, Dick, 61, 62
Daly, John, 234
Dandridge, Dorothy, 99
Daughters of Bilitis, 40
Davis, Barney, 51–52
Davis, Kenneth C., xv–xvi
Dawkins, Darryl, 199
Dawn of the Dead, 173
Dawson's Creek, 219
Day of the Dead, 173
Dealers of Lightning: Xerox PARC and the
   Dawn of the Computer Age (Hiltzik),
   179

Dear Abby, 28, 115
Deaver, Michael, 150
Decker, Wayne, 51
Degas, Edgar, 85
Delaware, 94
Democratic Party, 18–19
Denver Nuggets, 190–91
Derringer, Rick, 67
Detroit Pistons, 194
Diamond, Neil, 224
Diaper Changes: The Complete Diapering
   Book and Resource Guide (Farrisi),
   164
diaper rash, 160
diapers, disposable, xviii, 155–64
   engineering of, 156–57
   environmental dilemma and, 161–64
   pioneers of, 155–57, 160
   refinements in, 158–59
   storage of, 159–60, 161
Dichter, Ernest, 131
Dickson, James Tennant, 85
Diddley, Bo, 65
Diet and Health, With Key to the Calories
   (Peters), 24
Diet for Children (and Adults) and the
   Kalorie Kids (Peters), 30
diets, dieting, 23–32
   calories and, 26–27, 28, 29, 30
   early history of, 24–26
   fads and gimmicks in, 30, 31, 32
   psychological aspects of, 30–31
DiMaggio, Joe, 71
Disneyland, 220
Dixie Chopper Jet, 1–2
Dockers, 88
dogs, in Tacky Chic, 48
Dominican Republic, 98
Donahue, Phil, 108, 150, 152
Doo Dah Parade, 8
Doonesbury, 221
Douglas, Mike, 143
Dow Chemical, 156
Downey, Morton, Jr., 144, 150–51, 153–54
Downing, Andrew Jackson, 2, 4
Dracula, 165, 168
Drayer, Ralph, 161
Dr. Strangelove, 172
Duke University, 94
Du Mont, 70

Du Pont, 85–86, 110–11, 117–18
DVD videos, 185
Dylan, Bob, 67, 174

E
Earth Day, 161
Ebert, Roger, 171
EC Comics, 168
Eddy, Mary Baker, 29
Edsel, xviii, 129–42
    advertising and marketing of, 130–36,
        140
    development cost of, 129–30
    failure of, 131, 136–40
    features of, 130, 132
    naming of, 134–35, 141
    rollout of, 129, 135–36
Edsel Citation, 141
"Edsel Show, The," 136
Egypt, ancient, 14, 83–84
Einstein, Albert, xv–xvi
Eisenhower Medical Center, 209
Electoral College, 14, 18
electric guitars, 58–69
    history of, 58–60, 63–64, 66–67, 68
    manufacturers and brands of, 59, 61,
        62, 63–64, 66
    sound of, 60–61
"Electric Lawn, The," (Wigley), 8
Elevating the Game (George), 190
Elle, 215
Ellegirl, 222
Empire State Building, 214
Engelbart, Douglas C., 178–82, 183
    GUI demo and, 180–82, 186
    influence of, 183
Enron, xviii
Entertainment Weekly, 167, 221, 224
Environmental Protection Agency, 20
ephedra, 31
Epiphone, 59, 62, 69
Epstein, Joseph, 35, 42
Equal Rights Amendment, 206
Ertegun, Ahmet, 67
Erving, Julius (Dr. J), 189–201
    ABA slam dunk contest and, 189–92
    most memorable moment of, 198–99
    playing style of, 197–98
    product endorsements of, 200

ESPN SportsCenter, 192
Esquire, 93, 100–101, 102
E.T., the Extra-Terrestrial, 216–18, 223, 224
Extreme Ironing, 81–82
Eyes Without a Face, 174

F
Farnsworth, Philo, 124
Farrisi, Theresa Rodriguez, 164
Father Knows Best, 6
Federal Bureau of Investigation (FBI), 35,
    104, 105
Fender, Leo, 63–64, 66
Fisher, Irving, 29
Fitzhugh, Bill, 221
flax, 83–84
Fletcher, Horace, 26
Fletcherizing, 26
Flirt, 93
Flynn, Errol, 91
Food Engineering, 127
Foote, Cone & Belding, 134–35
Forbes, 229
Ford, Betty, xviii, 202–213
    autobiography of, 207–8
    background and character of, 205–7
    impact of, 210
Ford, Gerald, R., 203, 206
Ford, Henry, 64
Ford, Henry, II, 135
Ford, Mary, 63, 65
Ford Focus, 220
Ford Foundation, 139
Ford Motor Company, 129–42, 220
Forrestal, James, 105
Forster, Rebecca, 113
Fortune, 130, 201
foundation garments, 109
Francis, Steve, 192
Frankenstein, 65
Frankenstein, 165, 168
Freed, Alan, 65
Freon, 15, 120
Freud, Sigmund, 35
Friedman, Monroe, 215–16
"Friend in Need, A" (Coolidge), 49–50,
    55, 56
Frozen Food Industry Hall of Fame, 126
Furness, Betty, 143

G

Gabor, Zsa Zsa, 104
Gagne, Paul R., 171, 175
Galileo Galilei, 35
gall wasps, 33, 41, 43
Gant, Allen, Sr., 111–12
Gant, Ethel, 111–12
Gap, 215, 219
Garbo, Greta, 30
garters, 109, 111
gas-heated irons, 85
Gates, Bill, 177, 178, 180, 183–84, 232
Gathorne-Hardy, Jonathan, 38, 39, 41,
   43–44
Gebhard, Paul H., 41, 42
General Electric, 230
General Electric Pension Fund, 230
Genet, Jean, 55
George, Nelson, 190
Georgie Pins, 71, 75
Gibson, 62, 63, 64, 66
Gifford, Frank, 101–2
Gifford, Kathie Lee, 101
Gilmore, Artis, 190, 197
Ginobili, Emanuel, 194
Ginsberg, Allen, 65
girdles, 109, 111
Gladwell, Malcolm, 156, 161
Glen Raven Mills, 111–12
global warming, 20
Globe, 101–2
Goddess of Truth, The, 23
Godfrey, Arthur, 143
Golden Era of Golf: How America Rose to
   Dominate the Old Scots Game, The
   (Barkow), 233–34
Goldeneye, 218
Goldstein, Patrick, 151, 221, 222
Goldwater, Barry, 19
golf, xix, 3, 225–36
   social change and, 233
   statistics on, 226–28, 234
Golf, 236
golf balls, 233
Golf Magazine, 227
Gone With the Wind, 104
Gonzaga College, 96
Good Morning America, 2, 212–13
Gordy, Berry, Jr., 67

Gorgeous George (George Wagner),
   xviii–xix, 70–79
   antecedents of, 73
   background of, 74, 76–77
   death of, 77
   decline of, 76
   influence of, 72, 77, 78
   theatrics of, 70–72, 74, 75, 76, 77
   turkey business of, 76
Gorrie, John, 15
Gossip: The Inside Scoop (Levin, Arluke),
   102–3
Graduate, The, 115–16
Graham, Billy, 34
Graham, Martha, 203
Graham, Sylvester, 25
graphical user interface (GUI), 177–88
   birth of, 180–84
   disabilities and, 187–88
   impact of, 178, 184–85
grass, 1–11
Grauman's Chinese Theater, 103
Great Big Bertha Titanium Driver, 226
Great Britain, 3, 48, 66, 89
Great Exhibition of 1851, 48
Greeks, ancient, 24, 73
Griffin, Merv, 143
Guinness, Alec, 83
Guinness Book of World Records, 8
Guitar Player, 62, 63, 68
Gutenberg Bible, 96

H

Haggar, 87
Halloween, 175
Handley, Susannah, 85, 110, 117–18
Hanes, 112, 113
Hardball, 151
Harden, Doyle, 53
Hard Rock Café, 67
Harlem, N.Y., 61, 196
Harmon, Carlyle, 155–57, 160–61, 163
Harper, Billy Gene, 155–57, 160–61,
   163
Harris, Moira, 49
Harrison, George, 67
Harrison, Robert, 90–106
   character of, 92

Harrison, Robert (*continued*)
  death of, 101
  early career of, 92–93
Hartmann, David, 212–13
Harvard University, 20, 37
Hauser, Gayelord, 30
Hawaiian Guitar, 63
Hawkins, Connie, 196, 197, 199
Hay, William H., 30
Hayakawa, S. I., 138
H. B. Reese Candy Company, 217
Health Builder, 29
Healthy Choice, 126
"Heartlight," 224
Heffington, Ryan, 78
Hefner, Hugh, 33, 40
Helmstetter, Dick, 230, 236
Hendrix, Jimi, 58, 66
Hershey Foods Corporation, 217–18
Hershkowitz, Allen, 162
Hidden Persuaders, The (Packard), 138
Hiltzik, Michael, 179, 182
Hippocrates, 24–25
history, two kinds of, xvi
Hitchcock, Alfred, 167
Hoffman, Dustin, 115–16
Hollywood, Calif., 90, 94, 100, 102, 103,
  104, 119, 167, 174, 224
Hollywood Boulevard, 90
Hollywood Diet, 30
Hollywood Reporter, 173, 174
homosexuality, 35, 40, 42, 72, 78, 95, 97
Hoover, J. Edgar, 104, 105
Hope, Bob, 76, 136
Hopper, Hedda, 94
horror films, 166–67
Hosiery Association, 108
Houston *Chronicle*, 191, 198
Howard, Moe, 75
Hudson, Rock, 97
Hughes Act, 204–5
Hughs, Ina, 109–10
humidity, human comfort and, 14–15
Huntington, Ellsworth, 16

I
I Am Legend (Matheson), 169, 175
IBM, 178, 183

ice-making machines, 15
idiot lights, 132
Ike, 127
Illinois, University of at Chicago, 83
I Love Lucy, 6
Index, 78
Indiana University, 33, 37, 40, 43
Inside News, 101
*Instruments of Desire: The Electric Guitar
  and the Shaping of Musical Experience*
  (Waksman), 62
Interface Hall of Shame, 185
Internet, 185–86, 222
Internet Refrigerator, 185–86
interventions, 203, 208
Investor's Business Daily, 87
I Refuse to Wear Clothes!, 144
irons, ironing, 82–85
  Chinese innovations in, 84
  early types of, 84–85
  electric, 85
  steam used in, 85
*It's Only Talk—The Real Story of America's
  Talk Shows*, 145–47
It's Your Nickel, 145

J
Jack Daniels, 216
Jackson, Jackie, 191
Jackson, Michael (singer), 102
Jackson, Michael (talk-show host),
  153
Jagger, Mick, 67, 78
James, Henry, 26
James, LeBron, 215
James Bond, 216, 218
Japan, 110, 232
Jazz Golf, 234
J. Crew catalog, 219
Jehovah's Witness, 76
Jell-O, 126
Jenny Jones, 149
Jobs, Steve, 177, 178, 180, 182–84
Joe Pyne Show, The, 146
Johnson, Lyndon B., 19
Johnson & Johnson, 156, 158–59
Jones, Duane, 172
Jones, James H., 34, 39, 42

Jordan, Michael, 192, 196, 199, 200–201, 220
Jorgensen, Christine, 40
Journal of Commerce, 84
Journal of Pediatrics, 160
Juárez, Mexico, 53–54

K
Kaminer, Wendy, 211
Kamins, Michael, 216, 223
Karloff, Boris, 172
Kashner, Sam, 93, 97, 104
Kefauver, Estes, 93–94
Kellogg, John Harvey, 26
Kennedy, Jackie, 205
Kennedy, John F., 18, 147
Kenny G., 232
Kentucky Colonels, 190
Kerr, Johnny, 197
Kimberley-Clark, 158–59
King, Larry, 144, 152
King, Stephen, 8, 175
Kiniski, Gene, 79
Kinsey, Alfred C., 33–44
    childhood of, 36–37
    as collector, 43–44
    early career of, 33
    honeymoon of, xviii, 34, 36, 38–39, 42
    private life and sexuality of, 34, 42
    sex studies of, 34–36, 39–42, 64
    sexual liberation and, xviii, 35, 39, 65
Kinsey, Clara Bracken McMillen "Mac," 36, 37, 38–39, 41
Kinsey Institute for Research in Sex, Gender, and Reproduction, 40
Kinsey Scale, 40–41
Kiss, xix, 70, 78
kitsch, 45–57
Kitsch in Sync (Ward), 48
Klatt, Gustav, 48
Knabusch, Edward M., 124
Kolster phonograph, 60
Kostabi, Mark, 150
Kramer, Scott, 236
KTLA, 75
Kurland, Bob, 194–95
Kurtz, Howard, 151

L
Ladies Home Journal, 29
Lancaster, Burt, 7, 76
Landers, Ann, 28
Language of Clothes, The (Lurie), 109
Larks, 216
Larson Brothers, 61, 62
Last Man on Earth, The, 175
"Last Supper, The" (Leonardo), 46
Latent Image, 169
La Tour, Georges de, 50
"Lavender Skeletons in TV's Closet," 97
Lawn Institute, 2
Lawnmower Man, The, 8
lawn mowers, 1–2, 4
    first patent for, 5
    injuries from, 8
    racing of, xvii, 1, 8–9
lawns, lawn culture, 1–11
    clover and, 10–11
    in Europe, 2–3
    in films, 7–8
    suburban, xviii, 3, 5–6, 7–8
    in Victorian era, 3
    water and, 9–10
La-Z-Boy chair, 124
Leave It to Beaver, 6
Led Zeppelin, 58, 66
Leeteg, Edgar, 50–53, 55
    background and personality of, 45–46
    establishment rejection of, 46–47, 52
    success and wealth of, 51–52
LeFauve, Skip, 140
L'Eggs, 112, 113, 114
Legionnaires' disease, 14, 20
Leno, Jay, 144
Leonard, Sugar Ray, 232
Leonardo da Vinci, 46
lesbians, 35, 40, 97
Les Paul (guitar model), 64, 66
Les Paul: An American Original (Shaughnessy), 60, 64, 65
Letterman, David, 67, 144
"Letter on Corpulence" (Banting), 26
Letts, Quentin, 116–17
Levin, Jack, 102–3
Levinson, Barry, 125
Lexus, 219
Leykis, Tom, 150
LG Electronics, 185–86

Liberace, 72, 91, 95, 99
Librium, 203
Like Mike, 220
Limbaugh, Rush, xviii, 144, 149, 152
linen, 83–84
Linkletter, Art, 143
Lisa computer, 183
Listerine, 63
"Log" (Les Paul's guitar), 58–69
Lolita (Nabokov), 40
Londos, Jim "The Golden Greek," 73
Loose Balls (Pluto), 197
Los Angeles, Calif., 74, 75, 78, 94, 99,
    207, 220
Los Angeles Lakers, 195, 199
Los Angeles Open, 225
Los Angeles Times, 27, 29, 55, 79, 148, 151,
    207, 222, 235
Lost Weekend, 205
LPGA Tour, 232, 233
Luckingham, Bradford, 18
Lurie, Alison, 109
Lyle, Irvine, 15
Lynch, David, 7–8

M
McCarthy, Joseph, 104
McCarty, Ted, 64
Macdonald, Dwight, 53
McDonald, Fred, 75
Macfadden, Bernarr, 92
McGirk, LeRoy, 74
McGrady, Tracy, 192
Macintosh computer (Mac), 183–84
MacNair, Jennifer, 93, 97, 104
McNamara, Robert, 137–38
McNichols Arena, 189
McRoy, Deborah, 150
Maddox, Lester, 148
Mahdi of Baghdad, Caliph, 14–15
"Maiden with a Pearl" (Vermeer), 56
M&Ms, 217
Manet, Edouard, 56
Man From the Meteor, The, 168
Manhattan, 67, 105, 127
Manigault, Earl "the Goat," 196
Man in the White Suit, The, 83
Mann's Chinese Theater, 119
Manson, Marilyn, 78

Man's Turf: The Perfect Lawn, The (Schultz),
    10
Marine Corps, U.S., 145
Marsden, Michael, 149
Massachusetts, University of, 197
Massachusetts Institute of Technology,
    53, 179
Masters Tournaments, 235
Matheson, Richard, 169, 175
Mathison, Melissa, 217
Mattachine Society, 40
Maximum Overdrive, 8
Mead, Margaret, 34
Medici, Cosimo de', 51
Melendez, "Stuttering John," 144, 151
memex, 179, 182
Men in Black, 218
Menlo Park, Calif., 181
Mercury, 133, 137
Mercury Comet, 140
Metropolitan Museum of Art, 53
Microsoft, 178, 183–84, 187–88, 223
Mildred Pierce, 216
Millais, John Everett, 48
Milland, Ray, 205
Miller, Johnny, 231–32
Mills, Victor, 157–58
miniskirts, 111, 112
Minneapolis Lakers, 195
Minority Report, 219
Minute Rice, 125
Mitchum, Robert, 94, 95
Moe, Doug, 191–92
Mondo, 116
Monroe, Marilyn, 40
Moore, Garry, 143
Moore, Marianne, 141
Morgan, Todd, 55
Morris, William, 48
Mother Jones, 149
Mothers Against Drunk Driving
    (M.A.D.D.), 210
Motion Picture Association of America,
    173
Motorola, 18
Mount Vernon, 3
mouse (computer), 180, 181, 183
movie theaters, air conditioning of,
    15–16, 17–18
MS-DOS, 183, 187

MSNBC, 152
Muir, Florabel, 100
multitrack recorder, 66

N

Nabisco cookies, 200
Nader, Ralph, 107–8
Namath, Joe, 113–14
National Alcohol and Drug Addiction
    Recovery Month, 211
National Association of Hosiery
    Manufacturers, 108
National Basketball Association (NBA),
    77, 189, 192, 194, 195, 196, 197,
    198–99, 201, 220
National Council on Disability, 187–88
National Enquirer, 101–2
National Golf Foundation, 227–28
National Lawn Mower Racing Series, 9
National Medal of Technology, 186
Natural Resource Defense Council, 162
Navy, U.S., 121
NBA Shootout, 193
Nestlé Frozen Foods, 127
Newark *Star-Ledger,* 123
New Orleans, La., 87, 123
New Orleans *Times-Picayune,* 123
Newport Folk Festival, 67
Newsweek, 30, 71, 194
New York, N.Y., 59, 61, 62, 67, 85, 92, 94,
    104, 196
New York *Daily Graphic,* 92–93, 101
New York *Daily News,* 95, 100, 103
New Yorker, 95, 133, 156, 161
New York Jets, 113
New York Nets, 190, 197
New York Times, 31, 35, 50, 73, 149, 157,
    190
New York World's Fair (1940), 110
Nicholson, Jack, 219
Night of the Living Dead, 165–76
    critical reviews of, 167, 171, 174–75
    influence of, 167–68, 174
    production of, 169–71
Nike, 235
Nixon, Pat, 205
Nixon, Richard, 139, 206
NLS, 180
North, Oliver, 144

nylon, 112–13, 117–18
nylon stockings, 108, 110, 115–16
Nylon: The Story of a Fashion Revolution
    (Handley), 110, 117–18
"Nylon: This Chemical Marvel," 117–18

O

O'Hara, Maureen, 99–100, 103
Oklahoma State, 194
"Old Guitarist, The" (Picasso), 56
Olivier, Laurence, 75
"Olympia" (Manet), 56
Omaha, Nebr., 120, 121, 126
Omega Man, The, 175
Omega watch, 215, 218
O. M. Scott's & Company, 10
operating systems, 183
Out of the Red, 104
ozone layer, 19

P

Packard, Vance, 132, 138
Page, Jimmy, 66, 67
Palmer, Arnold, 231–32
Palm Pilot, 178
Palo Alto Research Center (PARC), 178,
    182–83
Pampers, 157–59
Pan American Airlines, 121
Panti-Legs, 112
pantsuits, 114
pantyhose, 107–18
    cotton crotch of, 111
    as fashion item, 109, 113, 114
    hosiery market and, 112, 115
    liberation from, 114
    sexiness and, 116
    unusual uses of, 115
Parrish, Maxfield, 48
Parsons, Louella, 94
Patrick, Matthew "Starch," 82
Paul, Les, 58–69
Paul, Ronald N., 127
PCs, 178, 184–85
Peele, Stanton, 209, 211
Pennsylvania, 165, 168
People, 102
Perkins, Tony, 97

permanent-press fabrics, 81, 82
Perot, Ross, 144
Perry, Frank, 7
Peter, Saint, 92
Peters, Lulu Hunt
 background of, 27–28, 30
 legacy of, 31
 on weight loss, 23, 24, 27–30, 32
Peyton Place (Metalious), 40
PGA, 231, 232, 233, 235
Philadelphia 76ers, 195, 198, 199
Philadelphia Warriors, 195
Philbin, Regis, 143, 146
Phillips-Van Heusen, 85–86
Phoenix, Ariz., 12–15, 17, 18, 20
*Phoenix: The History of a Southwestern
 Metropolis* (Luckingham), 18
Picasso, Pablo, 56, 91
pickups, 61, 62, 68
Pinker, Steven, 53
Pinnacle Foods, 126
Pioneers of American Landscape Design
 (Birnbaum), 4
Pittsburgh, Pa., 121, 167, 171
Playboy, 33, 40, 138
Pluto, Terry, 197–98
Polanski, Roman, 167
Pollard, Jim (Kangaroo Kid), 195
Polo, Marco, 50
Polsby, Nelson, 18
polyester, 85–86
polyethylene terephthalate, 85
polymers, 156, 160, 163, 164
Pope, Generoso, Jr., 101
Portland Trailblazers, 199
Potter, Beatrix, 49
pre-Raphaelites, 48
Presley, Elvis, xviii, 40, 46, 54–55, 65,
 101
Price Is Right, The, 219
Princeton Video, 219
Procter & Gamble, 157–58, 161, 162
Psychology Today, 128
Publishers Weekly, 221
Purkey, Mike, 227
Pyne, Joe, xviii, 143–54
 death of, 150
 early career of, 145–46
 talk-show formula of, 147–49
 verbal trademarks of, 145

Q
Quant, Mary, 111, 112
Quigley, Martin, 93

R
Rambler, 140
Rambo, 173
Rancho Mirage, Calif., 203, 207, 209, 212
Rand, Sally, 112
Rascals in Paradise (Day and Michener),
 46, 51, 52
Raven's Story, The, 111
Reagan, Nancy, 210
Reagan, Ronald, 14, 19, 150
"reality" TV, 103
RealVideo, 186
Rebel Without a Cause, 65
Red Scare, 35
Reese's Peanut Butter Cups, 217
Reese's Pieces, 210–18, 223
ReplayTV, 215
Republican Party, 18–19
Revlon, 219
Rivoli, 15–16
RKO Warner, 94
Robertson, Pat, 149–50
rock and roll, 65, 78
Rock and Roll Hall of Fame and Museum, 67
"Rock Around the Clock," 65
Rockefeller, Happy, 207
Rockefeller, John D., 26
Rockefeller, Nelson, 207
Rockefeller Foundation, 35
Rockwell, Norman, 48
Rodman, Dennis, xvii–xviii, xix, 72, 77
Roe v. Wade, 206
Rolling Stones, 67, 78
Rolls-Royce, 132, 138
Romans, ancient, 47, 84
Romero, George A., 166–76
 background of, 168–69
 critical praise of, 174–75
 influence of, 169, 174, 175
Roosevelt, Eleanor, 105
Rowenta, 83, 88
Rubenstein, Steve, 124
Rushmore, Howard, 98, 100, 103–4
Russell, Lillian, 23–24
Russo, John A., 169

S
Sade, Marquis de, 110
sad irons, 84–85
Safer, Morley, 206
Sager, Carol Bayer, 224
Salinger, J. D., 40
Salomon, Lawrence, 83
San Francisco Chronicle, 124
Sanger, Margaret, 37, 40
Santana, Carlos, 59
Saturn (car), 140
saunas, 12, 21
sauna suits, 32
Savage, L. C. Van, 110
Schlitt, Anne, 115–16
Schmitz, Jonathan, 149
Schnabel, Julian, 55
Schultz, Warren, 10
Schuyler, David, 3
Schwartz, Hillel, 28, 29
Schwarzlose, John, 212–13
Science and Health, With Key to the Scriptures (Eddy), 29
Scott, Frank J., 1–11
Scream, 167, 174
screen readers, 187–88
Seagrams, 220
Seattle space needle, 214
Seely, Henry W., 85
Seinfeld, 219
Server, Lee, 94
sexuality, human, 33–44
sexual liberation, xviii, 35, 39, 40
Shaughnessy, Mary Alice, 60, 64, 65, 66
Shaw, Phil "Steam," 81
"Sheik of Araby," 68
Shoemaker, Edwin, 124
Shore, Dinah, 143
sick-building syndrome, 14
silk, 110
silk stockings, 115
Simo, Melanie, 9
Simpson, O. J., 93
Sisk, John P., 96
60 Minutes, 151, 206
slam dunk, 189–201
    in ABA contest, 189–92
    colorful names for, 199
    popular culture pervaded by, 193–94

slam dunk (*continued*)
    school sports affected by, 192–93
    street virtuosos of, 195–96
Slam-Dunk Typing, 194
Smell & Taste Treatment and Research Foundation, 7
Smithsonian Institution, 59, 126
Smothers, Tommy, 232
Snead, Sam, 234
Sony, 193–94
Sony Ericsson Mobile Communications Ltd., 214–15
Sorenstam, Annika, 233
South Pacific, 152
Spacey, Kevin, 102
Spielberg, Steven, 167, 217–18, 219, 224
Sporting News, 195, 197, 199
Sports Illustrated, 198
Springer, Jerry, 144, 153–54
Springsteen, Bruce, 56, 67
Sputnik, 137
stain resistance, 88
Stallone, Sylvester, 51
Stanford Research Institute, 179, 180
Stanford University, 186
Star, 101
starch, 84
"Starr Report," 102
"Starry Night, The" (van Gogh), 56
"Star-Spangled Banner" (Key), 66
Status Seekers, The (Packard), 132
stealth marketing, 214–24
    astroturfing and, 222–23
    early examples of, 216
    in *E.T.*, 216–18
    in sports, 220
    on TV, 219–20
    on the Web and, 221–22
Stern, Howard, xviii, 144, 149
Straight Story, The, 8
Stratocaster, 66
Substance Abuse and Mental Health Services Administration (SAMHSA), 210–211
suburbs
    air-conditioning in, 16–17
    lawn culture in, xviii, 3, 5–6, 7
    in TV, 6, 70, 72, 75, 76, 79
Suicidal Tendencies, 208
Sullivan, Ed, 40

Sunbeam, 85
Sunbelt, migration to, 13–14, 17–19
Super Bowl, 113, 220
supermodel, 111
Supreme Court, U.S., 206
Susskind, David, 148
Swanson, Clarke, 121
Swanson, Gilbert, 120
Swimmer, The, 7

T
T, Mr., 54
Tacky Chic, 45–57
  mass production and, 47–49
  popular subjects of, 48–50, 52–53
  waning of, 54–55
  See also black velvet paintings
Tahiti, 45–46, 51
Talkers, 152
Talk Radio (Bogosian), 149
talk shows, xvii, xviii, 143–54
  celebrity hosts of, 149
  personal confessions and, 202, 204, 207
  political office and, 151–52
Taxi Driver, 173
Taylor, Bob, 182
Taylor, Elizabeth, 209, 213
Taylor Made Golf Company, 229–30, 232
"Ted Mack Family Hour, The," 120, 124
Telecaster, 63, 64, 66
television, 93, 101, 103, 104, 123, 125,
  143–45, 147–48, 151, 198
  first TV set and, 124
  1950s suburban ideal in, 6, 70, 72, 75,
    76, 79
  stealth marketing and, 219–20
Ten Commandments, The, 175
Texas, University of, 21–22
Texas Chainsaw Massacre, The, 171
"Theory of Mass Culture, A"
    (Macdonald), 53
"thermal-shape memory," 87
Thief's Journal, The (Genet), 55
Third World, CFCs in, 19–20
Thomas, David, 116
Thomas, Gerry, 119–28
Thompson, David, 190–91
Thorn, Rod, 198
Thunderbird, 133

Tilden, Bill ("Big Bill"), 97
Time, 34, 75–76, 91, 139, 147
Time Inc., 102
Times of My Life, The (Ford), 207
Titleist, 232, 233
TiVo, 215
Too Hot for TV (Deluxe Edition), 144
Toronto Star, 81
Travis, Merle, 63
Trudeau, Garry, 221
True War, 105
TV dinners, xviii, 119–28
  current technology and, 123
  invention of, 120–22
  obsolescence of, 127
  sales of, 126
  très chic diners and, 127
  TV and, 123–24
TV table-tray, 125
20th Century Fox, 220
Twiggy, 31, 111, 112
Tyler, Steven, 78

U
United Press, 95
United States Golf Association (USGA),
    233
United States Lawn Mower Racing
    Association, xvii, 1, 8–9
Universal Studios, 221
U.S. News & World Report, 157
U.S. Open, 231

V
Van Buren, Abigail, 115
van Gogh, Vincent, 56
Vanity Fair, 102
Vardon Trophy, 234
Variety, 167
Venice Beach, 74
Ventura, Jesse, 149–50, 152
Vermeer, Johannes, 56
Vibrola, 62
Victorian era, 3, 39, 47, 50
Vietnam War, 147, 171
Vigoro Lawn Food Company, 6–7
Virginia Squires, 197
Vogue, 157

Volkswagen Beetle, 139–40
Voris, Ralph, 39

W
Wagner, Cherie, 76
Wagner, Elizabeth, 74, 76
Wagon Train, 136
Waksman, Steve, 62, 66
Waldorf-Astoria, 67
Wallace, Ben, 194
Wallace, David, 133–34, 140
Wallace, Mike, 151
Walters, Barbara, 206
Ward, Peter, 48
Waring, Fred, 61
Warnock, C. Gayle, 130, 138
wash-and-wear, 82, 85
Washington, D.C., 205, 207
Washington, George, 3
Washington Post, 141, 173, 209, 220
Washington Wizards, 192
Waters, John, 55, 78
Watson, Whipper, 76
Waukesha, Wis., 58, 60, 62
Wayne, John, 71
Webb, Spud, 199
Web browser, 178
Web TVs, 185
Welch, Jack, 230
Westinghouse Electric, 16
Wheeler, Tom, 63
"Where Have All the Stockings Gone?"
    (Schlitt), 115–16
Whinfield, John Rex, 85
White, William L., 211–12
White House, 102, 205, 206, 207
Whittelsey, Frances Cerra, 108
"Whole Lotta Love," 58
*Why Women Pay More: How to Avoid
    Marketplace Perils* (Whittelsey and
    Nader), 107–8
Wild One, The, 65
Wilkins, Dominique, 199
Williams, Edward Bennett, 98
Williams, Montel, 147
William the Conqueror, 25
WILM, 145
Wilson, Theo, 103
Wilson (sporting goods), 218–19, 232–33

Winchell, Walter, 94, 97
Windows, 178, 184, 187–88
Winfrey, Oprah, 144
Wink, 93
Wisconsin, 58, 60
W. L. Maxson, 121
Wolfe, Tom, 93, 100–101
Wolfman, 168
Wolford, 114
"Woman Ironing" (Degas), 85
women's liberation, 107
Wonder World of Chemistry, 110, 117
Woods, Tiger, 220, 225, 226, 233, 234,
    235
Woodstock (rock concert), 58, 66, 225
World Basketball Championships, 194
World Series, 220
World War I, 230
World War II, 16, 30, 52, 110, 111, 121, 122,
    125, 126, 131
World Wide Web, 185
Wozniak, Steve, 183
wrestlers, wrestling, 70–79
    scientific, 73
    as show business, 70, 73–74, 78
wrinkles, wrinkle resistance, 81–89
    birth of, 82
    early attempts at, 84
    economic impact of, 86
    social status and, 88
    synthetic fibers and, 85–88
Wyeth, Andrew, 56

X
Xerox Corporation, 178, 182–83, 184

Y
Yale, 16, 29
Young, Leah, 211

Z
Zappa, Frank, 148
Zeronian, Haig, 84
zombies, 165, 166, 171, 172, 173, 175
Zombies That Ate Pittsburgh, The (Gagne),
    171
Zukor, Adolph, 16